# TOTAL CHESS

# TOTAL CHESS

*David Spanier*

E. P. DUTTON, INC.   NEW YORK

The lines from *The Defense* by Vladimir Nabokov are quoted
with permission from the publisher, G. P. Putnam's Sons,
and the author's estate.

Published in the United States by E. P. Dutton, Inc.
2 Park Avenue, New York, N.Y. 10016

Library of Congress Catalog Card Number: 84-72112

ISBN: 0-525-24302-X

10  9  8  7  6  5  4  3  2  1

OBE

# CONTENTS

# ACKNOWLEDGEMENTS

Chess is boundless and endless and that is part of its fascination. There will always be new things to say about it, and new insights into its skill and art as well as the social context in which it is played, in every generation. If there are mistakes and misjudgements in this book, they are my own. If these are, as I trust, few and far between, that is thanks to the vision and vigilance of the friends who helped me in my researches and in reading the work in progress.

I record here my gratitude, taking the chapters in chronological order, to Stewart Reuben; to Bernard Cafferty; to Rabbi John Rayner; to Raymond Keene throughout and likewise to David Levy; to Patrick Laver; to Robert Bellin and Bob Wade, and to James Rothman for statistical work; to Dr Joseph Berke; to Jonathan Speelman; to Harry Golombek for reading the book as a whole; to the writers and thinkers on chess whose work, down the centuries, has immortalised the game; to Rita Hughes for typing the manuscript so many times; and to my wife Suzy for putting up with all this chessomania.

Finally, I am indebted to Weidenfeld & Nicolson for permission to quote on pages 163–165 from Vladimir Nabokov's *The Defence*.

**Chess is a sea
in which a gnat may drink
and an elephant may bathe.**
*Indian proverb*

# I

# MOTIVATION

*I have a few peripheral friends here and there*
*who are non-chess players . . .*
Robert Lowell, The Winner

Heads bent, there are 130 people going right the way down the long room, facing each other in pairs. The concentration is so intense you can feel it burning in the air. Outside beyond the high windows of the new Barbican Centre, framed by tower blocks, sunlight plays across the plumes of the fountains. Inside, no sound penetrates. Occasionally a young man, eyes filled with secret knowledge, raises his hand briefly, moves a piece, taps his urgently ticking clock and scrawls an algebraic note. Now it is his opponent's turn to stare down. The room is still, cerebral, reverent in dedication. What are these kids, and not all of them kids either, what are they all doing, grinding through the golden afternoon, concentrating, concentrating? I mean, what are they really *doing*?

Ratings. The answer is ratings.

It's one of the things that make chess different. In no other sport can a player, any player from novice right up to expert, calibrate his ability so finely, so exactly, almost from day to day. The youths with their furrowed gaze, the girls, pop-eyed with the strain, the bearded veterans and hopeless hangers-on of the tournament circuit, they are all after the same, elusive, yet so immediately within grasp, higher rating – just one more point, that's all! – and they're there.

Never mind getting to the top. It's not like mountain climbing because they're never, ever, going to get to the top. Not up there with Karpov who's on an Elo rating of 2,710 points. That is the empyrean, the highest heaven, 'the sphere of fire or the abode of God', as my *Concise Oxford* puts it. Even little Anatoly himself, though of course he cannot admit to such mundane concerns, is aware of where he stands, would like to go just half a step up.

Because if he loses a game or two, his rating will slip and Garry Kasparov, lurking just below in the 2,690s will be drawing level. (Indeed he did overtake him, at the beginning of 1984.)

All right then, let's survey the prospect from below the summit, far below. What about the foothills? What about getting a first toehold in the rating list at the start of the ascent? That is already to stand high above the mass of chess players, who play the game now and again, who play for mere . . . *recreation*. A rating is achieved by getting a certain score against other rated players. The whole business was invented and codified by a professor of mathematics, now retired to Wisconsin, Arpad Elo. According to some people, Elo changed the nature of chess as radically as the Italian amateur in Renaissance times who gave the pawn the option of moving two squares on its first move instead of one, some five hundred years ago. The Elo system is based on players' performances in international and national events, and forms a network throughout the world, monitored and reported by FIDE, the International Chess Federation. FIDE publishes its standings twice a year and adjudicates on all disputes.

So as this silent, golden, afternoon fades, here at the Guildhall School of Music in the City of London, the players are struggling to improve their standing in the national grades, which can be converted, if they score high enough, into a FIDE rating. Half a point more, half a point less, it's crucial. The qualification for international honours is complicated but very precisely laid down. In this tournament, where each player plays nine different opponents to achieve a grandmaster norm, a player would need to score 7 points (1 for a win, ½ for a draw) against opponents who included at least three grandmasters, two other titled players and a minimum of four non-English players. That is just about possible, in theory. An international master norm, the IM, is more achievable; it could be reached by a total of 5½–6 points, with the level of opposition correspondingly reduced. Still hard enough. This is what is called a 'Swiss' tournament, which means that in each round each player meets an opponent with a game score as close as possible to his own. It is possible (especially in the early rounds) for an unfancied amateur to play against a grandmaster, a prospect incidentally which gives the GM the shakes. The unknown player has nothing to lose and everything to gain. If he secures even a draw there will be press photographers and news bulletins celebrating the event. Of

course the GM will win easily . . . ninety-nine times out of a
hundred. But mistakes do happen. In the second round, the late
Hungarian GM Janos Flesch went down to a fifteen-year-old
schoolgirl, Teresa Needham, a promising youngster but still, in
chess terms, a gossamer talent. Viktor Korchnoi himself, out of
form as he had been for some time, as the pressures of age and exile
inexorably gnawed at his powerful talent, lost to Dibyenda Barua, a
sixteen-year-old Indian boy who had travelled to London from
Calcutta especially for this event. The grizzled Viktor sat down at
the board later, faintly smiling, murmuring incredulously to himself
in Russian, replaying the moves. Yes, it happens.

Perhaps this is the point at which the author ought to make a
confession. Let me say it straight out. I am not, actually, a grandmaster. I never achieved, never even tried for, the 'norms', attain-
ment of which automatically confers on one what is, after all, the
most prestigious of all sporting accolades. Nor, for that matter, can I
claim to be of international master rank, the level below the highest
title in chess; nor even, some distance below that, a plain FIDE
master. After that the deluge, the wide spread of chess masters at
national level. If the truth be known, I cannot, do not, aspire to that
sort of title either. If the whole truth and nothing but the truth be
known, I am not a regional, county or club champion. I am not, in
fact, any kind of expert whatever. Though I did come second in a
chess tournament in the newspaper I worked for, none other than
*The Times*. It was the year when, as a gesture of staff solidarity,
pretty well everyone was obliged to enter whether they knew the
moves or not. Unfortunately, when it came to the final, my opponent was one of the very few members of the journalistic staff who
did, indeed, know the moves. For a short time, however, I was able
to bask in the reflected limelight of having been in the final of the
reporters' chess competition, in the very newspaper where the great
Harry Golombek was chess columnist. No, I am a bad player. How
bad, you ask? Somewhere between very bad and moderately appalling. And where, may I inquire, do you fit in? For below my level
come very appalling, absolutely appalling and finally, zilch. Put me
against a player in one of those categories and I shine. My opening is
swift, my middle game assured, sacrifices of high risk alternate with
saving resources; the combinations, as they unfold, seem irrefutable. Usually the endgame is never reached, so clearly won is the
position. So do not take on too superior an air. There is always

someone who plays a degree better than you. In all probability it is not the present author. But it could be, so beware.

Which prompts one to ask the basic question: Why play chess? I mean what for . . . it's 'difficult', it's endless as a matter of fact. The openings alone are beyond any ordinary player's mastery. *Modern Chess Openings*, in its latest edition, gives 400 pages of analysis. And even if one could come to grips with all that, there is the middle game. Ah yes, the middle game, the heart of chess: abstruse, combinative, working this way and that to achieve the transition . . . to the desired endgame. Which in turn is far more rigorous, yet less charted, than any other aspect of chess. The range of endings is dizzying – rook versus rook and rook's pawn; rook versus rook and knight's pawn; rook versus rook and two united pawns; rook and pawn versus rook and isolated pawns . . . no, that way lies madness. It is too much, too complex, can one ever – even at super-grandmaster level – get on top of it? Yes and no. There are principles, as in all aspects of chess, which filter out many of the possible lines of play as being unprofitable. So the good player can assess, at a glance almost, the nature of the position, and take action accordingly.

The fact remains, chess is an almighty sweat. Like love, like music, chess has the power to make men happy, as Tarrasch said in a famous phrase. Variously described as a game, an art and a science, it contains elements of all three, though as everyone knows it is too serious for a game, too transient for an art, too useless for a science. I like the description of chess in the *Great Soviet Encyclopedia* as an art manifesting itself in a game. Definitions are always elusive. When the Sports Council conducted a survey in Britain to find out what people thought sport meant, all sorts of answers came out, many of them contradictory – 7 per cent of people would not even accept that soccer was a sport, while 11 per cent thought cooking was. In charge of handing out government funds to needy sports, the Council took as its general requirement 'an acceptable balance between skill and effort', a definition which itself depends on value judgements. For most people who play chess (supposedly three million in Britain in the course of a week) it is a relaxation. But professional chess is a sport because it requires both physical stamina and mental effort to succeed. Some people will always believe chess is so 'intellectual' it cannot properly count as a competitive sport. In Eastern European countries they know better, which is why they are so good at it. The Dutch have a handy word, *denksport*, meaning a game with a lot of science in it. One might say, following Gertrude Stein, that chess is chess is chess, and leave it at that. But I have another formula based on the fact that chess does take up a lot of time, indeed it can absorb the whole of one's time.

Consider: getting up in the morning sometimes, after a long session of chess the night before, one's head is full of chess. The moves one did not make, the mistakes one did make . . . Or perhaps the game is adjourned. There is analysis to be done. Correspondence players (I am not one) no doubt wait in tremulous agitation for the postman. What next, what next? What has he done now? Correspondence games take months to play out, and correspondence championships take, literally, years to complete. Shall we assume you have to go to an office somewhere? Or catch a plane to another city? Well, on the bus, or in the taxi, or best of all, strapped into your airplane seat on a transatlantic flight, there is a perfect opportunity to go on playing. Either in your head, or, better, on a pocket set. All the great games are written down. Chess is also unique among sports in that for the past hundred years or so, all the master games are available, as if on a video tape. All you have to do is open up the book, and there before you, as fresh as the day they were first played, you can follow through the struggles of the titans, move by move, blow by blow. Those romantic names from the past – Morphy, Anderssen, La Bourdonnais . . . their names are magic, they have immortality insofar as immortality exists in this world. Or not necessarily names from the misty past. Modern tournaments, of which there are an abundance, new openings, new systems, new traps – there is a wealth, a cornucopia of material to work through and be entertained by. *Informator*, published twice a year in Belgrade, lists all the important or interesting games played throughout the international circuit, some 600–700 games an issue. As with musical notation, the work is international, it knows no frontiers but those of the mind. Or, more compactly, take problems. Chess problems, solving or composing them, are a world of their own: rarefied, 'artificial', legerdemain on the board. In other words, there is no need to sit down against another opponent – or a machine – to play chess. The process can be continued the whole time, day and night, in many different ways. 'Why are you so abstracted?' my wife sometimes used to ask. Now she skips the question, it's too obvious and simply taunts me with the answer: 'Your head is full of chess!' 'Oh no, darling, not at all, I was just thinking about . . . um . . .' Quite so, quite so.

So what is it all about, why do people play chess the way they do? The answer is: *Chess is a substitute for life itself.*

It is not more important than life, of course, it is not as 'real' as life, it is not practical to play chess without giving some attention to the problems of everyday living. (That's what Bobby Fischer did.) But it can be a very satisfying substitute for life, in the sense that over the board all the dramas and colours of living are continually being played out in imagination. Something like the effect of a gently powerful, pervasively consuming, hallucinatory drug. While the infinite possibilities of the struggle are being acted out, on the stage of the sixty-four squares, the players do have very little inclination or opportunity to consider the world, albeit the real world, outside those squares. Yes, chess is a substitute for life. But here's the secret: it is an extraordinarily good one.

Like Father Time, chess is old. It was invented, so far as is known, in north-west India during the sixth century AD. Its Sanskrit name *chaturanga* means four-armed, on the pattern of the four arms of an Indian army: infantry, cavalry, elephants and chariots. Invented is not quite the word – most likely it developed over many years from earlier games played with a board and dice, says Golombek in his *Encyclopedia of Chess*. The first written references are found in Sanskrit romances of the late sixth and seventh centuries. Early on, in the late sixth century, the game spread to Persia where it was known as *chatrang* – its ancient provenance in Persia makes the Ayatollah Khomeini's prohibition of the game all the more perverse – and thence to the Byzantine empire. After the Arab conquest of Persia around the middle of the seventh century, it became a Muslim game under the name of *chatranj*: and it was the Arabs, with their inquiring minds, who gave chess its first serious study, on a theoretical as well as a practical basis. Chess came to Europe, the *Encyclopedia* says, from four main paths, during the ninth and tenth centuries. First, by trade, from regions dominated by the Arabs, mostly via the Mediterranean, and from Byzantium to Kiev; another important way was through the crusades (but the story that Saladin taught Richard Coeur de Lion is probably mythical); a third route was via the Moors in Spain; and a fourth, only recently confirmed, was that the game spread, very early on, from the tribes in Central Asia to Russia. By early mediaeval times most of Western Europe had discovered the pleasures of chess: its flowering occurred in renaissance Italy, with the opening up of the game by such innovations as the pawn's initial advance by two moves, by castling and, most significantly, by the aggrandisement of the queen. This established the game in its modern form.

It was England, though, which can claim the credit for introducing the classic design of the pieces. Does the name of Howard Staunton, mid-nineteenth-century British champion, ring a triumphant peal? Yes and no: Staunton's ascendancy at chess was flawed by his ungentlemanly conduct in evading his strongest challenger, but his fame rests secure because it was he who gave his name to the standard 'Staunton' design of the chessmen. The curious thing is that it was not Staunton himself who designed the Staunton pieces. It is generally assumed that Nathaniel Cook, who registered a sketch of the chess pieces at the British Patent Office in 1849, was the original designer; Staunton authorised use of his own name on the boxes as a trademark in 1852, and the pieces have been thus known ever since.

Clean, clear, well distinguished without being ornate, why is the design so right? A technical verdict was well expressed by the author of *Chess Sets* (New York, 1968), F. Lanier Graham: 'The pieces are quite rewarding to the touch and responsive to the move. They are individually well proportioned, and formally inter-related by means of classical balusters, crowning balls and grooves that, in elevation, are either at the same height or at equally measured intervals. The graduated height of the pieces, although singularly unexpressive of relative power, contributes to the architectonic composition of the whole.' And beyond that, the natural symbolism is well expressed – the knight and the castle are obvious; the more abstract shape of a bishop's headdress suggestive of a mitre; the crowns of the king and queen imperiously clear. Chess players the world over take them for granted.

So here in London, at the end of this tournament at the Barbican, sponsored by a major clearing bank, no less, the scores are added up, not just for the masters but for all the competitors. The advantage of the Swiss system, as opposed to the smaller all-play-all tournament where, say, a dozen players each play all the others, is that a huge number of people can be accommodated in the same event. In each round there is a continual change about, as winners play winners and losers play losers. This is why it is possible for a grandmaster to find himself paired against a more or less untried competitor. The Swiss system also produces odd results. Going into the last round, Tony Miles (England), Vlastimil Hort (Czechoslovakia) and Ljubomir Ftacnik (Czechoslovakia) were leading; the first two drew with each other in a dozen moves, and Ftacnik was beaten by Gutman (Israel); so a couple of aspiring masters, who would in the normal run of things have no chance against such renowned GMs, slipped into first place. It didn't help their ratings, because en route to the final round they had played a number of players without sufficient grades to help them improve their own standings in the lists. But they did share the money, handed out in little brown envelopes by Sir Jeremy Morse, chairman (and chess problemist enthusiast) of Lloyds Bank. It's good business for an institution like a bank to sponsor chess events. It costs so little, relative to buying advertising in the media; and in return there is a continuous trickle of publicity, especially when, as in this event, some of the unknowns deliver an unexpected *coup de grâce* to internationally celebrated stars. Poor Korchnoi was in such dismal form that in the last round he lost to an Oxford student whom he had beaten the day before the tournament started in a simultaneous exhibition, and drew with Pia Cramling, the young Swedish girl. That was a very fine result for her, enabling her to achieve overall a male IM norm, the first woman outside the Soviet Union to manage it. 'Are you going to make chess your whole life?' I asked her. Looking like a schoolgirl who's been given a surprise half-holiday, Pia giggled: 'Oh no, I've got plenty of other things to do . . .'

And what about the mass of also-rans, forlornly totting up their scores? Most of them failed to get anywhere. Was it really worth all the effort, the relentless cerebration, the hours of analysis? Surely it was. There was the excitement of being involved in a major tournament, rubbing shoulders with the luminaries of the chess firmament . . . each loser hoping that in the next game, after the unfortunate little blunder committed in the last game, things would turn out better, would signal the lift-off to a higher rating. As I said, there are a lot of players better than oneself, but there are certainly quite a few who play worse.

What is the difference between good and bad chess players? One is tempted to say, adapting Hemingway's celebrated answer to Scott Fitzgerald's question as to why the very rich are different from the rest of us (they've got more money) – 'They've got more talent'. But a lot of work has been done in finding out what this talent consists of, how it works. It's not what you might think. Masters do not see ahead miles further than the rest of us. The classic answer, as I recall, to the question 'How far do you see ahead?' given by a master is 'One move further than my opponent!'

In his definitive and voluminous *Thought and Choice in Chess* (1978), the Dutch professor of psychology Adriaan de Groot perceived thought in chess to develop in two ways. He presented a number of positions from actual games to chess players, the group being made up of grandmasters, masters, experts and less skilled players. Each player had to produce a move as if playing the game and to think out loud as fully as possible. In this way a sort of diagram of how players made the choice of move was produced.

Initially, elaboration of the problem in the original state took place, followed by transitional phases. During the latter phases the results of elaboration caused radical transformation of the original problem – playing back from the branches to the main tree, as it were. What was interesting about these experiments – I follow here an introduction to a research project by Mary W. Goss done at the London Polytechnic in 1982 – was that de Groot found *no difference* in the thought processes and the search through possible moves of good and bad players. 'It was thought that masters might consider more alternative moves than weaker players. In fact the reverse was found and masters if anything appeared to consider fewer alternatives.' When considering a difficult position a master pondered on 15–25 moves to a search depth of about two or three before producing a decision. It was unusual for a master to search deeper than five moves or to consider more than one hundred. The results from weaker players were very similar. 'The only difference between skill levels that de Groot found was *qualitative*. Masters explored the same number of moves as weaker players but the moves themselves were much stronger. Weaker players appeared to spend a great deal of time analysing the consequences of bad moves.' De Groot concluded that masters do not 'see' any further than weaker players but that qualitative differences occur. 'A master possesses an ability for fast efficient problem formation and specialization which is gained from experience. Over the years a master builds up a superior system of experimental linkings which is wider, worth more and more differentiated than that of the expert.'

This is one of the great difficulties, by the way, in programming computers (see Chapter 6). The master's experience is related to his recognition of or familiarity with very many patterns on the board. A stock of 50,000 or more is the figure given by Neil Charness (one of the contributors to *Chess Skill in Man and Machine*, edited by Peter W. Frey, 1976). Practice at chess does not mean staring at and memorising 50,000 patterns. It means learning to recognise types of positions and the plans or playing methods which go with them. The reason why the information necessary to become a master does not appear readily in chess books, Charness adds, is that it is primarily *non-verbal*. Advice should take the form of: when you see this kind of pattern, consider trying such and such a plan.

In another kind of test, concerned with short-term memory, which de Groot conducted, players were given a chess position to observe for five seconds and asked to think about it a while before reconstructing it; likewise they were asked to look at positions where pieces had been placed not in a chess position, but just at random on the board. In this study not much differentiation between levels of skill was found. In other words, masters had about the same limitations on visual short-term memory as weaker players; they do not, it seems, possess a superior capacity in that respect either.

Further elaboration of these kinds of tests in cognitive psychology by Simon and Chase (*Skill in Chess*, 1973) revealed a very interesting distinction between the recall of chess positions and random distribution of the pieces. Whereas in reconstructing real positions, the master was better than the intermediate player who was in turn better than the novice, in random positions all skill levels were equally poor. How so? The answer is that good chess players see the board in 'chunks'. An analysis of the errors in memory tests showed that the majority were errors of omission, of which the greatest proportion were translation mistakes. Eighty-five per cent of placement errors still preserved some information about the location, identity and colour of the pieces – errors often occurred as whole units, so that several pieces were misplaced by a square or two but maintained the original configuration. The conclusion was that the absolute location of the pieces was not as important as the position relative to other pieces on the board.

The speed with which players perceived information on the chess board (judging from video tapes of these experiments) did depend on chess skill. It is the relation between the pieces – attack, defence, colour, identity, proximity – which gives good players what de Groot called dynamic perceptual ability. In random positions, in which the pieces do not contain any chess relationship one with another, all players are equal in observing and recalling what they see. Skilled players, according to these researches, appear to recall more chunks and larger chunks than weaker players. Indeed, they can recall whole games, many hundreds of their own and other players' back through the history of chess; or, in simultaneous play, recall exactly the order of moves in each game played, so that if during such a display one piece is moved out of its proper position on the board, the master (even if 'blindfold'), will spot it straight away. In short, grandmasters do not think faster or deeper, but because of this highly developed pattern recognition they do think about the right things.

A striking example of this phenomenon arose in the course of de Groot's experiments when former world champion Max Euwe was interrupted after ten seconds' viewing of a particularly active position. According to Alex Bell in *The Machine Plays Chess?* (1978): 'Euwe was able to reproduce the positions with only two errors insignificant to the play that was to follow. Further, he was able to identify the core problem in the position and had plans formulated for exploration. Most remarkable, he had already intuitively selected the winning move (which three masters, five experts and a number of average players had failed to do during a complete analysis) and was able to visualise a possible variation.' One must resist the temptation to throw up one's hands in despair at such virtuosity, because one can never imagine playing the board like that; Euwe was, after all, a world champion, and just because you can't serve a tennis ball like Borg or McEnroe it doesn't mean you can't play tennis.

Let's go back to chunks for a moment. Here is a typical chunk, which frequently arises in play, that everyone can recognise instantly (Diagram 1).

The implications are obvious: the fianchettoed bishop – a bishop developed on the diagonal by moving the knight's pawn – represents a permanent threat down the long diagonal (the two 'long diagonals' run from corner to corner of the board), while the cluster of pawns and rook protects the position of the king. The significance of such a chunk is so obvious, indeed so much part of a player's mental

1

stock-in-trade, that he doesn't even have to look at it: he sees it as a unit; it's programmed into his perception as if on a micro-chip.

Here's a more dynamic kind of chunk, which comes up again and again in slightly different configurations in endgames (Diagram 2). It's from Gligoric v. Fischer, Candidates' Tournament 1959 (No 12 in Fischer's *My 60 Memorable Games*). I explain algebraic notation, by the way, in the glossary on page 221.

2

Fischer, who can see these things a mile off, played 58 . . . Kb8! which draws immediately. As he noted: Black holds the 'distant opposition' (having the opposition means preventing penetration by the opposing king). For example, 58 Kc5 (or 58 Kd5 Kb7) Kc7 59 Kb5 Kb7 etc. Yes, it's simple really: but it takes a moment's thought, and many less skilled players would mess about by playing the king to b7 or c7 and possibly go wrong. Whereas to an experienced player, this, and many thousands of more or less elaborate patterns on the board, are so well imprinted in their thinking as to trigger a reflex response.

Here is an extremely complex pattern, though one that is easily recognisable as a very common kind of game position (Diagram 3). In this example, four out of five grandmasters chose the objectively correct move and the fifth included it in his analysis. By contrast, none of five experts picked the move, and only two of them even mentioned it in their analysis!

3

White to play. I give the best move at the foot of the page.*

Why did all the GMs consider the correct move? 'There were probably certain features in the position, which quite automatically, *when recognised*, elicited the appropriate move,' says Charness, commenting on this position. Moves are only 'obvious' when the patterns they spring from are recognised. As to why masters remember more chunks in memory tests than less skilled players, no doubt they were better at guessing which pieces should be on the board. But the most persuasive explanation offered by researchers is that the long-term memory of the master is structured so that information associated with particular chunks acts as a cue to retrieve other chunks from store (like a computer). Moreover, it seems likely that chunks are not all of a uniform size. A well-learned chunk that a master player would possess needs only a hold label; a chunk not so well assimilated by a weaker player would contain several pieces of information. By contrast the master instinctively or

* Bxd5! Don't ask me, try and work it out!

automatically homes in on the precise information he needs, without time-wasting distraction in other directions.

So how many chunks does a master have in view and, behind that, in store? Recognition of a position is done by short-term memory, i.e. a quick look at the board. The capacity for short-term memory, as suggested by G. Miller (*Psychological Review*, 1956), is about seven chunks (plus or minus two). In a position of about 25 pieces, the master makes sense of it by dividing it into about 4 pieces a chunk. As Bell puts it: 'His advantage is that, due to experience, he has amassed an enormous vocabulary; a rough estimate is that he can recognise about 100,000 clusters of pieces.' (Vocabulary, one may note in passing, is commonly regarded as the best single test of IQ.) Experiments on eye movements show that masters hardly look at any of these pieces, Bell adds. Their peripheral vision informs them of a pattern which they have seen thousands of times; the properties and purpose of this 'superpiece' are well known and the pieces are not, nor need to be, distinguished individually. Perception of the structural pattern occurs before the player starts to search out a good move.

How, in turn, is that done? Simon and Chase suggest that masters find a strong move without great analysis because they can build in the mind's eye an internal representation. This is where information from the long-term memory becomes associated with structural information about the pattern. Putting this into more homely language, I think it means that strange process which we all experience occasionally at chess known as 'feel'. One sees, as an average kind of player, a certain position, more or less complicated, one is not sure which way to move in it, but one feels – unconsciously recalling from the memory bank similar situations from past games – that it ought to go in a particular direction, and plots the move accordingly. (The only trouble for us *patzers* is that more often than not we get it wrong – even though the process of thought is akin to that of a master.)

Building up knowledge of patterns takes thousands of hours of play, it is stressed, hence the overriding importance, in attaining skill, of practice. It is the process of playing, looking at and learning from all the positions that arise in over-the-board play, that serves to imprint patterns in long-term memory and 'programme' a player's mind. However, there are no final answers yet as to how players' perception and memory work; and research findings differ on the extent of short-term memory, how the process of coding and retrieving information works, and much else besides. What seems evident, to quote de Groot, is that good players need a high degree of discipline to retain complex data structures, as well as a high degree of motivation.

'It's a funny thing,' mused Stewart Reuben, an international arbiter and organiser of the Lloyds Bank tournament in London, 'most players think that if they can get a higher rating, they become a better player. But it's the other way round!' The objective, Reuben explains, is to become a better chess player. 'A higher rating is a *demonstration* of this, not a *proof*.'

So how do you, casual player, with a bit of a sharp edge now and then, not averse to displaying a touch of 'art' when the occasion offers, how do you calculate your own ability? A master could no doubt assess your performance in a single game. But the right way is to play in half a dozen tournaments – local affairs – in the course of a year, and from the resulting three dozen or so games, the British Chess Federation will give you a grading. As Reuben explained the process (*Chess*, June 1981), it's a complicated affair: what the *British grade* reveals is an historically accurate fact as to how a player performed during the previous year. The *international rating* attempts to state a standard of play based on a lifetime's performance but with a weighting given to the most recent results.

International ratings are published by FIDE twice a year, on 1 January for events from the preceding June to November, and on 1 July for events in the preceding December to May. There are two lists, one for men over 2,200 and the other for women over 1800. The equivalent British grades are 200 and 150 (British grade × 8 + 600 = Elo rating). The rules are reviewed at the FIDE congress each year and usually tinkered with – the subject is fraught with prestige, argument and complexity and, not least, intrigue, because possession of a high rating is very important to chess players, being the passport to expenses and appearance fees, invitations to foreign tournaments and, overall, the opportunity to make a living.

Grandmasters are very ratings conscious, according to Reuben, even Karpov himself. What slightly rankles with the World Champion is that it is virtually impossible for him to equal Bobby Fischer's rating. He claims this is due to a difference in the system, but the explanation lies more in the fact that Fischer always played to win, to 'crunch' his opponent – *wham! pow-ee!* – so he always scored well. For Karpov it is sufficient to win the event, a relief to beat Korchnoi by a point. Fischer's peak was 2,780, Karpov's highest to date 2,720. Sixty points is a huge leap at that rarefied level, even if such comparisons do not have much statistical validity. The general level of play in the modern game is higher, not just because the amount of information available about what is going on in the international tournament circuit is so readily on tap; it is rather that, beyond this immediacy, *understanding* has risen. A new twist in the opening, an unfashionable line rehabilitated, a clever transposition in an old system, a hidden nuance in move order in the middle game . . . such hairline gleams of gold speed around the world in a flash, to become the common currency for everyone to spend.

Nor is it so surprising, given the value of results and prestige of ratings, that a certain amount, let's say a very small amount, of sharp practice at a personal level takes place. Cheating? Let's not mince words. *Buying* and *selling* is what it's about. Selling points for money: buying points to get a bigger prize or a higher rating. The only way to *cheat* is to look up established analysis during a game or to analyse a difficult position on a pocket set in the privacy of the loo; or to seek advice from someone watching the game.

The practice of offering and accepting a draw in the last round of chess tournaments is not in question. This reflects merely the entirely reasonable private understanding by the two players concerned that if the game has no significance for their standing in the tournament, and it's the final day when everyone is packing up to fly back home, then there's no point in beating their brains out to go for a win. Everyone does it. The so-called 'grandmaster draw' in the course of a tournament is rather less condonable; while it is true that such pacific draws do allow players to concentrate their energies on the crucial games in an event, it can be unfair to the other competitors. Certainly if a player needs a vital half-point, in going for a GM norm, then a compatriot would usually let him have it.

Makings deals at the chess board is nothing new; it goes back to the first international master tournament ever held, the great London tournament organised by Staunton in 1851 to coincide with the Great Exhibition. The book of the tournament states: 'Szén opened his match against Anderssen with infinitely more skill than he exhibited in the concluding games. It subsequently transpired that a compromise was effected in the middle of the contest, by which it was stipulated that, if either player were fortunate enough to gain the first prize, he should pay one-third of its amount to the other. Whether this arrangement had any effect upon the afterplay of the Hungarian it was impossible to say, but unquestionably his latter games in this match are vastly inferior to his best efforts.' It would seem that Szén had decided that Anderssen had more of a chance of winning the tournament than he did, comments David Levy, so he allowed himself to be slaughtered. I would imagine that Anderssen, who had a very open character, allowed himself to be persuaded (he was short of funds and had difficulty even in travelling to the tournament) since he could presumably have beaten Szén without too much trouble, and was indeed the best player there. He won, and Szén came fifth.

Bribery is something else. It does occur, and players know who is likely to try it on. Tournament organisers cannot do much about it, as Raymond Keene (one of England's first GMs) discovered when he protested at being pestered by an East European player to throw a game in Reykjavik, for a bribe of $50. 'I tried to get away from this man, who kept on begging me to take the money, and finally I managed to slip away on a bus tour of the Icelandic geysers,' Keene recalls. 'And then at the last moment this individual rushed out of the hotel and got on the bus too. The result was I had him wheedling away at my elbow all day long and when we eventually met at the board, I was so demoralized I lost the game.' Later, at a tournament in Spain, when this same Romanian player tried to buy another game, the contestants got up a collective protest to the organisers, and he was severely reprimanded. Publicity has cured him somewhat of his unsporting habits, so I won't name him here.

Keene, who takes an active part in upholding standards, as the founder of the Players' Council in FIDE, recalls a nice story of how a certain rather jovial Soviet grandmaster continually upped the ante against a young opponent who desperately needed a draw. Half-way through the game, when the younger player clearly stood worse, the price went up from 100 to 200 roubles. 'I can't afford it!' wailed the buyer. 'Too bad!' retorted his unyielding exploiter. 'All right, I suppose I'll have to pay up.' The game went on and the young man's position got even worse. The price was raised to 300. 'This is ruining me! I can't pay any more!' His greedy opponent shrugged, unmoved by all entreaties to stick to the original bargain. By the adjournment, when the game was absolutely lost the price had risen to 500 roubles. In despair, the luckless briber went away, looked at his lost position, examined his funds and informed the tournament arbiter overnight that he was resigning the game. When the news that he had won was given to the GM who was taking the bribe, he was outraged. 'What do you mean? He can't resign! *We're not living in the jungle!* Tell him we're playing on.' And the game was resumed next morning, willy-nilly, with the draw agreed. Bribery is not confined to Soviet bloc players, of course, but Keene points out that what with the premium on success and their difficulties in getting approval to travel abroad, the temptation for some East European players to fix results is a strong one.

One must admire Viktor Korchnoi for admitting so openly what once happened to him in reaching the master norm. It was back in 1951 in the Chigorin Memorial Tournament in Leningrad. 'I reached the master norm, though not altogether honestly,' Korchnoi writes in his autobiography *Chess is My Life* (1977). 'The point was that in the last round I needed to win, but I was against an experienced master. Our game was adjourned in a dead drawn position. But being a young player, I had a number of supporters, including some of the organizers of the tournament. They put strong pressure on my opponent, threatening not to hand over the cash prize due to him, if he did not agree to their demands. In the end my opponent succumbed to this blackmail, and he found a way to lose the drawn position. I must admit that throughout this unsavoury episode I behaved quite improperly. I made out that I knew nothing of what was happening, and laughed at my opponent. I now wish that I had had the determination to decline the services of my supporters, and to cut short this "charade".'

Many years after the 1960 Soviet Championship, which he won in a tremendous struggle, Korchnoi was told by Bronstein why on that occasion he gave away a point to Yefim Geller. 'Do you remember how on that February day in 1960 I "threw" my game against Geller?' David Bronstein confessed, in reminiscent mood. 'Why did I do it? Well, during the game I suddenly saw how unscrupulously and crudely Krogius was losing to Petrosian. I couldn't leave Petrosian as the sole winner of the championship. In an excellent position I made an incorrect piece sacrifice, and soon resigned.' 'But what about me?' protested Korchnoi. 'In that way you were betraying me as well!' 'You were in a bad way, I thought you were losing, and I couldn't leave Petrosian as the sole winner,' Bronstein explained.

It is necessary in throwing a game to do it with some semblance of chess skill, however. An occasion when the hidden plot appeared too glaringly obvious was in the notorious Interzonal (the play-off to select the Candidates for challenger to the World Champion) at Palma in 1970, when Mark Taimanov of the Soviet Union needed a win, playing against Milan Matulovic of Yugoslavia in the last round, to be sure of qualifying. As the tournament book baldly noted, 'Matulovic strolled in at least fifteen minutes late, sat down, filed his finger nails, looked at the newly issued bulletin that had been lying at his board side . . . Between moves Matulovic strolled around looking completely unconcerned – at variance with his normal tense, shortish paces . . .' Having wasted the best part of an hour playing the opening, Matulovic then proceeded to tear through the middle game at a whirlwind pace to a lost rook and pawn ending. The evidence, as William Lombardy and David Daniels observe, recalling this incident in *Chess Panorama* (1975), was merely subjective: the loser (whose vanity evidently impelled him to show that he was not being beaten on merit) was seen to spend most of the game wandering round the tournament hall chatting to friends, giving the impression that he was not involved in a real contest. Whatever Taimanov's culpability in this affair – the price was rumoured to be $400 – fate had a nasty surprise in store. He had to face Fischer in the Candidates' the following year and was *ker-runched* 6–0.

Perhaps the most elaborate case of a game being thrown in modern times, elaborate in the sense that the chess spoke for itself, was the game Vizantiadis–Ciocaltea, Athens 1968. It had been made clear to all and sundry by Trifunovic, the Yugoslav organiser of this tournament, that the notorious Greek Colonels who held power at that time required and demanded, as a condition for putting up the money to stage the event, that the Greek players should be rewarded. GM titles were beyond his scope but Trifunovic guaranteed two Greek IMs. This meant, obviously enough, that some players had to lose to them. It so happened that Victor Ciocaltea, the Romanian player, was an expert on a very interesting variation of the French Defence, known as the King's Indian Reversed. He had written a two-part article analysing the system at length in the Romanian chess magazine, including in his annotation a victory of his own showing how, by a clever knight sacrifice, he had trounced the Czech player Kozma, at Sochi 1963. 'Ciocaltea knew the defence inside out, backwards, forwards and upside down, with his eyes closed and his hands tied behind his back,' as David Levy, who wrote the affair up in an American chess journal, put it to me. So when the same variation, in every particular, was repeated in the Athens tournament, with Ciocaltea playing Black, i.e. on the receiving end of the knight sacrifice, he might have been expected to put his own analysis to good effect. Instead, surprise, surprise, he lost. His fortunate Greek opponent, not afraid of Romanians bearing gifts, took the point and got his IM norm. Such bizarre happenings, while the exception to the general rule, are well known to the inner circle of chess professionals.

An Indonesian player, so the story has it, needing a vital half-point for his title in a game in Bulgaria, dropped a bunch of car keys on the board, in the middle of his game! He got his title. If chess ever becomes a game of mass entertainment, with big sponsors and television hype, the temptations will no doubt increase.

To return to the main theme of what 'talent' consists of: the master homes in on the 'right' move, where by contrast weaker players skitter around pursuing false trails and dead ends. How is a player to choose a reasonable move in a few seconds? There is not the time to evaluate thousands of positions, or even a few dozen. According to Kotov in *Think Like a Grandmaster* (1971), 'it is better to follow out a plan consistently even if it isn't the best one than to play without a plan at all. The worst thing is to wander about aimlessly.' Planning is a problem for the amateur: after he has achieved what control he can in the centre, developed his pieces and castled, he is at a loss for a continuation. . . . Without a plan, says Kotov, he makes uncoordinated moves or merely waits for something to turn up.

I think the computer programmers can give us a useful hint here. 'Many outsiders regard the chessmaster as a kind of superman,' notes Eliot Hearst, not without irony, in an essay on *Chess Achievements and Chess Thinking*. 'He is presumed to be a person who possesses an extraordinary memory, can calculate many moves ahead with lightning rapidity and probably has an astronomical IQ . . . However, if pressed for clarification about the third characteristic, high intelligence, the layman (and anyone else, for that matter) would have some difficulty answering . . .' What chessmasters do have is 'the ability, at least in chess, to acquire new ideas rapidly, to solve novel problems, to recognise and quickly evaluate similarities and differences between various complex situations, and to isolate the core of a difficult problem without much hesitation . . . It is these latter qualities that probably come closer to characterising the master's skills, and the talents of good problem solvers in any area, than do exceptional memory capacity and calculational ability.' (*Chess Skill in Man and Machine.*)

Here (in another contribution) is a practical example of the chess player's mind in action, in selecting the right move by these criteria (Diagram 4). In the strongest speed tournament of all time held at Hercegnovi on the Adriatic coast in 1970, Bobby Fischer achieved the amazing result of 19 points out of 22, 4½ points ahead of Tal and the rest of the field. In five-minute games, lengthy analysis is not possible.

4

24. . . . Nh8!

'After it was played the point was obvious. Fischer wanted to post a knight on g5 where it would be poised to be sacrificed at the appropriate time for White's pawn on h3. The route is h8–f7–g5–h3.' The difficult part of that move, according to Russell M. and Kenneth W. Church, was deciding on the goal: its execution was straightforward. 'We do not know how many seconds Fischer thought before making that move, but it is likely that the move was made after only a few seconds of reflection. In that time it would not have been possible to trace the implications of all possible moves and replies to a depth of 8 ply [i.e. 4 moves and 4 replies] or greater. Other methods of analysis make this an intuitively appealing move, however, and the intuition was correct in this case.' (*Plans Goals and Search Strategies for the selection of a move in chess.*)

Alas, we can't all play like Fischer. In fact none of us can play like Fischer. On a more terrestrial level, the kind of advice given by Kotov and others, such as 'Be able to assess a position accurately' and 'Be able to hit the right plan' is a bit trite; the trouble with such precepts is that they represent ends rather than means, they state the desired objectives, not the way of achieving them. Thinking, as most of us do, along the lines of 'If I do this, then he does that, and I do this, then . . . he . . . might . . . do . . . that –' is not much use. 'The treatment of the legal move as the elementary unit of chess is concrete but undoubtedly misguided,' according to these analysts of search strategies. What is really required is to *recognise the patterns* – what do they mean? what is their value? how should they be handled? In the openings, particularly, players can recognise patterns from previous experience; in the middle game, while the overall picture may be too complicated to classify, elements of the position will disclose familiar patterns (pin, fork, skewer, discovery, overworked piece and so on). Likewise, endgame patterns (backward pawn, open file) are normally associated with goals and plans rather than specific moves. To simplify, the problem is broken up into manageable pieces; given a meaningful idea, the move may not be so hard to find – as in Fischer identifying the target and then finding a safe route for the knight to attack it.

It is the same sort of process that comes up in chess problems or tests of ingenuity in newspaper diagrams. Once one is told there is a mate in two or a winning combination, it is usually not so difficult to find the answer. In over-the-board play, a player needs to identify the problem first, and then try to find a solution to it. If only one could do that, one's rating would soar . . . up, up and away . . .

Maybe.

# 2

# THE SOVIET MIND

*There are many moves but only one mate.*
*Soviet proverb*

What have these eight players in common?

| | |
|---|---|
| **Gennadi Sosonko** | **(Holland)** |
| **Vladimir Liberzon** | **(Israel)** |
| **Leonid Shamkovitch** | **(USA)** |
| **Anatoly Lein** | **(USA)** |
| **Roman Dzhindzhihashvili** | **(Israel)** |
| **Viktor Korchnoi** | **(Switzerland)** |
| **Lev Alburt** | **(USA)** |
| **Igor Ivanov** | **(Canada)** |

Answer: they were all born, grew up and became masters in the Soviet Union. And between 1972 and 1979 they all left home.

The exit of good and even great players from the motherland of modern chess is one of the most extraordinary phenomena of our times. Why didn't they – privileged and often pampered as outstanding chess players in the Soviet Union are – want to stay there? These players as a team could, on their best form, match any country in the world and could give the Soviet Union itself a fair challenge. Of course they could not play together – they are scattered far and wide, meeting as chess players do in far-flung corners of the globe at tournaments or olympiads. When they meet, what they have in common is the Russian language.

Some of these players left the Soviet Union with permission, with emigration papers in their pocket. Others skipped the KGB 'minders' accompanying the players on their trip abroad and asked for asylum on the spot – Korchnoi in Amsterdam, Ivanov on the way back from Cuba, Alburt in a team match in Germany. It seems easy. It only takes a couple of days before visas are granted, and the exile finds a new country and a new life . . . But that is when the troubles really begin.

In the Soviet Union, as is well known, chess is regarded as a high and serious profession, and youngsters who show talent – green shoots – are cultivated through nationwide coaching so as to bring them to maturity as seasoned competitors. Chess players receive good pay which they draw each month from the State, something like three times higher than an average professional salary; they also get (by Soviet standards) good flats to live in, and sometimes cars to drive; they travel (with official approval) to foreign tournaments where they can earn hard currency and bring back (customs officials turn an indulgent eye) useful or decorative things (women's under-wear is much in demand) for their families. They are the stars of Soviet society. Their lives are favoured. Of course, if a chess player loses badly and, by extension, lets down the Soviet reputation, he may lose such privileges. This can take an extreme form. When Mark Taimanov was wiped out 6–0 by Bobby Fischer in their Candidates' match back in 1971, he became *persona non grata* and was put into cold storage – no tournaments, no travel, no teaching. It took a long time before he was given the chance to compete again and was finally allowed to play in tournaments in Eastern Europe (dinars, zlotys – not at all the same thing!) and gradually work his passage back to official approval. Even Tigran Petrosian, the most subtle operator of the system, though he was not banished after Fischer had crushed him by the not quite so overwhelming score of 5½–2½, had a lean time, and lost the editorship of the all-important chess journal *64*. Korchnoi himself, who committed other and graver offences, such as stepping out of line, answering back to the authorities, and having the temerity to call in question the genius of Karpov, became a non-person for a year. He had to trim and compromise to get back into circulation, though the bitterness of this experience became the breaking point for his defection.

The popularity of chess in the Soviet Union, given the seal of approval by Lenin himself, is nothing new. Chess has been a bright and dominant thread in Soviet culture, running back more than a thousand years to the *byliny*, the ancient heroic epic poems. The game seems originally to have been introduced from the East (as distinct from the Arabic influence in Western Europe), and was favoured by all classes, even obsessively. Here is a revealing entry in the journal of Peter the Great: 21 November 1716, 'Played chess with Bitka all day.' 29 October 1720, 'Played chess all evening', etc. He carried special soft-leather chess-boards during military campaigns, one of which has survived and is on show at the Hermitage museum in Leningrad. Catherine the Great liked the game very much; one of the most beautiful chess sets ever made, by the Tula arms factory, 'unique in its artistic craftmanship and finishing' (I. Linder, *Chess In Old Russia*, 1975) in burnished steel, also on display in Leningrad, was a gift to her. She even bought an automatic chess machine from Wolfgang von Kempelen (see Chapter 6). Ivan the Terrible supposedly died in the middle of a chess game. There are many reports from travellers in Russia, attesting to the popularity of the game, such as this late eighteenth-century vignette from an English historian: 'Chess is so common in Russia, that during our stay in Moscow, I scarcely entered into any company where parties were not engaged in the diversion; and I very frequently observed in my passage through the streets, the tradesmen and common people playing it before the doors of their shops or houses . . .' A latter-day comment, slightly exaggerated for comic effect, no doubt, shows that things have not changed in their essentials; the raconteur is none other than Harpo Marx.

We did two weeks in Moscow . . . One day when there was no matinee I ducked out and went looking for some kind of action. In front of a good-sized theatre, one I hadn't been in yet, there was an unusually long line of people. The line wasn't moving. No tickets were being sold. It had to be something sensational with this many people waiting for a chance to get in . . . I had apparently come in during the intermission. Yet the curtain was raised and the stage was lit. Oddest of all was the setting on the stage. There was a small table and a chair. On the table were two telephones, and a bunch of knick-knacks . . . Then a buzzer sounded. People damn near trampled each other to get back to their seats . . . A boy, maybe 10 or 11 years old, walks out from the wings. He sits at the table. He picks up the receiver of one of the telephones. He listens for a while, then hangs up without saying anything. He moves one of the little props on the table. The joint is so quiet I can hear my wristwatch ticking. The boy moves another knick-knack. A guy comes out, walks to the footlights, announces something to the audience, and the joint goes wild.

People jump to their feet. They yell and throw their hats in the air and embrace each other. The guy who made the announcement shakes hands with the boy, and the cheers are deafening. This is absolutely the craziest show I ever saw. . . .

The Marx Brothers' tour was in 1933. According to the compilers of the chess anthology *King, Queen and Knight* (Norman Knight and Will Guy, 1975), where I found this extract, the identity of the prodigy is not known; the scene itself, however, is entirely recognisable.

During his exile, Lenin played chess with his comrades. He was human enough to be irritated when he lost a game, according to Sir Robert Bruce Lockhart, the first British representative to the Bolshevik government. Gorki, writing from Capri in 1908, reported that Lenin played chess with Bogdanov and both showed great zeal. Lenin would get peeved and depressed when he lost, he noted, adding that it was remarkable that these childish moods never marred the fundamental oneness of his character. Marx (Karl, not Harpo) was rather more irascible, it seems, judging from a reminiscence of Wilhelm Liebknecht, one of the leaders of the German working-class movement: 'When Marx got into a difficult position he would get angry and losing a game would cause him to fly into a rage!' The official judgment on Lenin's chess was given by *Pravda* in the famous front-page article on Botvinnik's great victory in Nottingham in 1936: 'Lenin's chief interest in chess lay in the stubborn struggle, in making the best move, and in finding a way out of a difficult, sometimes almost hopeless situation. The fact of winning or losing meant less to him. He enjoyed his opponent's strong rather than his weak moves and he preferred to play with strong opponents.' After the Revolution, Lenin apparently could not find time to play chess.

It was Mikhail Botvinnik, World Champion, with two short breaks, from 1948 to 1963, who put Soviet chess on the map (in the same sort of way, one might say, that the first sputnik elevated Soviet science). Botvinnik's story, in his autobiography *Achieving the Aim* (1978), is an inspiring one, marked by courageous struggle and high endeavour. From it emerges, or rather it itself embodies, the Soviet ambition to achieve mastery in chess through the winning of the World Championship by a Soviet player. With the coruscating exception of Bobby Fischer's interregnum, the World Championship has indeed been held in Soviet hands for the past thirty-five years; before that Alexander Alekhine, whose questionable conduct during the war years when he more or less collaborated with the Nazi regime in France has left a distinctly bad odour about his name, does not really count. The point is that chess is the one sport at which the Soviet Union not merely excels but dominates and through it – this is in no way an exaggeration – the Soviet Union believes it gains admiration for its whole way of life. (As an extreme case, compare the niggardly East German attitude to sport, where the authorities will not send any sportsmen to compete abroad unless they have a realistic chance of getting into the first three, so reflecting credit on the regime.)

It was not Lenin but his comrade in arms N. V. Krylenko who should be honoured as the founder of Soviet chess. Botvinnik's story describes how in 1924 Krylenko formed a massive new chess organisation based on the Trade Unions and Physical Culture Councils (imagine that in Britain or America!). He loved chess passionately. 'He played chess by post, took part in team events, spoke at chess meetings, wrote articles, edited chess publications and had a touching care for chess masters . . . He could see right through people at the saying goes; it was hard to fool him. When he took over the leadership of the Soviet chess organisation he carried out a sort of revolution in Soviet chess life. The game became available to all the working masses, including beardless youths. Chess books and magazines appeared, and the most massive organisation, the trade unions, began to devote a lot of attention to chess. Everywhere chess circles sprang up – at work places, at schools and military units. The Councils of Physkultura and trade unions assigned the necessary funds for the development of chess; there had never been anything like it before in history.'

In the space of a few years, the new generation of Soviet chess players had grown up. The Soviet Championship of 1933 ended in complete victory for the younger players over the old (in their forties!). The task set by Krylenko, Botvinnik goes on, had been successfully carried out. Before the Revolution it was impossible to gain the master title in Russia, so Russian players went to Germany. Now, it was impossible to organise events between Soviet and foreign players. Hence the joy with which Botvinnik received the news that the celebrated Salo Flohr, the Czech player, was proposing a match with him. At that time Flohr was the chess hope of the West and, according to Botvinnik, was counting on an easy victory. In the 1930s 'chess players trembled before him and compared him with Napoleon'. The sports authorities wanted a tournament instead, doubting the Soviet champion's ability to meet Flohr directly, head on, but the doughty Krylenko prevailed. 'It will be a match,' he said. 'We have to know our real strength!' Botvinnik lost two games and Flohr was declared to be a genius; but in characteristic fighting style Botvinnik rallied to level the match in game ten. Before the twelfth and final game, because the play had been about equal, Flohr sent a message proposing a draw. As for his critics . . . 'they quickly readjusted', Botvinnik adds. This was international recognition of the developing Soviet school in chess. Krylenko came to the final banquet: 'In this match Botvinnik displayed the qualities of a real Bolshevik!' And eighteen months later, after an international tournament in Moscow, he became a grandmaster. He also got a car and had his salary raised from 300 to 500 roubles a month.

Next Krylenko got Botvinnik to the great tournament in Nottingham in 1936, accompanied by his wife – an unheard-of privilege. (He felt his results improved in her company.) Krylenko had had to get approval of the Head of State, Kalinin, for Botvinnik's trip – it was an official visit quite as much as any diplomatic mission. 'I was handed straight away passports, tickets and currency. It was a sizeable sum of money, a travelling allowance and something like £100 sterling, just like the People's Commissars got.' And on arrival, 'I came to our Embassy as if it were my home.' (I do not want to give the impression here that Botvinnik was spoiled – on the contrary, he had to struggle every inch of the way; but it was a struggle on behalf of the State.)

He tied for first place in the tournament with Capablanca, then past the height of his powers but still a very fine player. This was probably the strongest tournament every played in England, though the Phillips and Drew tournament (of 1984) was perhaps on a par with it. More to the point of the theme I am pursuing here, Botvinnik treated the Russian exiles Bogoljubov (then living in Germany) – who managed to draw with Capablanca in the last round – and Alekhine, with friendliness and courtesy. Players who had emigrated (or stayed abroad) without permission were reviled in the Soviet press as 'renegades'. On the way home Botvinnik learned that he was to receive an award, the Mark of Honour. At Moscow he was welcomed by a formal reception outside the Byelorussia station, a party at the theatre and a leading article in *Pravda* (as mentioned above), which, having noted that Marx and Lenin had devoted time to the game, claimed that 'the USSR is becoming the classical land of chess'.

Krylenko was very pleased. 'We sent your letter addressed to Comrade Stalin straight away to his dacha,' he told Botvinnik. At that time everybody wrote letters to Stalin about their achievements: Krylenko, realising that Botvinnik was not the kind of person to do this, had organised it all himself. Botvinnik was presented with his decoration at the Praesidium of the Central Executive Committee of the USSR. 'Botvinnik is awarded this order because his success at Nottingham furthers . . . (here the presiding official faltered momentarily) . . . the cause of the Soviet Revolution.'

And what about Krylenko? What was his reward? Commissar for War 1917, Commander-in-Chief Armed Forces 1918, Public Prosecutor for revolutionary tribunals, Commissar for Justice of the USSR . . . 'liquidated in 1938 as part of the Great Purge' (translator of Botvinnik's book, Bernard Cafferty). Krylenko also figures in Solzhenitsyn's *Gulag Archipelago*.

Botvinnik entered into lengthy negotiations to stage a world title match with Alekhine. In this he had official support. 'If you decide to challenge chessplayer Alekhine to a match we wish you complete success. The rest [prize money] can be easily guaranteed.' This telegram was signed by Molotov, but in all probability was dictated by Stalin himself. Soviet players as a whole needed a figure whom they could look to, to win the World Championship. The match with Alekhine never took place in the end, because the champion died. But the intervening difficulties were very considerable, partly through official opposition, because of Alekhine's reputation, partly perhaps through jealousy of other Soviet players.

I add one anecdote from Botvinnik's memoir, to show his dedication to the game. He had fared rather badly in the Soviet Championship of 1939 because of the terrible smoke and din in the playing hall and, he says, the scornful attitude to the creative side of chess. So in his training for the 'Absolute Champion of the USSR', i.e. the candidate who would be given the official blessing and backing for taking on Alekhine, he prepared in a rather weird way. He played training games with the radio on and, after the game, did not open the window and slept in the smoke-filled room. Yes, Botvinnik deserved the extra grant of 1,000 roubles given him earlier that year. And in the coming tournament, he cracked Keres in round three, and won the event by 2½ points. But such are the plans of mice and men . . . two months later Nazi Germany attacked Russia and chess receded far into the background.

Nevertheless, during the war years, Soviet chess managed to keep its resilience and strength in depth, despite the loss of many fine players in battle or on the civilian front. Botvinnik himself, who volunteered to work as an engineer in an isolated post in the permafrost far from the comforts of home, being unfit for military service because of his eyesight, kept alert. He knew the challenge was coming. At one stage he was excused three days a week, on direct orders from Moscow, the onerous task of felling timber, which he found completely wrecked his mental concentration for chess. During this time he annotated all the games of the Absolute Championship, his best work. The official wrangling went on, to play Alekhine or not to play Alekhine – the line which Botvinnik upheld was that while condemning him as a person, he must be given his due as a chess player – and the preparations slowly went forward. In the spring of 1945, with the whole country exultant after winning the war, Botvinnik won the USSR Championship in dominant style. 'The Soviet School of Chess had not only not weakened during the war but had probably became stronger from the creative point of view,' he summed up. 'Its research characteristics guaranteed the swift improvement of young talents; as already noted this was possible because of the support of the State.' His official grant was reinstated. In a famous radio match, the USSR beat the United States 15½–4½. Stalin's tribute was passed on to the players: 'Well done, boys.' At long last, in the spring of 1946, the arrangements for the match with Alekhine, to be staged by the British Chess Federation that August in Nottingham, were completed. And as the letter went off from Moscow, the news came . . . Alekhine had died in Estoril. It took just a decade for his native land to rehabilitate him: the former bourgeois renegade was soon to be hailed as co-founder, with Mikhail Chigorin, of 'the Soviet School of Chess' – a set phrase very common in the chauvinistic period around 1945–60, much less commonly employed nowadays.

For the first time since 1886 there was no recognised World Champion. It was agreed, via FIDE, that a match tournament between the top six players in the world should be held to decide the World Champion. Even then, there were still many slips, official prevarications and doubts, and much hard fighting, on and off the board, before the final tournament to decide the new World Champion could be held. Botvinnik rose to the occasion. He mastered Euwe, Alekhine's erstwhile conqueror; he beat his compatriots Smyslov and Keres; lost to Reshevsky (Fine had withdrawn) and then came back to beat him; finally after 16 of the 20 games he was so far ahead he only needed to draw to take the long coveted title . . . and on VE Day, 9 May 1948, he clinched it.

The House of Unions in Moscow was besieged by chess players . . . an ovation thundered out. The world champion was now a Soviet player. But Botvinnik adds at once: 'This was the success not of an individual but of a whole generation. It took the younger generation of Soviet masters something like a quarter of a century to win the world title and reach the heights of chess mastery. The principles of the Soviet school, the investigatory nature of the new direction in chess exerted an influence on the development of chess thought. The new champion was recognised by the whole chess world.'

Botvinnik's dedication to chess, which emerges from his story as very deep, notwithstanding his extraordinary efforts in sustaining, in parallel, original research in engineering, remained with him. But his attitude to the success he had won was ambivalent. 'After the tournament it became harder than during the actual event – meetings, the closing ceremony, concerts, official conversations. The most difficult thing was without a doubt the consciousness that I had become champion.

'This was an obstacle in living, but I managed to withstand the pressure. My instinct for survival asserted itself. Soon I forgot about the fact that I was champion, and when I did remember and felt somehow uncertain, then I reflected: What is it to be champion? All it means is you have won an event for the world championship, nothing more than that!'

Botvinnik's style as a chess player was marked by great depth and complexity. In his early days he complicated his games, in working out strategic ideas which – even now with hindsight – are hard fully to appreciate. Typically, he would achieve some minimal positional advantage in the opening part of the game which would be exploited, with patience and tenacity, to achieve over the long haul a won ending. Later in his career he chose to play in a simpler style, requiring less physical and mental demands, but always with a deep strategic sense. As an example of the complexity and precision of his conception, here is the long conclusion of a key game against Grigory Levenfish (Diagram 5), outstanding among the pre-revolutionary players in Russia and in Botvinnik's own words endowed with 'a fine mastery of technique, a superb competitive nature' and a long career, winning the Soviet Championship in 1937 at the age of fifty. Botvinnik had not played in that event, because he was presenting his engineering thesis; in the match that followed he was held by Levenfish 5–5.

In this game Botvinnik had doubled his a-pawns and isolated his e-pawn and his pawn structure was a horrible mess. Looking at this position, any half-decent player would take Black's game as won . . . Indeed one can play this game through many times and still not really understand how White managed to win it as he did.

5

| 25 | . . . | Nf6 | 35 | Rxd1 | Qc7 |
|----|-------|------|----|------|------|
| 26 | a3 | Nbd5 | 36 | Rd5 | Rc6 |
| 27 | e4 | Nb6 | 37 | Qd2 | Qe7 |
| 28 | Nd6 | Re6 | 38 | Rd7 | Qe6 |
| 29 | e5 | Ne8 | 39 | Qd5! | Qxd5 |
| 30 | a5 | Na4 | 40 | Rxd5 | Kf8 |
| 31 | Nc4 | Rb8 | 41 | Rd7 | Rc7 |
| 32 | Qf2 | Rxb1 | 42 | Rd8 | Ke7 |
| 33 | Rxb1 | Nc3 | 43 | Rd6! | Ra7 |
| 34 | Rbc1 | Nxd1 | 44 | Rc6 | Kd7 |

| 45 | Rb6! | Ke7 | 57 | Ra8 | Kf4 |
|----|------|-----|----|-----|-----|
| 46 | Kf2 | f6 | 58 | a6 | Ra1+ |
| 47 | Ke2 | Ra8 | 59 | Ke2 | Ra2+ |
| 48 | Rc6 | fxe5 | 60 | Kd1 | Rxa3 |
| 49 | Rxc5 | Nd6 | 61 | a7 | Ke3 |
| 50 | Rc7+! | Ke6 | 62 | h4 | Rd3+ |
| 51 | Nxd6 | Kxd6 | 63 | Kc2 | Rd7 |
| 52 | Rxh7 | Rc8 | 64 | g4 | Rc7+ |
| 53 | Rg7 | Rc2+ | 65 | Kb3 | Rd7 |
| 54 | Kf1 | e4 | 66 | Kc3 | Rc7+ |
| 55 | Rxg6+ | Ke5 | 67 | Kb4 | Rd7 |
| 56 | Rxa6 | Ra2 | 68 | Kc5 | Resigns. |

It meant a great deal to the Soviet State that the World Champion was a Soviet player, tried, tested and internationally recognised. Why was chess so important to the Soviet establishment, in those difficult days of the twenties and thirties after the Revolution, through the hardship of the war years, and beyond? . . . so that still today, holding the World Championship is as important as, perhaps even more important than, it was in that heroic struggle of '48? As Botvinnik shows, it *was* a conscious decision by the Soviet State, to back chess players, to spread the network of coaching, to devote time and money to bringing on young talent; alternating with this ambition, official anxiety was continually manifesting itself as to the competence of a Soviet player to take the championship – was Keres better than Botvinnik, surely Reshevsky was more talented than either, was it wrong to play Alekhine, and so on. In the committees of the sports authorities there was rivalry and disagreement. But from Krylenko on, individuals who loved chess, as well as supporting the official line, managed to get the necessary backing for the players. The successes of athletes, football teams and so on, which confer prestige on a country, were almost entirely absent in those days; the first Soviet participation in Olympic Games was not until Helsinki, 1952. Stalin himself, the man responsible for the purges of hundreds of thousands of innocent Soviet citizens, infernal architect of the whole apparatus of the Gulag archipelago, was associated with the virtuous process of bringing Soviet chess to the fore.

Interestingly enough, in our own day another major power has decided to throw its considerable weight behind chess . . . China.

What will the one billion Chinese achieve? Judging from early results, a great deal, especially in women's chess.

The Chinese did not come into international chess until the late 1970s. It was an official decision, recommended by the Chinese sports federation, to promote the game. Without such recognition from on high, it was very difficult to make any progress, so it was explained to me when I met Mr Niu Zhong of the All China Sports Federation. Apart from speaking English fluently, Mr Zhong had a very clear idea of what it was that made China take off as spectacularly as it has – money. In fact there is never enough money for the exchange of visits and organising of competitions that the Chinese want. The limited funds that have been made available are used for taking part in olympiads and Asian games. (The cost of airfares is a permanent handicap on developing countries' improvement.) The first olympiad that the Chinese took part in was at Buenos Aires in 1978. In the first round the Chinese top board Chi Ching crushed the Icelandic player Sigurjonsson, who was then reproached by Dutch GM Jan Donner with the words, 'How can a European grandmaster lose to a Chinaman?' The answer to the question came soon enough, when Donner met Weh Chi Liu a few rounds later (Diagram 6).

6

| White to play and win. | | | |
|---|---|---|---|
| 15 | Qh7+ | Kf7 | |
| 16 | Qxg6+ | Kxg6 | |
| 17 | Bh5+ | Kh7 | |
| 18 | Bf7+ | Bh6 | |
| 19 | g6+ | Kg7 | |
| 20 | Bh6+ | Resigns. | |

It is mate in two.

According to David Levy, who used to play for Scotland, reporting the event, Donner expected that this defeat would immortalise him in Chinese literature, just as Kieseritsky was immortalised by his famous loss to Anderssen in the mid-nineteenth century in the 'Immortal Game'.

'When you want to develop something, you must have funds. Domestically we organize national championships once a year. That also requires money, but not foreign currency,' thus Mr Zhong. The great leap forward in Chinese chess stems from this official recognition and also from the fact that the Chinese have another form of chess, Chinese chess, which is very similar.

The traditional Chinese chessboard (Diagram 7) consists of two sections of 8 squares × 4 which are separated by a river one square wide, says R. C. Bell in *Discovering Old Board Games* (1973). The pieces are placed on the intersections of the lines instead of on the squares, the board thus becoming one of 9 × 10 points. Each half of the board contains four squares marked with diagonals, known as the fortress. The king and *two* queens of each player are restricted to these nine points. The bishops are prohibited from crossing the river and are therefore confined to their own side of the board; the other pieces are free to move anywhere. The chessmen are circular discs with the ranks written on the upper face, in red for one side and in

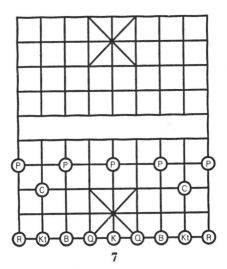

7

green for the other. There is also a unique piece found only in Chinese chess, the cannon, which moves orthogonally (in right angles) in any direction but which, when capturing, must jump over some other piece on the way to the point being attacked; the intervening piece is known as a screen and can belong to either side.

The ideas, the process of thought, the strategy in Chinese chess, are closely akin to Western chess, as they call it. The distinctive feature of the game, as an expert explained to me, is that it it is extremely open, because the pawns are separate from each other. This structure allows immediate and rapid advance of the pieces down the open lines, in the most dramatic fashion. In short, play goes straight into the middle game. In their own game, the Chinese are the strongest country in Asia. This experience makes it relatively easy for Chinese players to make rapid progress in a short time, and achieve some very surprising results. Miss Liu, who only learned Western chess in 1974, qualified for the Women's Candidates' in 1982. And in the olympiad of that year, the Chinese women came equal fifth with West Germany.

The Chinese also succeeded in narrowly defeating a British team (which contained two GMs and four IMs) in 1981, the first international tournament ever played in China. 'After a welcome which totally took us aback – the Chinese team, officials and spectators all stood and applauded as we filed into the room – we settled down at our boards to the gradual realization that the room was extremely chilly and unlikely to warm up . . . while our inscrutable friends sat impassively in heavy overcoats . . .' The winner of the tournament, Robert Bellin, reported that, stylistically, the Chinese are all tacticians, at their best when playing positions where the strategy is clear-cut and small-scale concrete operations predominate. Probably a consequence of playing Chinese chess.

I asked Mr Zhong how it was possible for a tiny minority of people, the chess players, to influence the sports authorities in a country of a thousand million people. His charming answer was: 'Sometimes minorities have correct ideas.' The aim now of this Chinese chess 'minority' is to push the game in schools, to make it more popular. There are only about 7,000 players in the whole country, according to Mr Zhong, so the task is colossal. But great oaks from little acorns grow (look what they did at ping-pong) and the time may not be far off when the first Chinese grandmasters appear in international tournaments. The emphasis will be on schools, because it would be too hard, Mr Zhong says, to involve the older generation. As in the West, the authorities do not understand that chess is a sport – they consider it a mental relaxation, not a physical activity. The Chinese women have made such spectacular progress because they play with men.

Still the question remains, why chess? To which Mr Zhong replied very seriously, 'From a cultural point of view, whatever the West does, we have to do, and learn to do it well.' We have been warned.

Soviet dominance in international chess became an established fact, an axiom. The names of the world champions after Botvinnik's long reign – Smyslov and Tal whom he defeated in return matches, Petrosian, finally Spassky – *were* the history of chess. It was not so much unthinkable as that it never seriously occurred to the rest of the chess community that this dominance could be weakened. True, there was the exception of Bobby Fischer, but no one could ever be sure that his wayward genius could be brought under the discipline of World Championship rules and regulations. Right up to the start, and even after the start, of the great Fischer–Spassky match in Reykjavik there was an awful doubt that Fischer might not go along with the official arrangements. So his individual case did not really challenge Soviet supremacy overall, even if it proved, in the end, that there was another and stronger player alive in the world, alive and kicking one might say.

What first changed the picture was not Fischer himself so much as another very surprising and indeed marvellous event, a match arranged between the Soviet Union and a 'Rest of the World' team in Belgrade in 1970. This was an epic event. I remember the thrill of coming across a little yellow book by the ubiquitous David Levy entitled *The Match of the Century*, which captured the sheer excitement of that occasion.

The teams were of heroic cast. On the Soviet side, in order (ages in brackets), Boris Spassky (33), Tigran Petrosian (40), Viktor Korchnoi (38), Lev Polugayevsky (45), Yefim Geller (45), Vassily Smyslov (49), Mark Taimanov (44), Mikhail Botvinnik (58) eighth board!, Mikhail Tal (33), Paul Keres (54); substitutes Leonid Stein (35), David Bronstein (46). Some team! Average age 43.

The Rest of the World fielded a hardly less impressive line-up: Robert Fischer (27), USA; Bent Larsen (35), Denmark; Lajos

Portisch (32), Hungary; Vlastimil Hort (36), Czechoslovakia; Svetozar Gligoric (47), Yugoslavia; Samuel Reshevsky (58), USA; Wolfgang Uhlmann (35), East Germany; Milan Matulovic (32), Yugoslavia; Miguel Najdorf (59), Argentina; Borislav Ivkov (36), Yugoslavia; substitutes Fridrik Olafsson (35), Iceland; Klaus Darga (36), West Germany. Average age 38.

The prizes were generous. Players and reserves received their travelling and hotel expenses as well as a $500 appearance fee. Fluorescent lighting had been especially installed at Fischer's request in the 2,000 capacity Trades Union Hall. The winner of the Spassky–Fischer match would receive a Fiat 1600, and in the event of a 2–2 tie, $1,000 each; the winner of the second-board Larsen–Petrosian match, a Soviet-built Moscovitch car, with $400 each for a tie.

Everything seemed to be proceeding on course when Bent Larsen decided that he should have been offered first board, in view of his outstanding tournament results during Fischer's eighteen months 'retirement'. He announced his intention of withdrawing from the team unless he was allowed to play the World Champion. The organisers tried to tempt Larsen by paying for his wife to come to Belgrade, but even so he remained adamant. (Well, everyone knows that temperament in chess players makes opera prima donnas look like doctors of logic.). Fischer, in a magnanimous gesture indeed, declared that he would play Petrosian on board two, because 'I want to co-operate.' The Soviet team was probably quite relieved, because Petrosian was then regarded as the hardest man in the world to beat. If Larsen soon had cause for second thoughts, it was a switch which Petrosian must certainly have regretted.

Based on the ratings of the players, Professor Elo forecast a 21½–18½ win for the Soviet Union. Everyone agreed that the match would be won by the Soviet side. Korchnoi thought the result would be as much as 23–17. Fischer was not optimistic about the outcome either.

Bobby's personality no less than his play dazzled the whole proceedings. A minor sensation was caused by Larsen's loss to Spassky in round two, when Larsen played his then celebrated opening pawn b3. He was effectively busted in seven moves. Rather than resign so early, he spent almost an hour on his 12th move, finally resigning in 17. Fischer's play was magnetic. In his first proper master game for eighteen months, he demolished Petrosian in a Caro-Kann – to a wild ovation from the audience – and in the second, when Petrosian chose the English, he repeated the process with Black. Petrosian managed to draw the next two. During one of the later rounds Madame Petrosian was heard to say that her husband was doing badly because he had prepared to play Larsen; a somewhat flimsy excuse, which conveniently ignored the possibility that Fischer himself might have prepared to play Spassky. (More of this redoubtable lady in Chapter 5.)

Fischer was hounded by journalists, photographers and TV interviewers throughout, and even during the night was pestered by people ringing up just to speak to him or ask him questions. He granted interviews more or less on request. 'On one afternoon,' as Levy's witty account has it, 'having nothing else to do, the Serbian Chess Federation took him to a jeweller's and had a gold medal made for him.' The applause he received each day when he walked onto the stage to play his games was only exceeded by the standing ovation he was given when he won each of the first two games. Not only do the Yugoslavs love chess more than life itself, they treated Fischer as if he were a god.

So to the results (Table 1). On the top five boards, the USSR lost 8–12! They lost the match over the first six, seven, eight and nine boards. Only after adding in the tenth and last board did they manage to inch ahead to 'win' the match 20½–19½. As Botvinnik, meanly demoted by his colleagues to board eight, observed in his memoirs, lack of harmony in a team is always punished. (Korchnoi in his account claims that during the play some of the Soviet players walked up and down the stage, rejoicing over the misfortunes of their own team members.) Soviet face was saved by those whom the 'authorities' had not been relying on. One of the Soviet masters summed up, in a significant comment at the end of the match (which was of course a tremendous success from the chess point of view), speaking of the public in the USSR: 'They do not understand. *They think there is something wrong with our culture.*'

*Was* there something wrong with Soviet culture? This Pyrrhic victory over the Rest of the World showed that the Soviet hold on chess was no longer absolute. Other players, other nations, could challenge it and were challenging it successfully. Fischer's genius apart, losing 8–12 on the top five boards . . . that could not be explained away as a fluke. I suppose that in most countries, not just

*Table 1    USSR v. Rest of the World*
*Results (showing the Russians' game scores)*

| Rounds | 1 | 2 | 3 | 4 | |
|---|---|---|---|---|---|
| 1) Spassky | ½ | 1 | 0 | | v. Larsen |
| Stein | | | | 0 | v. Larsen |
| 2) Petrosian | 0 | 0 | ½ | ½ | v. Fischer |
| 3) Korchnoi | ½ | ½ | 0 | ½ | v. Portisch |
| 4) Polugayevsky | 0 | ½ | ½ | ½ | v. Hort |
| 5) Geller | 1 | ½ | ½ | ½ | v. Gligoric |
| 6) Smyslov | ½ | 1 | 0 | | v. Reshevsky |
| Smyslov | | | | 1 | v. Olafsson |
| 7) Taimanov | 1 | 1 | ½ | 0 | v. Uhlmann |
| 8) Botvinnik | 1 | ½ | ½ | ½ | v. Matulovic |
| 9) Tal | ½ | 0 | 1 | ½ | v. Najdorf |
| 10) Keres | ½ | 1 | ½ | 1 | v. Ivkov |
| Team scores | | | | | *Total* |
| USSR | 5½ | 6 | 4 | 5 | 20½ |
| Rest of the World | 4½ | 4 | 6 | 5 | 19½ |

the United States, but in Eastern Europe too, a setback in a national sport would not be regarded as such a seismic event as all that. One can imagine the Americans losing at golf or basketball or boxing, one has seen the English lose at soccer (often enough, alas). Our countries conduct extensive post-mortems into the mistakes made and the sporting lessons to be drawn – fire the manager! sack the team! – and plan anew for the future. But a cultural decline? Hardly.

In the Soviet Union that is not how the authorities look at chess. Because of the immense effort made by the State to promote chess and cultivate chess players, the game is seen from an official point of view as a reflection of Soviet culture. The best players reflect the excellence of Soviet culture, they confirm by their play its high standards. The World Champion, ideally, personifies the qualities of Soviet man at his very best.

Soviet players *do*, of course, play chess most excellently. And in doing so have given the rest of the world's chess players and chess lovers a lot of pleasure. But from the official viewpoint, behind, or perhaps one should say above, the games themselves, stands the strong but incorporeal ideal of Soviet man . . . outperforming, meeting his norms, working harder, playing better, shining with the truth of a superior social system . . .

But . . . but . . . what if the model Soviet chess player, designated to personify the ideal of Soviet man, turns out to have an in-built flaw in him, from the point of view of his Soviet creators . . . What if he is *Jewish*?

I do not intend (you may be relieved to hear) to address the question of Soviet culture here. But Soviet chess as a reflection of Soviet culture is something else. It is perfectly obvious to anyone who cares to look at it that something is rotten in the state of the Soviet sports authorities who run chess. The supervision, the tentacles of control, the KGB officers who accompany players on foreign trips, the trouble players have in accepting invitations abroad, the system of privileges and punishments, the all-embracing apparatus of the State – isn't this a microcosm of everything else that the system represents? Of course there are certainly very many things that can be applauded in Soviet society, and very many things that can be criticised in our own – I am not making that kind of balancing judgement, simply talking about the organisation of chess.

It has produced impressive results but it has also taken a heavy toll. If the story of Mikhail Botvinnik's life and achievements represents the positive side of Soviet chess, then the dark side may be symbolised by the life and achievements of another great player, Viktor Korchnoi. He did not become World Champion, but he came as near to it as anyone could and in the eyes of many people, but for the overwhelming handicaps in his way, partly self-created, he would have become World Champion. As it was, Anatoly Karpov took the throne vacated by Fischer.

The story of Korchnoi's disaffection with his life in Soviet Russia is revealing. He was a 'difficult' character, no doubt, but was he more so than most of the top players in the history of chess? How did he come to flee the motherland? It's a rather petty, unedifying story that emerges, of official pinpricks and persecution, matched on Korchnoi's side by the ups and downs of his own temperament. It is a kind of autopsy of the Soviet chess authorities' attitude, or at least its sinister side.

At the Candidates' Tournament in Curaçao in 1962, the Soviet delegation included (as usual) a man who had nothing to do with chess. 'He was a colonel "in civvies",' Korchnoi recalls, 'as a prominent member of the KGB is usually called. On our return to the USSR, he wrote a report in which he pointed out my improper behaviour at Curaçao. The chief sin noted by him was that I had permitted myself to have a go at the casino!' Such peccadilloes of Korchnoi – this was not the first – were accumulating in his personal file. He began to experience some difficulty in arranging trips abroad. It happened in 1965 that he wanted to go to a tournament in Zagreb in April, but the authorities insisted he should go to Hungary right away in February. He could have played in both but normally a grandmaster is allowed a maximum of two international tournaments a year. He was called in by the Deputy Chairman of the USSR Sports Committee. Korchnoi recalls this conversation (*Chess is My Life*, 1977) very well. 'He told me that J. Kadar himself [leader of the Hungarian Party] had requested that I should play in Hungary. He said: "You know that in 1956 Soviet tanks smashed holes in the houses of Budapest. You have been selected to, as it were, plug up these holes – by your cultural co-operation!"' Korchnoi dug his heels in and refused to go. He was temporarily banned from going abroad altogether. That year he joined the Communist Party 'under the naive impression that, by my participation in party work, I could correct much that I did not like. I also realised that it would make it easier for me to travel abroad.'

Travelling abroad means, first and foremost, earning foreign currency – the (quite legitimate) aim of all Soviet chess masters. There is the nice little story of the Soviet GM at Hastings, who announces just before the tournament: 'I must have a woman!' Consternation among the tournament organisers – 'But Master, this is just an English suburban sea-side resort . . .' 'Yes! I don't know my wife's size and I must buy her some lingerie. I need to find a woman of the same size, please.' Travel means gaining norms, prestige, experience; it's everything for a chess player.

Korchnoi, on the occasion he recounts, was restored to favour, but Taimanov, after his drubbing by Fischer, was stripped, by a draft order of the Sports Committee, of his title 'Honoured Master of Sport' and excluded from the USSR team. 'This draft was given to all the other grandmasters to read, for their edification, and we all signed it in recognition of having absorbed the lesson,' Korchnoi adds. When the order was finally published, Taimanov was kept in the team for a while and so retained his monthly salary. But in his native Leningrad he was treated severely by the Party and suffered further retribution. His engagements as a concert pianist (he was an accomplished performer, another instance of the well-known affinity between chess and music) were cancelled. And in the strain his marriage, his first wife being the other half of his piano duet, broke up. Finally his salary as a chess professional was withheld too.

Korchnoi was growing increasingly irritated by the KGB supervision of his and other players' conduct when playing abroad, and finally, injudiciously no doubt, he found a way of answering them back. After the European Team Championship in Bath, the team reported on return to Moscow, as is the usual practice, to the heads of the USSR Sports Committee (which comes under the appropriate section of the Communist Party Central Committee which, in turn, comes under the Minister of Culture in the Politburo). 'The Leader of the group reports on the results and conduct of the participants. Then the authorities say their piece. It is a tedious procedure, that is repeated year after year . . . there finally came the question: "Does anyone wish to add anything?"'

To interpose a personal anecdote here, I recall a high-powered lunch of newspaper editors at which Golda Meir addressed the company. After defending her position with a voluble and trenchant stream of arguments, Golda paused and turned full-face to the assembled gathering. 'Am I wrong? Tell me! *Am I wrong?*' The cream of Fleet Street breathed not a word.

Not so Korchnoi, he had a prepared opening: 'Chess players, people who travel all over the world, should be trusted or else not sent anywhere at all. Why are these four people [Antoshin and three other official 'minders'] sent along to supervise us? With their meagre experience, all that they did was interfere, more than ever before. And when they were needed, they weren't to be found . . .' And here the intrepid Viktor introduced a really crafty sacrifice into his variation. He explained that playing in a simul in the City of London (in a simultaneous display, a master plays several opponents at once, moving from board to board, making one move at a time), a man came up to him and handed him a protest about Soviet Jewish prisoners . . . and where were those four chess officials who should have been defending him and rebuking this man? Korchnoi demanded. There was nothing anyone could do to Korchnoi because he had shown by his play in the Interzonal that he was a serious contender for the World Championship. Later, this episode was also remembered and counted against him.

With this kind of record and background it was hardly surprising that Korchnoi's relations with the State should deteriorate until they reached breaking point, even though he perhaps did not realise during this time the inexorable conclusion to which events were leading. The climax came with his match against Karpov in the final of the Candidates'. Korchnoi lost, and fairly decisively. His claim, and it is one that must bear serious consideration though in the nature of things it is impossible to 'prove', is that the Soviet authorities wanted Karpov to win. He claims that everything was arranged to his opponent's advantage – trainers, the venue for the match, the hours of play. Korchnoi adds significantly: 'Karpov had been chosen as the favourite, and it was clear why. He was born in Zlatoust, in the Urals, in the centre of Russia. One hundred per cent Russian, he compared favourably with me, Russian by passport, but Jewish in appearance. He was a typical representative of the working class, the rulers of the country according to the Soviet Constitution, whereas I had spent my life in the cultural centre of Leningrad, and was contrasted to him as a representative of the Intelligentsia.'

Let's say straight out that Karpov played better than Korchnoi, in this match and in their two subsequent encounters at Baguio and Merano. Nevertheless, Korchnoi was, as the older man, as the chess dissident, as a highly emotional individual, quite obviously a less desirable world champion from the official viewpoint. In short, the future lay with Karpov.

After the match, which he had won 3–2 with 19 draws, Karpov, naturally enough, was eulogised. The highly embittered loser was not asked in the press interviews for his thoughts on the match. So when invited to say a few words for the Yugoslav press agency, he couldn't resist. What was published was toned down, but Korchnoi left no one in any doubt that he considered Karpov no more talented than other grandmasters he had beaten in the cycle, and that he agreed with Fischer's idea that draws should not be counted. When news of the interview filtered back to Moscow, the flak hit the fan. The Sports Committee demanded a written explanation. According to Korchnoi, his criticism of Karpov was 'of course a crime, but was nevertheless an internal matter', whereas his support for Fischer was considered an act of treachery.

There followed an attack by Petrosian in *Sovietsky Sport* under the heading 'Unsporting, grandmaster!' (sweet revenge for Tigran, who had had a bitter spat with Korchnoi after losing to him in the previous round), condemnation by the USSR Chess Federation, then publication of so-called 'workers' letters', calling for punishment of the offender. Other letters, says Korchnoi, comparing the current persecution campaign with the anti-semitic 'Doctors affair' of 1952, were not published. He was called to face a committee in Moscow, but pleaded illness. Finally, he could delay no longer and had to present himself. The charge: 'Irregular conduct'. Punishment: exclusion from the USSR team for a year, likewise from playing abroad; salary to be cut.

Back in Leningrad, where Korchnoi was as public a personality as a pop star, he became for some months a non-person. The authorities tightened the pressure. Their aim was to break his resistance, to get him to recant, support the official line against Fischer, and work his passage back to respectability. And Korchnoi was induced, in part, to give way – to his credit, because he realised that Karpov, in his heart of hearts, wanted to face the supreme test, to play Fischer. Korchnoi felt ambivalent about the new World Champion: personally, he says, he bore him no grudge; as a symbol of Soviet reaction, he still bears him a grudge. Karpov, for his part, seems to have acted to assist Korchnoi's rehabilitation. The months passed, invitations came in, which had to be declined, finally he was allowed, after a year away, to take part in an international tournament, not abroad, but in Moscow. It was Korchnoi's turn, assisted in his adjournment analysis by the other dissident in disgrace, Spassky, for revenge against Petrosian. He scored 4½ out of 5 at the finish to take third place behind Geller and Spassky – not bad after a year of anxiety.

But the iron had entered his soul. He realised that with his obstinate nature he would have to make a radical change. A chess player's span is limited, the time would come when he would be playing less strongly, and then the authorities could demote him. Should he submit an application to emigrate to Israel? For the moment, in anticipation of the next World Championship cycle, he was sent abroad. Neither his friends nor his wife could understand completely how he felt, even though those close to him, notably his son, were also marked by the bitterness and disgrace which attached to him. He no longer phoned the people who had dropped him during the darkest days, he did not write for chess periodicals. When the Chess Federation pressed him to know whom he intended working with in preparation for the Candidates' matches, he gave no reply. Korchnoi did not want to risk putting anyone in the authorities' bad books, he says, in the event of his leaving the country for good. In July of that year, 1976, he played in the IBM tournament in Amsterdam. (He had already sent off his chess books and photo albums for safe keeping.) Speaking out again, he gave an interview to Agence France Presse, in which he opined that it was disgraceful that the USSR should refuse to play in the olympiad in Israel. On another occasion he said he considered this was a continuation of the traditional policy of anti-semitism. It was only too obvious what sort of reception he could expect if he returned home. On the last day of his stay in Holland, when he should have reported back to the Soviet embassy in the Hague, he finished a simultaneous display and went off to friends in Amsterdam. He requested political asylum.

This was not the end of Korchnoi's story as a chess player – on the contrary, he went on to achieve great things (even though he never quite vanquished Karpov) thus showing, in his late forties, at the age when most chess players are over the hill, that his creative talents had been at least partly stifled inside the Soviet Union. His conclusion was prophetic: 'I am not the first, and will not be the last, to seek a release from the far from creative atmosphere inside the Soviet Union, and to resort to running away. But in the Soviet Union I enjoyed a degree of perfectly official popularity that neither Solzhenitsin nor Sakharov could boast of, nor even Rostropovich or Barshai, public figures who are much better known in the West than I am. I was seen on the television screen by tens of millions of people. I was greeted, and my speeches listened to, by hundreds of thousands. For dozens of years the papers talked about me – Stalin, Malenkov, Krushchev and Brezhnev gave way one to another, but my name did not disappear from the press . . .'

There was, there is, of course, a case for the prosecution, a counter-explanation to all this. By one of those funny coincidences that sometimes happen, Karpov's and Korchnoi's autobiographies both have exactly the same English title: *Chess is My Life*. Karpov's story, written in the main by his collaborator, Soviet chess journalist Alexsandr Roshal, attributes Korchnoi's character and conduct to the 'Salieri complex'. It's an interesting idea, especially for anyone who has seen *Amadeus*, Peter Schaffer's clever play about the relationship between Mozart and Salieri. The Salieri complex, I take it, is the jealousy felt by the man who merely has talent for his rival who has genius.

This is how Roshal puts it: 'If one makes a comparison between leading chess players and great musicians – Paganini, Tchaikovsky, Mozart . . . one cannot but compare Korchnoi with Salieri. And it is by no means simply a matter of a kind of similarity in performance – in other instances too this would be highly conventional. The analogy is suggested more by the way that Salieri is depicted in Pushkin's drama, and by the way that Korchnoi reveals himself to us when he gets up from the chess board. When talking with Korchnoi after a game, one is staggered by his forthrightness and the way he reproaches himself. But it would be all right if that was all. He opens a valve for his prickly emotions, which he professionally restrains (though even so, less well than the majority of grandmasters) during a game, and gives vent to his lack of objectivity. And if it comes to talking about his young and highly-talented conqueror, Korchnoi rarely manages to conceal his envy, which takes the form of searching for the other's deficiencies. It may be objected that Salieri acknowledged Mozart's genius . . . At heart Korchnoi also acknowledges it, but outwardly disclaims it. And therefore we have an instance merely of a variety of the "Salieri complex" augmented by non-objectivity.'

Pushkin's jewel-like 'little tragedy' *Mozart and Salieri* has Salieri confessing (in the translation by Antony Wood):

> Born with a love of art, when as a child
> I heard the lofty organ sound, I listened,
> I listened and the sweet tears freely flowed.
> Early in life I turned from vain amusements;
> All studies that did not accord with music
> I loathed, despised, rejected out of hand;
> I gave myself to music. Hard as were
> The earliest steps, and dull the earliest path.
> I rose above reverses. Craftsmanship
> I took to be the pedestal of art . . .

And then, in the jealous accusation which leads to Salieri taking Mozart's life:

> O where is justice when the sacred gift,
> Immortal genius, comes not in reward

> For toil, devotion, prayer, self-sacrifice –
> But shines instead inside a madcap's skull,
> An idle hooligan's? O Mozart, Mozart!

In chess terms, Roshal draws a distinction between players of amazing natural talent – Smyslov, Tal, Petrosian, Spassky, Fischer, Karpov, who suddenly burst into the world of chess like rockets – and on the other side Korchnoi, who required years of intensive work and polishing of his professional ability to make him a very strong grandmaster. It was always his qualities as a strong-willed competitor that have been most prominent, Roshal argues, and never his natural ability. 'That which came to Korchnoi with enormous difficulty was frequently surmounted with ease by the Champions, as if they were simply playing: they came, they saw, they conquered. He would devote all his strength to overcoming one, when another would appear . . . And now, when it appeared that he was close to his goal, a new star flashed onto the scene – Karpov.'

What else could Korchnoi do? Roshal asks. 'He couldn't do the same as Pushkin's character. So as loudly as possible he slammed the door.' Dismissing Korchnoi's complaints against the Soviet system as 'simply ludicrous', Roshal then puts the boot in good and proper: 'Korchnoi's morbid pride, inordinate vanity, and self-assurance in his relations with his colleagues and opponents at the chess board were well known, and were frequently pointed out to him . . . after his defeat, in bitter and irresponsible interviews to the foreign press, [he] spoke disrespectfully about the winner, and did everything possible to disparage his play and the result of the event as a whole . . . The USSR Chess Federation came to the following decision: for actions unworthy of a Soviet sportsman, Korchnoi was disqualified and deprived of his titles of Honoured Master of Sport, Grandmaster and Master of Sport of the USSR.'

Right or wrong? Or was there right and wrong on both sides? I leave this question to the reader as juror.

When a sailor jumps ship, that is the end of it. Korchnoi was not just any dissident, whose disappearance could be ignored by officialdom. The public had to be informed. First, claiming his whole course was due to wounded pride and vanity, Tass reported it, for publication abroad, not in the Soviet papers. Then, after three weeks, the Chess Federation made an official announcement. And shortly after that the campaign started to exclude him from the next round of Candidates' matches for the World Championship. To this end a letter from all the Soviet grandmasters was fabricated, citing his treachery to the motherland and emphasising particularly that he was unable to conduct himself properly at the chess-board. It was painful for Korchnoi to read on this list the names of men with whom he had exchanged ideas, and their daily bread and butter, for twenty years past. Some probably never even saw the letter to which their signatures were affixed, others were 'persuaded' to sign. Korchnoi adds that this crude attack by the Soviet authorities was not supported by Karpov himself.

Here another side of the story emerges, which would be funny if it were not so *nye kulturny*. Korchnoi's fame and presence in the chess world could not be wiped away, as by a cloth over a blackboard. Despite strenuous Soviet efforts in FIDE to have him excluded from the Candidates' Tournament, he had the international community behind him; and he went on to beat Petrosian, then Polugayevsky, and finally Spassky, to earn the right to challenge Karpov again. These games had to be reported, somehow, in the Soviet sporting press. But it was gall and brimstone to have to print such a detested name. He was in Soviet eyes a non-person. So the chess reports simply left his name out, wherever they could, referring to 'the opponent' or some such circumlocution. Occasionally his name got past the censors, perhaps depending who was on duty that day. All though the long-drawn-out, fluctuating marathon at Baguio, the authorities had to live with the awful fear that Korchnoi might win.

That contest, as everyone knows, was an abusive and degrading affair, in which Korchnoi's paranoia was the dominant emotion. In my humble judgement, he beat himself. His frustration, the sense of grievance and resentment and anti-Soviet feeling which he displayed, got the better of his chess and affected his play. Which is another way of saying that, in the end, the Soviet system got him. All this time, of course, the authorities were hanging on to his wife and son, refusing to let them out.

But the censorship, as I say, is funny in its own ghastly way. 'The whole point of Soviet coverage of the event,' noted Bernard Cafferty, editor of the *British Chess Magazine*, and a close student of Soviet affairs, 'was that before the match it received practically no publicity, during the match the attention given to it varied according to how Karpov was doing, and at the end the result was greeted with the rapture accorded to winning a war.'

*64* had a full-page article devoted to Karpov's departure, but failed to say who he was playing! In the early games, the space given to the match in *Pravda* and *Izvestiya* was minimal, just the bare game score. In all earlier matches many column inches were given over to annotations by leading GMs. Once Karpov took the lead coverage improved a little; when Karpov went ahead 4–1 press publicity rose accordingly; but then when Karpov started losing, the announcements became terse to vanishing point.

When Soviet exiles are involved, Soviet chess fans frequently have to deduce what happens by the absence of information, or by referring back to the list of the players at the start of a tournament and working out who was due to play whom in a particular round. Thus when Jacob Murey went back to Moscow for the Interzonal in 1982 – since he was an emigrant to Israel, not a defector, the Russians in the end had no choice but to comply with FIDE rulings in accepting his presence – they did not report his games. He had also committed 'the cardinal sin', as Leonard Barden, the English chess writer put it, of joining Korchnoi's team for the Baguio marathon. His results were reported deadpan, without comment.

The reporting of Ivanov's meteoric play in the Interzonal in Mexico that year was even weirder. Igor Ivanov – what could be more Russian than that? He was not one of the Jewish exiles – far from it. In appearance a chunky, tousled all-North-American guy, he jumped the aircraft at Gander and settled in Canada in 1979. When he started to play in the Mexico Interzonal *Sovietsky Sport* gave his name (for the first time since 1979) and results normally, even when he beat Soviet players. Then, as Barden reported, 'two rounds from the end, there appears to have been a panic in the censor's office. Ivanov's name disappeared, and instead of detailed reports there was no complete list of finishing scores.' Attentive readers had to work out from the tournament pairings what was happening, and draw the appropriate conclusion, that Boris Spassky failed to qualify because he was unable to win his 'hardest match' in the final round. Hardest match against *whom*? Thus does the beady-eyed head of the Soviet censor have to swallow its own tail.

No doubt we make our own misjudgements in the press in the West, and I cite one of my own. During the Baguio and Merano matches, when I was working on the London *Times* as diplomatic correspondent, I took up the cudgels on Korchnoi's behalf in one or two leaders on the subject of his wife and son, held in Leningrad.

The case on humane grounds was overwhelming and unanswerable. In chess terms, Korchnoi claimed he started every game 'two pieces down'; but at such a distance from events, I did not appreciate Korchnoi's mixed feelings about his family, and the rather special interest Korchnoi's friend and helpmate Petra Leeuwerik had in exploiting the game for her own anti-Soviet crusade. Some time after Korchnoi's final defeat in Merano – having again sweated through the long haul of the Candidates' matches, he was exhausted, a burnt-out case – the Russians finally let his wife and son go. He did not meet them at the airport.

During these years, may I confess, I felt a certain hero-worship for Korchnoi. His fighting qualities were so strong – swimming every day to keep fit, training to keep his mental powers alert, taking on the whole bloody system single-handed – his struggle seemed so admirable. But he too, in time, fell a victim to the system which he was fighting. How else can one explain – and balance requires this in itself trivial incident to be recorded too – his extraordinary lapse in respect of one of his own seconds at Baguio, Raymond Keene? All this time Korchnoi was ostracised by the Russians, who refused to play in any tournament if he was present. So a petition was sent to FIDE, organised by Ludek Pachman, the exiled Czech GM, protesting on his behalf and calling for the principles of sportmanship to be defended. But by then, after failing so narrowly to beat Karpov, Korchnoi had turned on his former aides and begun to blame them. This animosity went to such extremes that at one point he managed to exclude Keene from an international tournament in Switzerland (where he had taken up his new residence). The organiser of the tournament wrote to Keene that 'as a consequence of the circumstances that you and V. Korchnoi . . . are not on the best of terms any more, I see myself forced to withdraw your participation . . .' – a bitter twist.

By the start of 1984, largely thanks to the efforts of Keene and others, the unofficial boycott of Korchnoi – which was really a consequence of the kowtowing attitude of tournament organisers – seemed to be coming to an end. Karpov played him in a tournament in London: and for the first time in six years they shook hands.

To spell out the theme which has been only implicit in the account I have given thus far: the modern chess exiles were Jewish, yes; but so were most of the great Soviet players, and so most of them still are, in the decade of the 1980s. How can it be claimed that the Soviet authorities were anti-semitic, when you look at the long line of players who have some Jewish parentage, who have done so amazingly well in the world of chess? Botvinnik himself has never denied his Jewishness, though as in many cases it seems it was more an inescapable chance of birth than practice or belief. He recalls an incident just after, as a schoolboy, he had beaten Capablanca in a simul, and the boys were good-naturedly ragging him. He was keen on one of the girls. "'You won't get anywhere there," a boy told him. "Murka won't go kissing you, you're a Jew." I was flabbergasted, not so much by the fact that she wouldn't go kissing me, as by the reason why she wouldn't. When I was born my father gave me a Russian name. "He's living in Russia," he said to Mother," so let himself feel Russian."' Later in his autobiography he makes a fine comment. 'I was asked once [in Israel], "What do you consider yourself to be from the point of view of nationality?" My reply was, "Yes, my position is complicated. I am a Jew by blood, a Russian by culture, Soviet by upbringing."'

And after Botvinnik, the players of Jewish origin, in whole or in part, form the heart and soul of Soviet chess: Bronstein, Smyslov, Tal, Geller, Stein (who died young, one of the most brilliant talents), Spassky, Averbakh, Polugayevsky . . . They have not fled the Soviet Union. (Spassky is often described as a 'one-legged dissident' because, uniquely, he seems to have combined a life of extended residence abroad with return visits to the motherland.) They have prospered. They are household names. They are the heroes of Soviet chess.

And yet no one can seriously suppose that the Soviet Union is not deeply anti-semitic, in an ingrained, hateful, officially-inspired way. I do not think one needs to argue the case. So the success of so many Jewish players is something of a paradox. Or perhaps the point is better put the other way round. Jews happen to be very good at chess, as the whole history of the game shows, and have made an enormous, indeed overwhelming, contribution to it, and Soviet Jews are no exception. In that sense, they could not be held back.

But that is not to say that the Soviet authorities liked the fact that almost all their champions until the rise of Karpov had some Jewish connection. The principal reason why Anatoly Karpov is so lauded and applauded by the State, it has been suggested, is that he does conform, for the first time in the history of Soviet chess, to the ideal of 'Soviet man'. Karpov is a conformist – no, that word implies an overly negative image. Rather, as a member of the Communist Party he endorses the Soviet system, through his chess, at many levels. He is always ready to open new clubs, give lectures, appear on party platforms, sign petitions, stand up and be included with the prevailing majority. He always says and does the right thing, like finding the right move! He is, as one of the Soviet exiles Leonid Shamkovitch put it, a representative of the 'poor Russian man' – the expression, in Russian, is redolent of pathos and struggle – the poor Russian man as opposed to, shall we say, the 'rootless cosmopolitan' citizen whose internal passport is stamped 'Jewish'.

If one is looking for a snapshot of the pervasive significance of chess in the Soviet Union, here is a striking instance, from the early weeks of 1983. As the conference on European Security and Co-operation was resuming in Madrid – a very difficult conference which had been dragging on and off for years – the chief Soviet negotiator brought in, for a flying visit, Anatoly Karpov. The World Champion stood before the photographers wearing a bright (too bright) grin. An intriguing moment: very much in Karpov's style of doing the right thing by the authorities. But why bring in the World Champion? Can one imagine the Americans bringing in the heavyweight boxing champ? I couldn't help feeling (without wishing to over-state the case) that Karpov's visit was a way of saying, 'Look! The World Chess Champion is a Russian player, we know all about war and diplomacy, our culture is one which produces the strongest players in the game of war and (by implication) the strongest negotiators in the diplomatic game too . . .' The incident brought to mind the famous lays of the old Russian *byliny*, going back hundreds of years, where the heroes always did battle not only with swords, but over the chess board . . .

> Dear guest, fierce envoy
> Let us play a game of chess,
> And the envoy walked up to Prince Vladimir,
> And they sat down at an oak table,
> The chessboard was brought to them.
> Vladimir, Prince of the Kiev capital,
> Moved, but he did not move far enough.
> He moved again, overstepped himself,
> And the third time made a fool of himself.

And the young guest, the fierce envoy,
Beat Prince Vladimir.

These richly evocative poems show how far back in folk memory
the chess-struggle reaches. All the heroes and their brave comrades-
in-arms of the epic poems play chess. In the national imagination,
says Linder in *Chess in Old Russia*, the game was raised to the same
level as archery and combat. As a test of intellect, it frequently
preceded the joust.

In the case of the rising new star, Garry Kasparov, a potentially
awkward dilemma was avoided. Kasparov is a phenomenon – a
schoolboy wonder, an attacking genius, an obvious world champion
to be. The name he was born with happened to be Weinstein.
Weinstein, Weinstein? What kind of name is that for a Soviet
world champion? Kasparov maintains (in an interview published by
Spiegel-Buch in 1981) that his change of name was not (as suspicion
had it) instigated by the Soviet Chess Federation.

'My father died when I was seven years old and I lived from then
on with my mother and her parents. In her family, everybody's
name was Kasparov, my mother's, my grandfather's, my grand-
mother's. It was therefore totally natural for me to assume that
name too.' He did not, however, do this until some years later,
when he was twelve and had already shown his outstanding talent at
chess. 'This was my own personal affair and I didn't really ask
anybody for approval.' No need to make too much of this: Garry
will set the chess world alight under whatever name.

But it is not quite true, as I suggested in explaining the paradox of
Jewish players' success in the Soviet Union, that they were *all* so
strong that they could not be held back. And here we come back to
the starting point of this particular inquiry: why do these chess
players leave their homeland? To be Jewish in the Soviet Union is
not easy. 'It's a minus,' is the apt summing-up of another exile, Lev
Alburt, 'it's a minus.' That conveys the sense of it all. All Jewish
chess players have, in some measure, to overcome that minus.

As an example of what this means, here is a little news story
clipped from the London *Times* of 2 March 1983. The point is not so
much the report itself as the last sentence.

Seven years for Soviet dissident
Moscow. A dissident intellectual who said there was dis-

crimination against Jewish students at Moscow University was sentenced yesterday to seven years in prison by a Moscow court, Richard Owen writes.

Valery Senderov, aged 37, was co-author of a study which showed that Jewish students were given harder questions and lower marks in entrance examinations for the mathematics department. With Boris Kanyevsky, also 37, who was sentenced last month to five years internal exile, he conducted a detailed survey in secret over several years.

Mr Senderov's harsher sentence reflects the fact that he was charged not only with anti-Soviet activities but also with having maintained 'criminal contacts' with an emigré anti-Soviet organization. Reporting the trial, Tass did not refer to the question of anti-Jewish discrimination.

Alburt and others like him do not stress the Jewish aspect so much, or even at all, in their reasons for choosing life in the West. After all, it's not easy for very many people of whatever ethnic or religious persuasion to lead their own lives in the Soviet Union. Jews happen to be the most publicised minority. So far as Jews are concerned, it is a mistake for outsiders to suppose that they want to lead a normal religious life, with teaching, worship, wearing yarmulkas in synagogue (what synagogue?) and so on. Their Jewishness is something less overt, something they are born with, not necessarily or even tangentially religious. 'The Russians made me realize it,' as Sosonko told me. In chess terms this comes down to the feeling among Jewish players that, all things being equal, the authorities would far prefer a Russian Russian, a poor Russian, to go forward. Murey recalls an incident in a training match where he had clearly demonstrated his superiority over a Russian player; but the latter went through to the higher division. And he had to play forty-three match games to clamber up to that level – that sort of thing. Murey, as mentioned earlier, went back to Moscow for the Interzonal. The other Soviet players whom he met greeted him kindly. But he had another experience in Moscow, which illuminates (as with Korchnoi falling victim to the system) how the Soviet authorities take their toll in the end. Murey is a quiet, slightly sad-looking figure. He had not seen his mother for two years. She was in hospital. 'I went to see her . . . and she didn't recognise me.' Before his next game in the Interzonal he wept at the board.

Such are the individual human tragedies of exile – for those who get away. And for those who want to go and cannot leave, the situation is harsher. Boris Gulko, a former national champion, went on hunger strike to draw attention to his case. He is married to the leading Soviet woman player Anna Akhsharumova. They applied to go to Israel together in 1979. Their application was refused and a series of harassments, including physical roughing up of Gulko, began. The Gulkos were denied, as is usual, all work and all opportunity to earn a living of any kind. In October 1982, after further attacks on him, the KGB took him to a police station and told him he was to be prosecuted for 'parasitism'. They went on hunger strike together.

But chess plays funny tricks on its persecutors. Having previously qualified for the Soviet women's championship, Anna was entitled to take part and play, despite being a non-person married to a non-person. She gave up her hunger strike, travelled a thousand miles, and with only a week to prepare herself entered the championship. And despite having endured the kind of mental and physical strain which chess players in the West can scarcely imagine, she performed brilliantly. She led through the tournament, outpacing the officially approved candidates such as the pre-tournament favourite Nana Yoseliani, a world title semi-finalist. In Moscow, the prospect of a dissident, whose husband was also in open conflict with the authorities, winning the women's championship must have been a nightmare.

Still the authorities wouldn't cheat, would they? Well, of course not! There is doubtless some other explanation for the unfortunate – I choose that neutral word – dispute which arose during the critical eleventh-round game between Akhsharumova and Yoseliani. What happened was that Yoseliani lost on time and the result was duly recorded and reported on Moscow radio (though as usual in 'political' cases only the name of the loser was given). The following day the loser complained that there had been a malfunction of the clock which led to her flag falling early (at the time White still had ten minutes left, Black presumably just a few seconds). Three days later, the All-Union Board of Chess Arbiters in Moscow ruled in favour of Yoseliani and ordered that the game be continued from the point where the local judge and local tournament controller in Tallinn had registered the time loss. White refused to continue, pointing to the breach of the Soviet chess code which lays down that complaints of clock malfunction have to be made 'before the end of play' (not the day after). The sports newspaper duly reported the result: adjourned game – Akhsharumova 0, Yoseliani 1.

Whether in all this Yoseliani herself played a direct role – if she did not, so much the better for her – is irrelevant. For the point is that such a protest, such a ruling and such a result could only have been brought about by the political controllers of chess, by the Inquisition itself. And one can see their point. It would be just too much for the authorities to stomach, for Akhsharumova to be allowed to win the Soviet women's championship after all that had happened to the Gulkos, husband and wife. From leading in the championship, Anna finished up third, a magnificent achievement. As the *British Chess Magazine* noted in a stern editorial, condemning this 'disgraceful incident', the affair was not even mentioned in the two-page report in *64* on the championship. The report quoted eleven separate pieces of play from the event, covering games by nine of the top ten players. One prize-winner's name was not covered at all. The FIDE motto is 'Gens una sumus' . . . but some gens are less equal than others.

It is not being Jewish which drives the chess players into exile. Nor is it the quest for a better standard of life in the West. The idea is current among some tournament organisers that the Russians are mad for money and will gladly travel any distance if the prizes are high. Not necessarily so. True, Soviet players do like to win cash (as who does not?) and in a consumer-goods-starved society the opportunity to pick up items in the West unobtainable at home is a high incentive. But as Lev Alburt, who once lost the most expensive game on record (see Chapter 9), explained to me, money is not the motive. Actually it's very difficult for most of the Soviet exiles to earn a living from chess in the West. In the Soviet Union a professional chess player is used to a salary three times as high as a doctor or an engineer, a flat, foreign travel and other perks, 'and all he has to do is play chess!' In the United States, where Alburt now lives, a chess player earns only a third (if he's lucky) as much as a doctor or an engineer, has little or no status, and is living in effect on his candle-ends. The huge sums which Fischer could in theory earn from chess give a completely false impression of the general run of fortunes in the game. One or two exiles appear to have given up their chess (Liberzon and Kushnir in Israel).

No, the exiles leave because they do not like always having to obey the authorities. Having to travel when and where they are told, having to represent the State in ways which seem odious, having to conform in all kinds of little ways. I think that chess is their life still. During the Lucerne olympiad I had a strange, almost surreal, experience of walking through the town one sunny afternoon in the company of four exiles, Shamkovitch and Alburt, and then we were joined by Murey and Gutman. As they chattered in Russian, shrugged and gesticulated in their talk, it was like a scene from some Russian novel, set in a provincial town, where four Russian friends, rather down at heel, slightly feeling the cold, discuss something urgently and excitedly, which makes them forget the rather depressing circumstances of everyday life . . . and what were they discussing so urgently? The draw for the Interzonals.

To sum up the reasons for leaving I take a non-Jewish exile, a very Russian Russian with a very Russian name, Igor Ivanov. 'I wanted to be free, to make my own life, to do what I wanted without asking permission for everything. For a Jew it is easier to go. For me it was impossible.' One might not perhaps cite Ivanov, known to his mates in the Canadian team as 'the big I', as the ideal representative of libertarian values – he left behind him in Moscow a wife and children and apparently has no desire to see or hear of them again. But that's his business. He is a chess player, who had everything going for him, non-Jewish, no hang-ups, who just wanted to lead his own life. So on the way back from Cuba he did not reboard the plane at the stopover in Gander. The plane waited two or three hours while the Aeroflot people asked him if he really wanted to stay there or change his mind and come home. Rather decently, they slung out his luggage for him, less his games and papers, so he had some clothes . . . and three years later in 1982 he was Canadian Open Champion. As Ivanov might put it, looking back at his young life, win some, lose some.

# 3

# JEWS

*For a game it is too serious, for seriousness too much of
a game.*
*Moses Mendelssohn, 1729–1786*

Jews like to think of themselves as mild and peaceable people, but
the frequency of doctrinal disputes and rivalries suggests otherwise.
'Chess,' observed Reuben Fine in *The Psychology of the Chess
Player* (1967), 'is a contest between two men which lends itself
particularly to the conflicts surrounding aggression.'

Strange, given the way Jewish parents so often fulfil their fondest
hopes in the achievements of their children, that one has never
heard the maternal refrain, 'My son the chess player!' Because the
involvement of Jews in chess is extraordinary. It goes back to the
middle of the nineteenth century, according to the *Jewish Encyclopedia*, though various references to chess in Jewish writings
appear well before then during the Middle Ages. There were
diverse views among Jewish scholars (well, of course!) as to whether
the playing of chess should be encouraged. Maimonides (1135–
1204) expressed disapproval of chess when it is played for money,
coupling it with backgammon. The *halakhah* (Jewish legal teaching)
disapproved of chess as time-wasting, an attitude paralleled in
Byzantine and Canon Law. On the other hand many scholars,
Jewish and Christian, appeared to express approval, and several
popes played chess. Gradually opposition to the game abated
among both communities, as it was distinguished from gambling
games and time-wasting games.

Discussing 'Chess among the Jews', the great chess historian
H. J. R. Murray (1913) begins by making the interesting point that
there is no evidence to support the view that Jews obtained a knowledge of chess in any other way than from their Christian neighbours,
or that they played an independent part in the development of the

game in Europe. One might have supposed that there was a more or less direct link with the East, with chess in Muslim lands. But Murray says that the frequently expressed belief that chess is mentioned in the Babylonian Talmud has no basis in fact, and arose from blunders on the part of commentators. Chess very early attained to considerable popularity with the European Jews, Murray continues, and as a result had to pass through a period of suspicion on the part of the rabbis. Maimonides, who seems to refer to a forced mate, declared professional chess players to be unworthy of credence in the law courts. (One can imagine, even at this modern date, what he meant!) But judging from this relatively mild and virtually isolated censure, there was nothing corresponding to the swingeing condemnation of chess which occurred at one period in the early Christian church. A prime example is the famous letter, probably dated around the end of 1061, from Cardinal Damiani of Ostia, attacking the clergy who took part in lay sports and amusements.

'I restrain my pen, for I blush with shame to add the more disgraceful frivolities, to wit hunting, hawking and especially the madness of dice or chess . . .' Damiani relates how he took to task the venerable Bishop of Florence for playing chess with his companions, when they stopped to rest overnight during a journey: 'was it your duty at evening to take part in the vanity of chess, and to defile your hand, the officer of the Lord's body, and your tongue, the mediator between God and His people, by the contamination of an impious sport, especially when canonic authority decrees that Bishops who are dice players [*aleatores*] are to be deposed?' In reply, the Bishop made a very good defence: '*Scacchus* is one thing, *alea* another; that authority, therefore, forebade dice-play, but by its silence permitted chess.'

But Damiani was not a man to be put off by such a liberal interpretation. He asserted flatly: 'The decree does not mention. "*scacchus*" but includes the class of either game under the name of *alea*. Wherefore, when "*alea*" is forbidden, and nothing is said expressly of *scacchus*, it is established beyond the shadow of a doubt that each game is included under the one name, and condemned by the authority of one decision.' The Bishop, a prudent man, humbly assented. Some writers have identified him as Gerard, who was himself elevated to the papacy as Nicholas II immediately after Alexander II, to whom this letter was addressed, which would be a nice irony. But Murray says this identification is only a guess. The only way Damiani's argument makes sense, he explains, was if he was referring to chess-playing with dice, as it often was in those days. More likely (I suggest) Damiani was exhibiting the full force of the intolerant mediaeval mind. His prohibition led to a number of similar decrees but they ceased before 1400 as the Church, following the nobility, came to take a more enlightened view of the game.

Chess plays a curious part in the mediaeval legend of the Jewish Pope Andreas. As Murray gives the story: 'The Pope is described as devoted to chess, and this brought him into contact with many Jewish players, among others with Rabbi Simeon (Simeon ha-Gadol), an historical character who lived in Mainz at the beginning of the eleventh century, who was esteemed as the first player of his time. The Pope defeated the rabbi in play, but the rabbi recognized him as his son Elhanan through his making a particularly strong move which he had taught the latter in childhood.'

Four Hebrew works on chess survive from the Middle Ages, three of them in verse. One is a poem of seventy-six lines, ascribed to the celebrated Spanish rabbi Abraham ben Ezra, born in Toledo in 1088. In its English translation, the poem is a lively description of the rules of chess obtaining in Spain at that time, with the nice touch that the black pieces are described as Ethiopians and the red as Edomites (*edom* being Hebrew for red). Note that Black makes the first move.

I sing a song of an arranged battle
Ancient, invented in the days of old,
Arranged by men of prudence and intelligence,
Based upon the eight ranks . . .

. . . The Ethiopians stretch out their hands for the struggle,
And the Edomites move out after them.
The Pawns come first of all
To the battle in a straight march,
The Pawn marches straight forwards
Yet he turns aside to capture the foe . . .

. . . And if by chance the King is caught
And ensnared pitilessly in the net
And there is no way out to save himself, and no refuge
And no escape to a strong city of refuge,
He is doomed and removed by the foe;
There is none to save him, and by death he is mate . . .

The poem has a rather pleasing ending:

Yet doth the battle begin over again,
And the killed ones once more stand up.

– a conclusion likely to appeal to the frequently persecuted Jewish communities of those days.

The overwhelming involvement of Jews in modern chess is most simply indicated by listing the names of celebrated players given in the *Jewish Encyclopedia*. In the mid-nineteenth century Daniel Harrwitz (challenger of Morphy) and Bernhard Horwitz; followed by such players as Semyon Alapin, Ernest Falkbeer (exponent of the Falkbeer counter-gambit) and Simon Winawer; Wilhelm Steinitz, the first player to use the title World Champion and Emanuel Lasker his successor; Siegbert Tarrasch ('Praeceptor Germanorum'), Savielly Tartakower (writer and wit, e.g. 'The player who wins is the one who makes the mistake before the last') and Aron Nimzovitch (*My System*, 1925). And as the twentieth century advanced the names increased and multiplied: Akiba Rubinstein (endgame authority), Carl Schlechter, Jacques Mieses, Rudolf Spielmann, Richard Réti (*Modern Ideas in Chess*, 1923), Julius Breyer, Salo Flohr; in the United States, Isaac Kashdan, Samuel Reshevsky, the psychoanalyst Reuben Fine, Arthur Bisguier, and of course Bobby Fischer; just as in Russia players like Ilya Khan and Grigory Levenfish preceded the modern generation led by Mikhail Botvinnik and the constellation of stars like David Bronstein, Mikhail Tal, Vassily Smyslov, Boris Spassky and all the others mentioned in the previous chapter on Soviet chess who have some Jewish link by birth. In the famous radio match between the USSR and the United States after the Second World War, the Soviet team included five Jewish players in a team of ten and the Americans seven; and the British five in their match, including the liveliest spirit in British chess, Harry Golombek. One is not suggesting in the above list (in which more names have been omitted than included) that all these players were Jewish in any committed way, but simply to demonstrate the obvious truth that it is impossible to imagine the history of chess without the Jewish connexion; and to inquire why this should be so.

The usual explanation for Jewish talent at chess is that it has something to do with the habit of mind engendered by Talmudic study. (Rubinstein and Nimzovitch both emerged from *yeshivot*, schools of Talmudic training.) And when you come to look at it, chess thinking *is* like Talmudic dialectic. In exposition, the argument of the Talmud is stratified, it goes by a series of precedents, one stratum of thought being challenged by a divergent perception, and then a contrary opinion, each one enriching and playing back and forth over the others. Here is an example of how a question is discussed in the Talmud:

> During what time in the evening is the reading of the *Shema* [the basic affirmation of Judaism] begun? From the time when the priests go in to eat their leave-offering (see Lev.xxii.7) until the end of the first watch of the night, such being the words of R. Eliezer. The sages, however, say until midnight, though R. Gamaliel says until the coming of the dawn.

Answering this point, the Talmud has three sections which correspond to the three opinions. The first, *inter alia*, designates the appearance of the stars as an indication of the time, examines the division between day and night and the meaning of twilight, and proceeds to an exegetic discussion of the number of night-watches. Here is section two, in brief summary:

> Assi in the name of Johanan: 'The ruling of the sages ("until midnight") is the valid one, and forms the basis for the counsel given by Jose (4th cent.) to the members of the academy'. Baraita on the reading of the *Shema* in the synagogue; a question bearing on this matter, and Huna's answer in the name of the Babylonian amora Joseph, an illustration being given in an anecdote regarding Samuel b. Nahman, together with a haggadic saying by him. A contradictory view of Joshua b. Levi, together with pertinent haggadic sayings to the effect that *Shemoneh 'Esreh* must follow immediately the after-benediction of the *Shema* . . .

And so on and so forth.

And here for comparison take, because it happens to be one of my favourite notes, the commentary by Bobby Fischer to the fifth move of the exchange variation in the Ruy Lopez (or rather just a tiny extract from it) in game 56 v. Gligoric, Havana olympiad, 1966, given in *My 60 Memorable Games*.

Black can defend his KP in numerous ways . . . A) 5 . . . B-K2? (played by Reshevsky) B) The ballet dancer Harmonist showed good sense by trying 5 . . . Q-B3 C) . . . B-Q3? . . . as in Schallopp–Blackburne, Frankfurt 1887. D) A reasonable try is Bronstein's 5 . . . Q-Q3!? E) The most ambitious continuation is 5 . . . B-KN5!? . . . Em. Lasker used to win such positions . . . Hort–Kolarov, Poland 1967 . . . Keres in his old book . . .

And so on and so forth. Not so different in style from Talmudic dialectic really, is it?

At the domestic level, perhaps in closed communities and more especially close-knit family circles, chess has a special appeal. Like playing the violin. Why for that matter should there have been so many Jewish violinists? Is there perhaps something about this instrument – warm and vibrant and for a child quite demanding – which made it so appealing to the Jewish hearth and home? Why not another instrument like the flute? It just didn't happen. A piano might be too expensive but anyone could pick up a fiddle somewhere. It seems a not unfair assumption, to put it no stronger than that, that as Jewish families took to the violin, they also took to chess. Easy to acquire, pleasing for children to play, requiring a certain mental effort with more than a dash of art and imagination thrown in; clearly an improving pastime. And from quantity, the sheer numbers of Jewish families which had a liking for chess, emerged quality. Chess, music and mathematics are the vocations of child prodigies. There is something about each of them which enables gifted children to perform far beyond their years; probably because experience, in the sense of experience of life, plays no part.

Taking a more cerebral point of view, two kinds of affinity between music, mathematics and chess are suggested by George Steiner in his reflective essay on chess, *White Knights of Reykjavik* (1972). All three, he notes, being non-verbal, seem to depend on the interaction of highly abstract dynamic relations with a very strong emphasis on spatial groupings. Thus, the solution of a mathematical problem, the resolution of a musical passage, the elaboration of a winning chess position, can be envisaged as regroupings, as releases of tension between energy levels. In each instance, he says, tensions set up by the nervous system operating on highly cerebral use of rules and codes are released, 'affording a palpable muscular-nervous sensation of repose'. The second interrelation he proposes may be neurophysiological in a more obvious, perhaps even genetic, sense. It seems likely that all three activities may trigger powerful but narrowly specialised areas of the cortex which, in a young child, can develop apart from the rest of the psyche. This would explain the child virtuoso or pre-teen chess master who in all other ways is sexually and socially immature. There is evidence, too, that the capacity for highly abstract spatial imagining may be inherited, he adds. 'The large Jewish presence in topflight chess, as in modern mathematical physics and in the performance (though not in the composition) of music, does not look accidental.'

The Dutch psychologist and chess researcher, Adriaan de Groot, recalls discussing the phenomenon of Jews' talent at chess with Herbert Simon, the physics Nobel prize winner. They came up with two hypotheses. First, the phenomenon goes back to a predisposition for the game in Jewish people; secondly, it is a consequence of Jewish intellectual activities, the tradition of learning.

The idea of a genetic bent is not one which scientists like de Groot would care to underwrite. The most that might be said is that for historical reasons, there may be a different distribution of this sort of talent among Jewish people – people intermarrying, the daughter of a rabbi being betrothed to the best pupil of the rabbi, and so on. In any case, since skill at chess is not directly correlated with intelligence, the tradition of learning seems a far more cogent explanation. Commenting on this, GM Robert Hübner offers the perceptive thought that chess was an especially good activity for Jews to excel at, since it was totally independent of society, like a neutral space in which they took nothing from anyone, nor anyone took anything from them. I also think that chess must have been, and still is, a wonderful outlet for Jewish aggression. No better example could be found to demonstrate this trait than Steinitz. 'He fought on the chess board, he fought in chess columns, he argued endlessly with his friends,' says Fine. 'To his enemies he attributed anti-semitism (in this there was certainly some element of truth), and at one time began to write a book on Jews in chess, in order, as he said, to confound the anti-semites.'

Going back to the later Middle Ages – the game was widely played in the ghettoes and became a recognised pastime for men on the sabbath and on festivals, though as a rule on these occasions the stake was omitted, and special silver chessmen were used. In our own day it seems entirely acceptable for orthodox Jews to play on the sabbath. The Chief Rabbi of Britain and the Commonwealth, Sir Immanuel Jakobovits, pointed out to me, rather, that in playing chess on the sabbath the game should not be made to seem too ordinary, too like an everyday pastime.

In his classic account of *Jewish Life in the Middle Ages* (1896) Israel Abrahams lays great stress on the joyousness, 'the coping stone of piety', of Jewish life, and says that few pastimes of the period were excluded. The sabbath was a day of rest, not a day of gloom; games were permitted, a tone of 'elevated joy' prevailed. Despite this enthusiasm – 'To walk abroad in the fresh air on the Sabbath was a favourite delight . . . On the festivals they strolled by brooks and streams, and watched the fishes disporting themselves in the water . . .' – one may question how far the isolated, often impoverished and frequently persecuted Jewish communities could really join in the world of play. Obviously, Jews did not hunt, ride, shoot or fish, the great country pursuits. Nor could they join in the village or town sports which followed the seasons or saints' days. Normally they were not allowed to bear arms. Indoor amusements were, naturally, the closest to hand; Jews rarely invented a game but adopted a good thing when they saw it, Abrahams says. Dancing was most popular, but the sexes were not allowed to mix.

Another class of pastime, Abrahams goes on, was of a more intellectual nature. Arithmetical tricks known as *gematria* were much favoured in the Middle Ages and formed the recreation of rabbinical scholars. The Hebrew letters have a numerical as well as phonetic value, which led to endless ingenuity and entertainment in making humorous or moral connexions (a sort of crossword mentality). Riddles were the most popular form of table-game. Who is mighty? Who is a fool? Who is happy? In their origin riddles were an attempt to solve the mysteries of life, pieces of primitive science dependent on somewhat remote analogies. Many riddles of the Middle Ages were serious intellectual exercises, the most famous of which, a grammatical enigma, was written – as it happens – by the same ben Ezra to whom is ascribed the mediaeval poem on the Ethiopians and the Edomites playing chess, quoted above. He is also said to have composed a pretty arithmetical riddle on chess.

It is not difficult to see, in this domestic setting of piety and high spirits and mental acuity, how chess might have caught on so well.

Chess seems to have first made its way into Jewish circles as a women's game, as did most of their indoor games in the Middle Ages, Abrahams continues. Games were not played every day but women were privileged in these pastimes. And with whom should women play, one might ask, if not with their children? The same prohibition of the sexes which applied to dancing meant that even young boys and girls were not allowed to play together outside, but in their homes it was surely quite natural. And whereas word games and so on must have been beyond children, a game like chess could have been easy to join in. And of course on the sabbath, the men also played. The men had themselves learned as children; and the example to a child, seeing his father playing – with silver pieces – on the day of rest, heightened family admiration for the game first taught at mother's knee.

This sort of speculation of mine fits well with another aspect of Jewish life, the prohibition against gambling. Chess presumably involved far less dangerous consequences than cards, merely 'time-wasting'. It was only chess played for money that drew Maimonides' censure. One authority, opposing all games, complained that chess players spent many hours a day at the game. 'I am not sure that when their minds have – as they claim – been sharpened, these men display their keener wits over serious intellectual pursuits.' Such criticism implies how much chess was favoured. In short, may not Jewish talent for chess, insofar as it is distinctive, simply reflect the Jews at play?

So can one expect that Israel will produce a higher proportion of grandmasters for its population than any other country? You might suppose so: but probably not. Because once the whole range of sports and games is open to a people, any genetic or traditional bent for chess will be bound to lose that concentrating focus which nurtured it, in the first place, generations ago.

# 4
# POLITICS

*I know the knights walke in this game too well,*
*Hee maye skip over mee, and where am I then?*
Thomas Middleton, A Game at Chesse, *1624*

A wooden board, thirty-two chessmen, what could be simpler? You
might not suppose that there was any need for an elaborate international organisation to arrange anything so uncomplicated as playing
chess. But you would be wrong. The politics of chess is enormous,
proliferating, horrendous.

The reason is that chess arouses deep and violent human pas-
sions. The history of the World Championship with its rows and
tantrums and clashes of strong personality is evidence enough of
that fact. Whenever it comes round to organising the World Championship – which is the prime task of FIDE (Fédération Interna-
tionale des Echecs) – the rows come to the surface. The press,
reporting such stories for the general public, is usually surprised at
the bitterness of these rows. But not chess players themselves. They
know 'twas ever thus.

It follows that the President of FIDE is quite an important
personality. Indeed FIDE, with its 120 member countries, has come
to resemble – almost exactly – the United Nations itself. Squabbles,
power blocs, international rivalries, lobbying of votes and behind-
the-scenes intrigue – the whole diplomatic way of life is there. It's a
far cry from the first World Championship match in 1886 when
Zukertort brusquely dismissed what he considered excessive rule-
making: 'When once these gentlemen have consented to meet each
other over the board, it must be taken for granted they will behave
like gentlemen.' The 1886 regulations amounted to less than 1½
printed pages. Now the apparatus of the Championship provokes
continuous argument. Why? The prestige of being World Champion is such that the contestants, or their national chess federations

who back them, want to extract every last possible advantage and interpretation in their favour, a modern extension of Ruy Lopez' immortal dictum, 'Sit your opponent with the sun in his eyes.'

Founded in 1924, divided into twelve zones which run the tournaments which form the basis of the World Championship, FIDE consists of an elected president and general secretary, plus five regional vice-presidents (one each for Africa, America, Asia and Europe and one at large), backed by an official secretariat; advised by an executive council, which meets two or three times a year; supported in turn by a central committee; the whole apparatus responsible to an annual general assembly; with a host of technical and specialist sub-committees in its train. Membership of these various bodies gives the individual concerned influence and importance back home, offers the chance to travel and participate in chess meetings round the world, and generally adds lustre to people who (while they may do much useful work) are not as a rule any longer in the front rank as chess players. But *real* power rests in the hands of the President personally, hence the status of this post. And the news in the 1980s is that the balance of power (just as in the UN) has tilted sharply away from the old guard in Europe over to the developing world. It happened at the congress in Lucerne in 1982 and its effect may be long-lasting.

Fridrik Olafsson, a strong grandmaster and, like most of his Icelandic countrymen, a man dedicated to chess, had run FIDE through a stormy period. It was the time after Bobby Fischer's self-immolation in his over-heated interpretation of the rules for the World Championship, when Viktor Korchnoi emerged as the challenger to Karpov. During the Baguio drama the former world champion, Max Euwe, had somewhat struggled to hold the line as President of FIDE. After that traumatic event international chess obviously needed a period of calm and consolidation and Olafsson to some extent provided it. He applied the rules firmly and clearly and, in particular, upheld the right of Korchnoi to seek the release of his wife and son from Russia – not a course of action, however diplomatically pursued, calculated to ingratiate him with the Soviet authorities. In a similar stand of principle, Olafsson insisted that the exiled Soviet player Jacob Murey should be allowed to return to Moscow to compete in the 1982 Interzonal (see Chapter 2). Above all, Olafsson as an experienced grandmaster had the confidence of chess players themselves. Quiet, firm, self-effacing, he ran FIDE unobtrusively and well.

In deciding to run for a further four-year term in 1982, he could count on the support of the West Europeans and the United States and perhaps a wide arc of newly emerging countries who had benefited, one way or another, from his handling of international chess. In his summing up of his record to the assembly of FIDE, when each candidate was allowed a final two minutes to put his case, Olafsson could point to some solid achievements. The federation had grown to a record membership (second only in sporting organisations to football); he himself was an independent candidate from a country which, though small in population, had produced numbers of GMs and IMs, which showed other aspiring countries what could be done. The income of FIDE had risen by 50 per cent during his term as governments put more resources into chess; improvements had been made so as to award ratings to all players in the olympiad; discrimination against women was being stopped. And so on. It seemed an impressive record.

Bozidar Kažić of the Yugoslav chess federation had been around the chess circuit a long time. Nominally he had the backing of the Eastern bloc, but his candidacy was not taken very seriously and seemed designed more as a tactic to draw the fire of Olafsson's votes on the first ballot. His final address to the assembly was confined to reiterating, in four or five languages, his twenty-five years of service to chess.

The third candidate, Florencio Campomanes from the Philippines, universally known as Campo, was something else. He made no secret of his ambition; as vice-president of FIDE he was quick to take the credit for most of the good work that had been done and not slow to express his scorn about the capacity of the incumbent president. In the days which led up to the general assembly, Campomanes campaigned on the ticket 'A time for change'. He handed out booklets and pamphlets and leaflets, posters proclaimed his name, pledges and promises were given, and on the day of the vote enormous Philippine cigars were scattered around like confetti. In short, if there were any babies to be kissed, Campo would certainly have clasped them in his warm embrace, only making sure that the camera was at the right angle. All this work on the hustings had been preceded by extensive visits to the developing countries, where Campo had presented himself as the shining knight of the

Third World. As his campaign leaflet put it, he had 'travelled to various parts of the world from the mountains of the Himalayas to the innermost recesses of Africa and the sprinkled islands of the Caribbean and Oceania to learn of the problems of chess federations though not members of FIDE in the hope of soon recruiting them into its fold'.

Campo's campaign was graphically illustrated by a series of arrows on a map like a chess board, showing the movement of the presidency of FIDE – from its foundation in Paris in 1924 (first President Rueb, a Dutchman, 1924–49) to Sweden (Rogard 1940–70) to Holland (Euwe 1970–78) to Iceland (Olafsson 1978–82) and thence in a great sweep clockwise across the Pacific Ocean to the Philippines. How could such a campaign be sustained? His candidacy was seen in his own country as an event of national importance. 'When I ask President Marcos for two million dollars,' Campo would boast, 'at worst he wants to know whether he should bring the money straight away or whether I can wait for a cheque in the post.' Indeed the Philippines takes chess seriously, second in popularity to basketball. Campo organised the Baguio match between Karpov and Korchnoi and many other events in Manila over the years, all of which required some degree of official backing. And in the emergence of Eugene Torre as a leading grandmaster, Asia had its own champion in the chess arena. Torre had just underlined the point by qualifying for the 1983 Candidates' Tournament. Campo himself played in five olympiads, describing himself as 'a gifted woodpusher', and was non-playing captain in seven others.

For two decades chess has been dominated by its West European nucleus. New countries who joined FIDE made up for their lack of masters by their enthusiasm for the game. Their support became polarised in geographical groupings, as in the UN itself. The symbolic nature of chess as a pseudo-war, as chess columnist Leonard Barden put it, sparked off a great eagerness to identify victories, both on and off the board, with national superiority. Chess is played in all major nations (Japan though a member of FIDE has its own form of chess, Sho-gi, probably derived from Chinese chess). The Palestine chess federation (the Palestine Liberation Organisation by any other name) was elected to membership, with Israel's the sole vote against, at the start of the Lucerne assembly. South Africa's suspension was not lifted.

In such a context could Campomanes possibly lose? Olafsson's supporters were surprisingly confident. Immediately before the vote, one of the most experienced British delegates whispered to me, 'Have you ever seen a man put down fifty thousand dollars on red, and then see black come up? That's what's going to happen to Campo!' If so, Campo looked remarkably spry, bobbing around all over the place with nods and winks and virtually running the meeting. One by one the delegates cast their countries' votes. (One of the minor absurdities of FIDE is that while the Soviet Union has only one vote, the British Isles have four! England, Scotland, Wales and the Channel Islands. The Russians have never seemed to bother about this anomaly.) The East Germans, who had lacked the courage to play in the olympiad because of their national phobia of not ending up in the first three, had the temerity to vote. Each delegate who dropped his ballot into the box was checked off by the tellers, under Campo's watchful eye. But then one of those things happened which show that life can overtake fiction. Just as the votes were counted but before the result could be declared, the chairman of the proceedings rose to his feet: 'I regret to announce the death of President Brezhnev! We will stand and observe two minutes silence.' Everyone shuffled to their feet. The death of the Soviet leader upset many diplomatic plans but not the FIDE election. Kažić was wiped out on the first ballot. And on the second Campo obliterated Olafsson by the overwhelming tally of 65 to 43. Shortly after, the entire FIDE secretariat resigned their posts, to be replaced by Campomanes' nominees.

It seemed premature to talk of a split in FIDE, as some commentators did. For one thing, having attained his goal in such commanding style, Campo had the chance to deliver on the promises he had made. He intended to be an active president, one who enjoys the limelight. For another thing, if the split was between the new world of chess, now Asia-centric, and the 'minority' of Europeans, there was no need for it. Everyone is on the same side of helping the developing world to achieve more in chess, in terms of encouraging tournaments, creating masters, competing around the world.

At the grass roots, proselytising for chess means distributing chess sets and clocks, organising coaching and helping finance players' travel. The cost of taking part in tournaments abroad is the biggest handicap facing developing countries' players. For example, at the meeting of CACDEC, the Commission for Assistance for Chess-Developing Countries, the West German federation reported such worthy activities as handing over twenty chess clocks to Sri Lanka, providing a seminar for arbiters in Tunisia, making gifts of equipment to Senegal and Zaire worth a few hundred dollars a time. It is pleasant to reflect, is it not, that such small donations probably benefit the recipients quite as much as grandiose aid schemes. The Soviet Union's own contribution, drawing on its pool of grandmasters, was to send players out to the Third World, to give simuls and exhibitions and lectures. Taimanov, treading the penitential path back to grace after his defeat by Fischer, went to Indonesia, Suetin to Nigeria, Kondratiev to Zimbabwe, Geller to Ireland and so on. CACDEC, according to Campo, has broken the ice as no other chess commission. 'It has opened the eyes of the world that chess is played not only in important central areas like Europe but it is played all over and that every man of any race, colour or creed has the capacity to play chess well. And if every man is given the facility of equipment and literature, chess can be developed well in any area of the world.'

One aspect of this worth mentioning is the use of chess as a stimulus to education. In Venezuela, thanks to the enthusiasm for this project by no less a personage than the President himself, Luis Herrera Campins, chess was put on the syllabus of a number of schools in Caracas. The basic idea is 'the democratization of intelligence' which means, according to proponents of the scheme, an educational effort to filter the benefits of scientific knowledge through all levels of the population. The method chosen, with the objective of 'eliciting creativity and intelligence in the masses in a bold and revolutionary initiative', was to apply the processes of chess to everyday activities. Chess thinking was classified into six chess ages, from rudimentary learning to intellectual abstraction, and tests were then conducted on classes of children of six to nine years old, then higher ages, including the teachers themselves, over a period of several months. The findings showed that 'the methodological teaching of chess helps elevate the intelligence quotient . . . chess develops a new form of thinking . . . In addition the development of intelligence through the practice of a game creates a new form of abstract exercise which is self-motivating'. Perhaps the longer term political test is whether this interesting experiment survives the enthusiasm and personal support of a chess-playing national president.

On the day of the FIDE elections there seemed no likelihood

whatever of a clash over Soviet demands, notably the running battle between a Soviet champion and a Soviet challenger in exile. In the past FIDE's effort to uphold the rules, regardless of the player's passport, was the source of rancour in Moscow. But now, with the Lucerne olympiad, Soviet chess leaped forward again. The results spoke for themselves: the men's team achieved the crushing score of 42½ out of 56 points (losing only three games throughout the whole event), way ahead of Czechoslovakia with 36 and the United States with 35½. The Soviet women were hardly less dominant, taking first place with a score of 33 out of 42 followed by Romania 30 and Hungary 26. In such circumstances the next phase of the political dialogue in international chess was bound, in its essentials, to be a Soviet-run affair, all the more so – and this was the key point – because the challenger, the putative second best player in the world, happened also to be a Soviet player, Garry Kasparov. His tremendous form at the olympiad and in the Interzonals demonstrated, before a global audience, that he was the player of the future.

I mention Kasparov particularly because this was his olympiad. During the tournament he played a game which may stand (it is too early to tell) as marking the passing of the generations. It was against Viktor Korchnoi, playing first board for Switzerland. Karpov, nominally first board for the Soviet Union, diplomatically taking a rest, allowed his young compatriot to pick up the gauntlet. For this was a needle match, a 'political' match, for obvious reasons.

'When a new star appears, the firmament moves,' as I wrote in the London *Times*. Medium height, slightly sallow, with a shock of dark fuzzy hair and a white turtle-neck sweater, Kasparov has the look of a West Side rocker, ready for action. He sits nervously at the chess-board, continually shifting around, frowning under thick eyebrows, staring narrow-eyed at the pieces. Or he stomps up and down, waiting for his opponent's move. The players did not shake hands at the start of the game (that was only to be expected) though Kasparov, to his credit, made a half gesture to do so; it was Korchnoi who refrained, hurrying in from the cafeteria where he had been talking to some of the English team – if it was last-minute advice that was being offered, it was by then far too late. Korchnoi played a queen's pawn opening and Kasparov responded with the Modern Benoni, his usual choice. It did not take Kasparov long to set off in a new direction, whether prepared in advance or devised over the board hardly mattered for the fireworks that followed. He left a knight *en prise* for seven moves; he moved his queen into the enemy back rank where it was apparently totally cut off from safety; he held the spectators, following the game around the board and on television monitors, spellbound. Yet so provocative and complex were his ideas that even the experts could not analyse if or how he was winning. Instead, there was an overwhelming sense of mastery, of inevitable fate, as I say, of the passing of the generations. Too much to claim for one game? Here it is, with Kasparov's own notes. (*Fighting Chess,* 1983.)

1 d4 Nf6 2 c4 g6 3 g3 Bg7 4 Bg2 c5 5 d5 d6 6 Nc3 0-0 7 Nf3 e6 8 0-0 exd 9cxd a6 10 a4 Re8 11 Nd2 Nbd7 12 h3 Rb8 13 Nc4 Ne5 14 Na3 Nh5 15 e4 Rf8 16 Kh2 *'In principle I understood this position and yet despite this my next move was inexact.'* 16 . . . f5?! *'Bd7 was probably better.'* 17 f4 b5! *'Black burns his boats.'* 18 axb axb 19 Naxb5 fxe 20 Bxe4! Bd7 21 Qe2! Qb6! 22 Na3 Rbe8 *'At this moment my opponent made a serious error. He could have played 23 Qg2 to consolidate by taking the e5-knight and following with Ne2.'* 23 Bd2? Qxb2!! *'Korchnoi had overlooked that the intended Rfb1 to trap Black's queen is met by the winning blow 24 . . . Nf3+!!'* 24 fxe?! Bxe5 25 Nc4 Nxg3! 26 Rxf8+ Rxf8 27 Qe1 Nxe4+ 28 Kg2 Qc2 *'White is clearly lost!?'* 29 Nxe5 Rf2+? 30 Qxf2! Nxf2 31 Ra2! Qf5! 32 Nxd7 Nd3 (Diagram 8).

**8**

'After the game I devoted an enormous amount of time to analysing this position,' Kasparov declared in his book. Yet even he missed the final twist, which was pointed out by the young English player Nigel Short in his analysis (*British Chess Magazine,* January

1983), namely a forced perpetual (a repetition of checks, which the King cannot escape from, resulting in a draw) by White.

The game continued: 33 Bh6? Qxd7 34 Ra8+ Kf7 35 Rh8? Kf6 36 Kf3?? Qxh3+ and White lost on time. Short showed that White had a draw by 33 Ra8+ Kg7 34 Ra7! Qf2+ 35 Khl Qxd2 36 Ne5+. Black is unable to escape the confines of the back two ranks, eg. 35 . . . Kf6? Ne4+ forks or 36 . . . Kh6 37 Ng4+ leads to another fork; so 36 Kf8 37 Ra8+ Ke7 38 Ra7+ Kd8 and (what Kasparov missed) 39 Ra8+ for if 39 . . . Kc7? 40 Nb5+ Kb7 41 Ra7+ mates or wins the queen. 'A memorable clash' as Kasparov summed it up.

In his final speech at the election, Campo declared that we were on the threshold of a new era for FIDE, which was still stymied by what he termed the approach of the 1920s and, in a further backward flight, a nineteenth-century tempo of work. It was time for change (his manifesto), time to harness 'the chess explosion' around the world, time – now panning fast forward – to meet the challenge of the twenty-first century. There was something slightly comical about these large claims, but that is the politics of chess, new eras and global challenges. What does it come down to? Organising the World Championship is the touchstone of the health of international chess. If FIDE can uphold fair play in that – a modern version of Zukertort's conception of behaving like gentle-men – it will be doing what is required of it. Trouble, however, came faster than anyone could have predicted. But before relating that, let's replay an earlier crisis.

The most fateful decision taken by FIDE in modern times was at the Nice olympiad in 1974, when the delegates voted to reject the terms demanded by Bobby Fischer. It's a controversy which is still dis-puted even now. For whatever the rights and wrongs of the case, the end result has been – alas – to deprive lovers of chess of seeing the best player of our day defend his world title. Fischer will not, it seems, ever play serious chess again. And the loss is one that every chess player cannot but feel, such was the magnetism of Fischer, as a personal blow.

In case anyone does not remember those heady days, Bobby was the *enfant terrible* of chess. From the age of 13, when he won what was called – slightly grandiloquently – 'the game of the century' against Donald Byrne in a tournament in New York in 1956, he seemed destined to become World Champion. He won the US

Open Championship, his first major title, the following year, aged 14, and demonstrated in winning the US Championship each time he competed, seven in all, that he was so far superior to any other American player as to set him a whole world apart. It was not just his unstoppable talent, his aggression, his utter dedication to the game which raised his fame. It was how he set himself against the Russians as a latter-day knight-at-arms, doing battle for the new world against the Soviet dragon, and vanquishing it, which made him a star, a figure to marvel at, and – when he defeated Spassky for the world title at Reykjavik in 1972 – a household name for a mass audience which had no knowledge whatever of chess. He seemed unaware of or uninterested in any way of life other than chess. During his rise to the top he was insistent in demanding (rightly) far better terms and conditions for playing chess than anyone had ever dreamed of; passionate in his denunciation of the Russians' conduct, whom he accused of cheating and fixing; as ready to walk out in protest from an Interzonal tournament (Sousse 1967) as to play a masterpiece; by turns crude and graceless (though always 'correct' at the board), overbearing and voluble, consumed with righteous anger, high ambition and, above all, genius for chess. Single-handed, he transformed the modern game.

Despite all this, the question remains: did he ever intend to defend the title that he so outrageously and summarily snatched from Boris Spassky? Were his prevarications all a complicated ruse designed to provoke the official rejection in public that in some way he deliberately sought in his unconscious mind? I can answer that question at least. He did intend to play. The evidence lies in his preparations. He commissioned Bob Wade, the former New Zealand master who had helped him with similar research before his match with Spassky, to track down and collect all the games that Karpov had ever played. Not such an easy task – Wade managed to find several hundred. Fischer evidently preferred to contact him rather than an American compatriot to do the job. The motive for such exhaustive preparation, according to Wade, is to go beyond the well-known published games in order to study the whole *oeuvre* of an opponent.

'Somewhere in the past people have weaknesses,' as Wade put it, 'which they have been successful in concealing. It's not so much in their losing games, but quite possibly the games they have won. When a player wins, he's pleased, and may not look at his games critically. This is extremely important, it's a truism. It's your victories you've got to watch out for.' As a coach, Wade has found this applies particularly to juniors. Young players sometimes get away with their weaknesses, because they are strong in another direction. It's important for juniors to get their weaknesses knocked out by stronger players, provided the lesson is not too severe. As an example of Fischer's application, Wade recalls a game in Yugoslavia, when Fischer had beaten Matanovic. Afterwards he spent the entire evening pulling his game to pieces, because he was dissatisfied with his play.

Players are sometimes quite canny about keeping their early games secret. At one time Wade sought permission to publish 120 games of Spassky as a junior. 'Niet!' said Boris, humorously wagging his finger in admonition. Bobby Fischer was a very clever fellow, he said (this was after their Reykjavik meeting when Spassky thought he would emerge as the challenger next time; unfortunately for him, he met Karpov in the Candidates'), and would learn something even from these early games. Indeed Fischer's *My 60 Memorable Games* almost never saw the light of day, as three-times US champion Larry Evans, his editor, has revealed, chronicling the fall of Fischer (*The Chess Beat*, 1982). 'Bobby withdrew the manuscript before it went to press. No reason was given. He just bought his way out of the contract, and in those days Bobby needed the money.' Two years later the publisher asked Bobby if they could destroy the plates, otherwise he would have to be charged storage. Well, why not just ship the plates to his apartment in Brooklyn? Evans pointed out that they weighed several tons and all that lead might come crashing through the floor. 'Wow! I didn't think of that! Maybe I should publish the book. The world's coming to an end anyway.' The real trouble was that Fischer was worried about revealing his opening strategy. He was too much of a perfectionist to omit the best lines, and too much of a competitor to publish them, Evans adds. So he suppressed the book for almost five years until 1969. By that time it had to be updated, so *My 50 Memorable Games* became *My 60 Memorable Games*. (Pity he didn't wait a few more years! If I had the choice of just one chess book to take with me on a desert island, I think it would be this, for its sheer exhilaration.)

Fischer planned to play Karpov. So what went wrong? The terms on which the match was to be played were discussed by the chess community at the FIDE meeting – with one conspicuous gap in the delegates' ranks. Fischer himself had failed to show up. He declined to play in the American team, for the same kind of reasons, illogical or neurotic as you wish, which had dissuaded him from playing any competitive chess since Reykjavik. If he had played at Nice he would have met Karpov on the first board, which would have been an interesting hors d'oeuvre to the title match. In his absence, Fischer was represented by the persuasive and personable director of the American chess federation, Ed Edmondson. He also communicated his own wishes directly through a succession of peremptory telegrams. It is nothing new for world champions to set conditions in their favour. It was thanks to Botvinnik's foresight in stipulating that if the challenger only drew the match, the title remained with the champion, that he twice held on to the world title. Alekhine staved off meeting Capablanca in a return match after he won the title.

The trouble this time was that Fischer seemed to want rather more than a drawn result to count in the holder's favour. He made a number of difficult conditions, the most controversial of which was, in effect, that the challenger had to win by *two* points.

Fischer's first telegram to FIDE proposed that the World Championship be decided when one player had won ten games. Historically, six wins was deemed sufficient and a longer match, in which draws did not count, could become a marathon lasting four or five months, running on without limit. So the proposal was hardly likely to be received with enthusiasm by those responsible for organising the event. Fischer further demanded that if the score was 9–9, the champion should retain his title, which meant that the challenger had the burden of having to win by at least two points, 10–8. According to Larry Evans, the idea that the champion should have an edge originated with Steinitz, who tried to impose the same conditions as Fischer when he met Lasker. Fischer's stipulation was designed to prevent a player who took a lead in the match protecting his position by going for draws the whole time. Since 1950 every title match has called for the best of 24 games, the champion retaining his title on a tie. This is an advantage, but a minimal one, of half a point, i.e. at a score of 11½–11½, the champion only has to draw to hold on. Fischer's proposals, draws not counting, had the effect of extending this advantage to a full point, i.e. at 8–8 or 8–9 the champion only needed one win to keep his title.

The American GM Robert Byrne, who qualified for the Interzonals in 1973 and 1976, poured scorn on Fischer's demands: 'Absolutely stark naked cheating', he wrote in his *New York Times* column. 'I think Bobby would rather retire undefeated than risk the possibility of losing. Karpov maintained that to play on until ten victories was awful . . . the match would turn into forced labour.' In a letter to Evans's own newspaper column, Fischer defended his position: 'The champion must also win by at least 2. When the champion gets 9 points that match isn't automatically over, although at that stage his title is secure. It continues until he wins 10 games unless the challenger wins 9 first to tie him . . . Then the money would be split equally and the match declared a draw.' (Conveniently ignoring the fact that the title itself is priceless!) All right, to uphold Fischer's point of principle, why not, in the event of a 9–9 tie, continue until one player gets two ahead? Fischer refused to consider any such compromises, according to Edmondson.

Looking at the problem from the other side of the great divide, did the Russians want to play the match against Fischer? The answer is YES, and for a rather special reason. What would the title be worth if it was won by a Soviet player through default? Such a triumph would be ashes in the mouth. And I believe that Karpov himself wanted to play Fischer. Most grandmaster opinion took the view that in such a match, the Fischer of those days would have beaten the young Karpov, would indeed, in Evans's words, have 'slaughtered' the player who squeaked past Korchnoi. Maybe so. What one can certainly say is that Karpov would have given a decent account of himself, would have prepared for the match very thoroughly, and would have been temperamentally calm and clear-headed, far less likely to cave in under Fischer's psychological bombardments than did the lugubrious troubadour Spassky. Fischer evidently recognised in Karpov a challenger who would test him seriously.

An absorbing account of the Soviet attitude to the FIDE debate is given in Karpov's *Chess is My Life* by his co-author Alexsandr Roshal. This biography by an 'official' Soviet journalist (Karpov's contribution is mainly an analysis of his games on the way up) gives the approved Soviet view of events. At the end of this Nice olympiad as the delegates were celebrating with a dinner-dance in much noise and revelry, Roshal bumped into Edmondson – 'tall and young looking, he stands inside a wide circle of admirers, a glass of white wine in his hand. A former Lieutenant-Colonel in the United States Air Force, strong, clever and cunning . . .' is how Roshal saw him. 'What does the USA chess federation intend to do, so as not to lose the title of the World Champion without a fight?' he enquired. 'Pray!' replied Edmondson.

Edmondson declined to give an interview, but Fred Cramer, Fischer's legal advisor, short and energetic, tie askew, was in voluble mood. 'Just ask me, and I can give an answer to all your questions. This is a stupid Congress. They have killed the World Championship Match. I know grandmasters who have cried on account of the fact that they won't see Fischer at the board . . .'

'Is it your opinion that the match won't take place?'

'Fifty-fifty.'

'You mean there is still a fifty per cent chance that Fischer will change his mind?'

'No. There is a half chance that FIDE will reconsider its decision.'

Fischer had sent another final telegram to the Congress after it had taken its fateful decision rejecting his stipulation of a tie at 9–9. It ran as follows: . . . 'I have been informed that my proposals have been rejected by a majority of votes. By doing so the FIDE has decided against my participation in the 1975 World Championship. I therefore resign my FIDE World Championship title.'

Not his *world title*, be it noted, which Fischer still regards to this day as his, but his FIDE title.

By assiduous lobbying among the Latin Americans and others, Edmondson had persuaded the congress to approve the match being played to ten wins, as opposed to the traditional six. The vote was close: 26 to 24 with 12 abstentions. A compromise was adopted on playing the match without limit; it was set at 36 games, the winner being the player leading at that point; in the event of an equal score the World Champion to keep his title.

So far, from Edmondson's point of view, only half good enough. Then Fischer's telegram about the 9–9 score had arrived. This the congress could not be persuaded to accept, despite all Edmondson's blandishments and Cramer's harangues (delivered from the added height of a little plastic stool).

Karpov himself had behaved with dignity. The other central figure in the drama, but off-stage, he had spoken out in the debate, briefly, against changing the rules. Late that night, one of those starry Côte d'Azur nights, Karpov and Roshal fled the razzamatazz of the party; they came up to a deserted bench on the seafront. It was by then five in the morning. 'My life is unsettled with all this travelling and preparation,' Karpov blurted out to Roshal. 'Oh, for some Ural ravioli like my mother makes!'

The Americans had lost. But Edmondson had not given up. He had one final tactical resource: to convene a special FIDE congress, to get the delegates to think again. Fischer had until 1 April 1975 to accept the regulations as agreed. In March, an extraordinary congress was held at Bergen in Holland. It lifted the limitation on the number of games in the match. But on Fischer's sticking point of the two-game margin, Edmondson could not prevail. Almost all the major and most influential chess federations, Roshal noted, which included in their ranks the overwhelming majority of GMs and IMs, voted to reject the 'Fischer amendments'. Thus of the 16 federations which comprised the top group in the olympiad only three – the USA, Philippines and Wales – voted for; all the others were against. The final resolution read: 'The winner of the match for the World Championship will be the first player to win ten games, the total number of games to be unlimited.'

Karpov accepted the decision of the extraordinary congress, though strongly opposed to the abolition of the limit on the number of games in the match. (He had had to play sixty games to get to the point of official challenger.) How did he assess his chances? 'In my opinion, for a long time we underestimated Fischer, and said, just wait – when he comes up in a match against a real Soviet grandmaster, everything will be put in its place – Fischer will be beaten without fail. We then went to the opposite extreme. Even our strongest grandmasters would sometimes make statements to the effect that it would be a hopeless matter to try to defeat the World Champion, and they would merely estimate the score by which they would lose a match against Fischer. I am convinced that the truth lies somewhere in the middle. Against the present World Champion, as against any player, even the most outstanding, it is possible to put up a not unsuccessful fight. But only with genuine, all-round preparation. It is realised that this does not give any guarantee of victory, but it is essential to guarantee full mobilization of all one's powers.'

Max Euwe, the President of FIDE, waited a further day on 1 April, in case Fischer's reply might somehow be held up . . . but it was no surprise to anyone when no message came. On 3 April Karpov was proclaimed World Champion, and in a formal ceremony in Moscow later that month, Euwe bestowed the laurel wreath on the shoulders of the young man in person, the 12th World Champion in the history of chess.

The question whether he was a worthy champion, which troubled many people, seems to me beside the point. He was in the circumstances the right and proper person to be champion in the absence of Fischer, whose withdrawal from chess was patterned by his retreat into far-out religious movements in southern California. In short, FIDE proved stronger than any one individual. And Karpov set out (he had trained as if he was to meet Fischer) to *prove* that he was a worthy champion, by playing in a series of high-level events, which he won clearly and decisively (prompting Edmondson to swallow his previous jibe of 'paper champion'). No champion has ever displayed a better record. While some critics saw him as a rather colourless, unexciting personality, he happened to be the best chess player in action – and that was that.

But of course the Russians were tormented by the anxiety that he might not be regarded as worthy – especially as, by the bitterest of ironies, the man whom he had beaten, and again had to beat in Baguio, had become a Soviet non-person. In casting aspersions on Korchnoi, they were, unavoidably, belittling the victory in the final round of the Candidates' of beloved Anatoly himself. This anxiety reinforced his determination to compete in the international arena and demonstrate beyond any shadow of doubt his fitness, his supremacy. Indeed a large part of *Chess is My Life* is, in effect, a laborious effort by Roshal to sanctify his hero.

On receiving Euwe's tribute, Karpov responded in typical Komsomol style: 'I am happy that the supreme chess title, or, as it is generally called, the "chess crown", has returned to our country, which is rich in historical chess traditions, and is known worldwide for the depth of its chess culture. It was these traditions of the Soviet Chess School which have been promoted by a whole series of World Champions, both male and female, that enabled me in a comparatively short time to acquire my chess mastery . . . I am ready to collaborate with the FIDE as regards strengthening its unity and authority, and the further development and propagation of chess in my own country and throughout the whole world.' Compare this with the story I heard at Reykjavik, not altogether apocryphal, of Fischer's comment on arriving – late as usual – at the final tournament banquet: 'Okay, where's the money?'

Later, Karpov confided some revealing comments on Fischer's

conduct: 'Fischer found himself in an unfavourable psychological situation. For him it would have been simpler to meet any one of his former opponents – since he had already defeated everyone apart from me, and they were all older than him, which is also significant. But as it was, everything turned out to be more complicated. We had never met at the board – we had never played in the same tournament, but had somehow missed each other. This meant that nowhere had he defeated me or finished ahead of me. I emerged on the world arena just at the time when he stopped playing in tournaments. There had been the "Fischer years", but then it was I who began producing the best results . . . and I am eight years younger than Fischer. This situation made a painful impression on Fischer. After all, he is accustomed to having everyone for him, and everyone supporting him. And perhaps it was this "change of climate" that he was unable to cope with . . .'

Enter Campomanes. It was no accident that one of the countries which backed Fischer in the final vote was the Philippines. Campo, then a FIDE vice-president, knew Fischer personally and had striven, behind the scenes, to arrange the match. In the months that followed, he tried again to find a way round the ex-champion's obduracy. Karpov had announced that he was still keen to play Fischer, under 'sensible' conditions, not a battle of endurance. And next year, Campo managed to bring the two together in Tokyo, after Karpov had been playing in Manila. Hardly had Karpov entered the hotel room than Campo staged his conjuring trick. 'I have a surprise for you,' and through the opposite door came Bobby himself (without his recently acquired beard). Despite promises to Fischer that nothing would be said to the press, the next day 'details' of the conversation were given by all the news agencies – Bobby was by now a superstar without light, a chess Garbo – reporting 'agreement' on a match for a five million dollar prize . . . What, in fact, was said? According to Roshal, 'Fischer said he would like to play an unofficial match with Karpov. He didn't want to play against "ordinary grandmasters", since he had already defeated them, and he wouldn't be paid much for winning against them again. He added that he had reached the age of a businessman, and that he no longer wanted to "play for nothing". Karpov replied that he had agreed to play an unofficial match with Fischer, back at the time when he had just been proclaimed World Champion, that he was not concerned about the financial conditions, but that what was important was a sensible schedule for the event. The present year was already taken up . . .'

A month later, when Karpov was playing in Montilla in Spain, Fischer flew to Cordoba. Again they met over dinner. 'The American grandmaster placed on the table his former cards: the number of games in the match should be unlimited, and the winner should be the first to win ten games (in a sub-variation of his "project" he suggested that with the score standing at 9–9 they should play on to another three wins). Karpov asked with a smile how long such a match might go on. Fischer, after some thought, replied that there were two ways of looking at this. They both won frequently, so that the match could finish quite quickly. On the other hand, they rarely lost, so that it could also drag on. "But on average, if everything should go normally," Fischer summed up, "we should spend five to six months at the board . . ."'

Karpov spread his hands in disbelief: to play without a break for half a year, and against one and the same opponent, was simply not possible. 'And then exactly at midnight on the eve of Karpov's departure from Madrid for Moscow, Fischer knocked at Karpov's door. He apologised for calling at such a late hour, and said it had been a pleasure to make his acquaintance, and asked him not to be offended if he, Fischer, should begin playing against someone else. At that they parted.' It remains to add that Fischer declined to take the place open to him in the next World Championship cycle. He did not want to play against 'ordinary grandmasters' and the vacant place went to Spassky.

It is a sad story. What it shows, I think, is that Fischer did want to play against Karpov, and went a long way towards trying to persuade himself to do so. But the inhibitions in his character (see Chapter 7), stemming as much from fear of starting as from fear of losing, held him back. Karpov, one may be sure, was guided by the Soviet chess federation's cautious approach. Personally he would have liked to take on Fischer – and by that stage, being so much in form, in regular practice, he had good chances of holding his own. Politically, the Soviet school of chess had everything to lose and little to gain from such an encounter. Practically, Fischer's obsessive conception of the match put it out of the question.

The moment, like a 'window' in space, closed. As the years passed it became clear not merely that Fischer would not play serious chess again, but – worse – that his absence was irrelevant.

Chess had moved on. Stories still abounded about Fischer. He was seen occasionally by a few friends in southern California, friends whose silence he could count on absolutely. Perhaps one or two helped him with money, since he had no visible means of support beyond the royalties on his book. Or he could be seen at a certain time each week in Pasadena public library. Or, admittedly a bit far-fetched, that he had all the fillings in his teeth removed, so as to avoid being attacked by hostile 'rays' . . . And people still tried to get him back to the board.

As recently as 1982 the Dutch newspaper *De Telegraaf* attempted to arrange a match with Jan Timman, for a prize of one million guilders (about £240,000). Fischer's representative wrote back: 'The world chess champion [sic] Mr Bobby Fischer says that he feels the amount of the prize is insufficient and therefore he feels the offer is so low he is somewhat reluctant even to make a counter offer . . .' The letter added: 'PS. For what it is worth, he was and is intrigued by the idea you mention of playing such a match in private and only publicise it later on.' *De Telegraaf* persevered, however, and over the months the ante was raised to the point where Fischer was to receive $1.5m starting money, with prize money for the match itself set at $1m. Amazing as it may sound, the paper managed to find sponsors willing to raise this vast sum. Naturally Bobby had a few other stipulations to make. Simply to meet and discuss them, he wanted $5,000 a meeting, the Dutch representative out in Pasadena to have the cash ready in an envelope. So far as the chess was concerned, he reiterated his demands made to FIDE, namely a match of unlimited duration, the winner being the first to score ten wins, draws not counting; also no adjournments (quite a good point) designed to prevent a player consulting seconds or taking expert advice in the course of a game. Play was to be in a hall without photographers or other disturbance but he was apparently prepared to allow a one-way mirror for television cameras to hide behind – a share in TV rights was of course mandatory. Beyond all this, his hosts were advised that it was of the utmost importance that Fischer be given the impression that his stay in Holland would be made as pleasant as possible. KLM first class would be acceptable, the ticket to be made out to Mr Fischer *the* World Champion, which was the way he insisted he should be addressed in all correspondence.

As I wrote at the time, this was a case where in matters of

commerce the fault of the Dutch, was asking too little and giving too much. And having got thus far, the newspaper had second thoughts. The whole idea faded away into the sands of what-might-have-been. Timman might have been a good opponent to test Bobby's mettle, a strong grandmaster but not too strong, and good-humoured with it. Can a top player stay away from the board for years and years and come back match-sharp? The answer would normally be no, in every case, except perhaps the one-and-only much regretted, if not the late-lamented.

The new storm broke in an entirely unexpected quarter: a Soviet quarrel with Campomanes. Their objections to the man whom they had so recently voted for in the final ballot at the election rose during 1983 from mild disagreement to fierce argument to open hostility, orchestrated on an international scale as only the Russians can (or would). What was the cause of this falling out? Simply that the Russians refused to accept Campomanes' choice of Pasadena for the eagerly awaited Candidates' semi-final between Kasparov and Korchnoi.

Why did the Russians take so against Pasadena? And why did Campomanes insist, to breaking point? The politics of chess, as I observed at the start, are horrendous. The players' wishes are only one of the criteria which FIDE applies in deciding where such encounters are to be staged: financial considerations are another. In this case, the players differed in their preferences for the venue. Bids had come in from three places: Las Palmas, Rotterdam and Pasadena, the last offering the best terms, including – a factor which weighed heavily with Campo – a grant of $40,000 for assisting chess in the developing world. With no common first choice by the players, Campomanes opted for Pasadena; and with the declared aim of 'diffusing' chess among the member nations of FIDE, he accepted an offer by the United Arab Emirates to stage the other (far less attractive) semi-final between the Hungarian GM Zoltan Ribli and former world champion Smyslov in Abu Dhabi. (Smyslov, hitting the comeback trail at the age of 62, had himself qualified, after tying a long and uninspiring match against Hübner, on the spin of a roulette wheel!)

Pasadena . . . neon and smog-ridden . . . residential excrescence of Los Angeles . . . it's not everyone's dreamtown, admittedly. But what was *wrong* with it? (Bobby Fischer had made his hide-out somewhere there, so perhaps Campo hoped to persuade him to make a personal appearance.) After all, the American chess federation was holding the national championships in Pasadena at the time, so it was a natural focus for the Candidates' semi-final. In all the argy-bargy the one certain fact was that the Russians took against it, and the veto came from a very high level, higher than the mere Soviet chess federation. Campo, having made his choice, went to Moscow to try and straighten things out and was treated, during two sessions of talks, to an extended litany of Soviet objections. The meetings were attended by the President and Vice-President of the Soviet Sports Federation, the reigning Soviet World Champion and the two Soviet semi-finalists themselves. High-powered diplomacy! Through a long day they individually and collectively rehearsed their objections to Pasadena. They were worried about 'security' – though what that meant was not quite clear, for Soviet swimmers had competed in LA only that summer. They were concerned about the visa problem – Pasadena being an off-limits area for Soviet diplomats. But again, access could certainly have been arranged via the embassy easily enough. Whatever it was, and Kasparov joined in the thunder and lightning, Pasadena was o-u-t. Campo on his side was adamant. The rules of FIDE laid down the way that the President should choose the venue and he was sticking to the book. Would it have been wiser for Campomanes to pay more heed to this Soviet barrage? Rules are rules, but Russians are Russians. When it comes to chess, they are, as a superpower, more equal than others. But no, Campo remained inflexible. When I saw him on his return, at my favourite chess café in London, he was convinced that in the end the Russians would give way. And at a special meeting of the FIDE executive he got his ruling upheld by 8 votes to 2 with 3 abstentions. Korchnoi was by then in late July already in Pasadena, waiting.

On the morning of 6 August, Korchnoi, wearing a grey suit, drove across to the Pasadena City College auditorium, shook hands with the referee, seated himself at the chess table in front of an audience of journalists and chess buffs, and played pawn d4. He then pressed his opponent's clock. For the next hour, as *The Los Angeles Times* reported, Mr Korchnoi paced about, hands clasped behind his back, head down, expression sombre. In the absence of the Soviet *wunderkind*, thirty years his junior, Korchnoi was awarded victory, a quarter of the purse, and a place in the final. (Staying on, he won *en passant* the US open.) To make matters worse, the Soviet chess federation refused to participate in the other semi-final (claiming Abu Dhabi was too hot) and Ribli was given the match. The world of chess was thrown into total confusion.

Some people suggested darkly, Korchnoi among them, that the Soviet authorities wanted to 'protect' Karpov, their favourite, from the challenge of the younger man; and that the authorities, in any case, were worried lest Garry might defect. I myself gave no credence to such arguments. Apart from the fact that the outcome of a Karpov–Kasparov match was entirely unpredictable, a player could defect anywhere in the world, if he had a mind to. I think Harry Golombek was nearer the mark when he wrote in the London *Times*, 'I despair at the utter failure in the present imbroglio of any understanding on the part of the opposing factions of the point of view of the players, and of the whole of the chess world who are so anxious to see these matches played.' Given that both players would have been happy to play in Rotterdam, he went on, Campomanes was wrong in allowing a feeble monetary consideration to carry such weight. The air became thick with accusations and counter-accusations, and the whole fracas was referred to a meeting of the FIDE congress in Manila in October.

The general expectation was that Campo, having over-reached himself, would be humiliated, and in the climbdown would very likely be obliged to resign. For if the Russians refused to accept the situation and denounced FIDE, Karpov would remain champion. What value would Korchnoi's 'win' have then? Answer: nil. But politics can be an even stranger game than chess.

During the summer, several attempts were made at mediation, including a special visit to Moscow by Raymond Keene, who as chairman of the new Players' Council had an influential role in such discussions. Keene advised the Russians that if they wanted the Korchnoi–Kasparov match to be rescheduled, in another venue, they would have to make a deal: an admission, formally speaking, that the President of FIDE was within his statutory rights to act as he did, in return for an agreement by all concerned to replay the match that Kasparov had lost by default. During a tournament at Niksic in Yugoslavia, the Players' Council, Karpov included, issued a call for the disputed semi-finals to be replayed, in the interest of chess. And this statement, read by Keene, was filmed for Soviet television. A senior Soviet administrator, Vice Sports Minister Ivonin, flew post-haste to Lucerne and started negotiations with Campomanes. Most significantly, Kasparov met Korchnoi over the board in a blitz tournament at Hercegnovi (repeating Fischer's triumph at blitz there thirteen years previously) and the two of them expressed their readiness to replay the match. In this Korchnoi showed good sportsmanship (and good sense). He wanted the Soviet boycott against him to be dropped. And the very fact that Kasparov himself ignored the unwritten Soviet rule against playing with the arch-defector was an encouraging sign. Meanwhile, in a week of discussions at Lucerne, Ivonin gave in all along the line. Financial compensation would be paid to Korchnoi for the match he had 'won'; the expenses incurred by the organisers of the aborted match in Pasadena would be defrayed; and, not least, FIDE would be recompensed for the revenue it had lost – a grand total, so it was reported, of $180,000! One cannot really explain such a change in Soviet policy, except to say that when a high-level political decision is taken on a certain course of action, in this case to re-stage the match, then all the signals are flashed to green, regardless. Expense is not in question. (The funds were to be raised by Soviet players foregoing hard-currency prize money in future events they might win and taking roubles instead!)

It was an amazing result, and Campo gloried in it. At the Philippines congress he rubbed the Russians' noses in his victory without a shade of remorse or tact. The congress voted by acclaim a resolution extolling 'the sportsmanship of Grandmaster Korchnoi and Grandmaster Ribli [though not an important figure in the drama, he was also a winner by default, against Smyslov] in agreeing to play their semi-finals matches, and in the spirit of reconciliation the General Assembly urges that all boycotts especially that of Mr Korchnoi should be lifted forthwith'.

Campo had got everything he wanted. How remained a mystery. But he also had, so it was whispered in dark corners, a secret weapon up his sleeve, in chess terms an atom bomb. If the Russians had refused to accept his ruling and denounced FIDE, then Campo planned to *invite Bobby Fischer out of his retirement* as 'undefeated World Champion' to defend his title against Korchnoi! One may speculate how far this was really likely. But the threat being worse than the execution, such a master stroke must have concentrated Soviet minds wonderfully.

Keene finally managed to get the semi-finals staged in London, at the end of 1983. The prize money was put up by Acorn Computer. But what swung the deal was Keene's offer to Campomanes – a shrewd stroke, this – of a gift of chess books, via his publishers, for helping promote chess in developing countries; at a face value of 40,000 Swiss francs, this doubled the aid already pledged in cash. *Snap*!

The match itself had its moments but was, to my mind, an anti-climax. Korchnoi won the first game against Kasparov, but cracked in the middle of the match, eventually losing the event he had previously won by default, by the decisive margin of 4–7. The best chess, by far, was played by the evergreen Smyslov, who at the age of 62 showed tremendous flair and energy in defeating Ribli, a player half his age. His victory showed that, like politics, championship chess is not always a young man's game.

In the original Bobby Fischer affair, the Russians played a difficult game and came out of it with a hundred per cent: in the Korchnoi affair they were markedly less successful, though they won in the end by preserving the Soviet title. Which raises a wider question: is there a link between chess and diplomacy? Foreign affairs are sometimes described as 'moves on the diplomatic board'. Politicians are much enamoured of expressions like 'treating people like pawns' or 'Soviet moves to prevent a stalemate'. Is diplomacy really like chess? Ye-es. The main difference is that chess is an adversarial relationship, in which one side is doing its damnedest to beat the other; whereas in diplomacy, a country can play as though to 'win', but may be seeking other kinds of result. Diplomacy is normally conducted to produce agreements, though it is significant that ultimately Soviet policy seeks to 'bury capitalism'. Further, the adversarial element is a one-against-one encounter, whereas in the real world a whole host of other players may be involved (perhaps a chess tournament provides a closer parallel). Secondly, chess is played sequentially, one move at a time. Again, this does not happen in the real world, where countries or governments often have to do several things at once. And finally, most important (actually this is the real mystery of chess, which makes it so hard to understand why we bad players cannot play like good players), chess is played entirely in the open. All the moves are immediately visible and the power of the pieces precisely regulated. There may be an intention to deceive, of course, but chess is the opposite of secret diplomacy.

It is not a particularly Russian habit of mind to view diplomacy in chess terms. But the analogy of chess with Soviet behaviour is revealing. 'A Soviet diplomat, like a skilled chess player, does not expect his opposite number to give up something for nothing, not even a pawn,' noted a veteran of many US–Soviet negotiations, Arthur H. Dean. He was making the point that unilateral concessions by the West, in the interest of stimulating reciprocal concessions, served only to arouse Soviet suspicion and concern. And a former British ambassador to Moscow, Sir William Hayter, has commented on the 'mechanical' nature of negotiations with the Russians and their (chess-like) reliance on a 'calculation of forces'. 'They rely on what Stalin used to call the proper basis of international policy, the calculation of forces. So no case, however skilfully deployed, however clearly demonstrated as irrefutable, will move them from doing what they have previously decided to do; the only way of changing their purpose is to demonstrate that they have no advantageous alternative . . .' (like a forced sequence of moves).

Below this, at the tactical level, the Soviet belief in the use of surprise and retaining the initiative is well documented. As Foreign Minister Andrei Gromyko put it, in a speech on the 50th anniversary of the Soviet diplomatic service in 1967, 'Being the master of events, retaining the initiative in foreign policy, knowing how to go onto the offensive but also how to defend oneself and manoeuvre – none of these methods of diplomacy should remain unused if it can benefit the Soviet State and the cause of Communism.' Substitute the word 'chess' for foreign policy in the above and you have a perfect formula for the Soviet school.

Whilst Soviet diplomatic training owes nothing to the direct study of chess, many of the qualities which go to make a strong chess player are put to good use by Soviet diplomats – patience, concentration, a capacity to put 'duty' before personal feelings, profound analysis and cool appraisal of 'objective realities', the ability to think ahead. The key quality, probably, which distinguishes Soviet diplomats is their readiness to study all the relevant material and precedents. The permanence of Soviet officials, many of whom reappear again and again in Soviet delegations (like Gromyko himself) provides a chess-like continuity of study and an invaluable memory bank for the substance of previous encounters. They are, in the judgement of Western diplomats, ruthless exposers of an unprepared, inconsistent or weak opponent. The Russians are also very adept at exploiting *zeitnot* in negotiations, i.e. in marking time as a way of holding the position, in view of a later objective. But of course if the struggle between capitalism and communism is historically pre-determined, then there can be only one ultimate winner (no draws), so it is not a game. I think it is because this struggle is *not*, in 'objective reality', pre-determined, that it *does* bear a resemblance in some important sense to chess.

# 5

# WOMEN

*She plays very well for a lady.*
Thomas Hardy, A Pair of Blue Eyes, *1873*

Women can't play chess, can they? They can, they can, they can! All right, let's rephrase that . . . Women can't play chess *as well as men*. I point to the obvious and up to now incontrovertible fact that there are no women among the top echelon of grandmasters.

Yes, but, that is not the whole story. In fact it's not the point at all, according to women players. The reason that women's results are not in the same class as those of men, they say, does not stem from any inherent sexual differences – as it does in, say, tennis or athletics or swimming, where the physical disproportion between the sexes is unalterable. Unless we include some Eastern bloc giantesses fed on a diet of hormones which effectively de-sexes them, and we're not (I hope) talking about that kind of thing.

Women's results are not in the same class as men's, so the women claim, because of an inherent environmental handicap. That is, girls don't learn and play chess at school as boys do. And if a girl shows any sign of promise, she's likely to be squashed. After all, no self-respecting high-school kid wants to be beaten by a girl, does he? To put the case more forcefully, for a girl to do well at chess is just about like expecting a boy to excel at . . . sewing. Ridiculous. The whole spirit of our upbringing is against it.

Granting this argument, which seems to me entirely valid as far as it goes – and has nothing to do with male or female chauvinism as such – there is surely no reason why women should not in the near future play as well as men do, and no reason really why a particularly gifted woman should not one day aspire to become world champion. True, the demands on physical stamina in chess at the grandmaster level are tremendous. But women can surely manage it, as they manage other intellectual or imaginative feats, such as writing fiction.

The reality is that there is a bias against women in chess. They've had a bad press, typified by Bobby Fischer's dismissive comment that he could give any woman a knight odds and still wipe her off the board. Not today, Bobby. There are some fairly formidable women players around.

For that matter, even in the past some women players have been more than good enough to hold their own against male opponents. Vera Menchik, born in Moscow in 1906, who came to live in England at the age of fifteen, was the first woman to compete against men at the international level. The men she beat included Euwe, Reshevsky, Saemisch, Sultan Khan, George Thomas, Yates, Colle and Alexander, which was not bad going. She received her major training from none other than Géza Maroczy, the famous Hungarian theorist, inventor of the Maroczy bind, who became teacher in residence at the Hastings Chess Club after the First World War. Menchik won all the women's world championships from 1927 to 1939. Women's olympiads began in 1957 – not until thirty years after the first men's olympiad! The reason was that up to that time there were so few women playing that the idea of a separate olympiad had never been considered. The women's olympiads have been dominated, from the start, by the Soviet Union.

Since Menchik's time, the USSR has produced all the world champions – Rudenko, Bikova, Rubtsova, and the wonderfully named Georgian girls, Gaprindashvili and Chiburdanidze. What is the reason for the dominance of the Soviet women, as distinct from Soviet men who may be superior *en masse* but have been successfully challenged every day by Western players? According to Susan Caldwell, the young English player, discussing women in chess (*British Chess Magazine*, November 1981), the Russians have maintained their position 'by allocating trainers to women and campaigning to popularize women's chess. This initiative has been responsible for keeping up interest in women's and girl's chess in the USSR and for encouraging young girls to take their chess seriously.'

That is surely correct, it's a question of money, or economic priorities, and it bears out the general point that Western women players don't have all that much going for them. Given the need of most British or American women to earn a living somehow, either in an office or in a profession, it takes a lot of effort to become a good chess player. The time is simply not available. Even to take part in an olympiad, a woman needs special leave of absence. And anything more than a weekend tournament has to come out of her annual holiday. Men have the same problem, but there are more chances for men to earn a living through chess, by writing and competing, just as on the whole it is much easier for men to get to the top in the modern commercial world. 'Far from being encouraged to compete in mixed championships girls are given separate tournaments and offered significantly lower prize money, thus asserting from a very early age that they are not as good as the boys.' Caldwell goes on to complain that newspapers report more of the girl's looks than her chess-playing ability and that some players have been known to display the same sort of interest . . . Tut tut. The 'fatal distractions of the opposite sex' as the father of English prodigy Nigel Short once lamented. Or rather, boys will be boys. Still, in the prevailing circumstances it is going to take a really exceptional woman player to break through to the men's level, as an equal, as Gaprindashvili and Chiburdanidze have (almost) done. Currently there is no woman graded as high as the top 300 men.

As in other areas of endeavour, women have a long row to hoe to be taken seriously in chess. 'We see no objection to ladies entering the tournament by correspondence but should recommend them to use the name of some male relative (a father or a brother), unless her opponent is a lady also. Many ladies are clever chess players, and good housewives too,' runs a reply to a reader in the *Household Chess Magazine*, published in 1865. Such whimsical comments were commonplace in chess journals from the mid 1860s onwards, according to another report in the *British Chess Magazine* (September 1981). 'During the late Victorian period the majority of chess magazines printed increasing numbers of humorous stories, poems and anecdotes about the agonies and idiocies of women chess players, presumably as an antidote to the alarmed reaction of men to the fact that women were encroaching on their "territory".'

In 1848 the first chess column in a women's magazine appeared in the *Ladies Newspaper* in London and in 1860 the first chess book written by a woman was published in London, an elementary handbook entitled *The ABC of chess, by a Lady*, identified as H. I. Cooke, though nothing more is known about her, according to Jacqueline Levy who compiled this report. The book ran into ten editions by 1868. Problems composed by Russian ladies first appear in print in the 1870s. Despite these signs of increasing interest among women, the number who competed in club matches or tournaments was extremely limited until the mid 1880s. 'Indeed,' Levy goes on, 'the participation of women was so rare that a woman only had to win a few chess games against a reasonably strong male opponent to be hailed as a "female Morphy", or more coyly as the "Queen of Chess".'

In the late 1870s an American player, Mrs J. W. Gilbert, became famous in the world of chess because she had won a number of correspondence games in international matches against male opponents. Her victories included two wins against an English player, appropriately named G. H. Gossip, in one of which she announced mate in 21 moves and in the other mate in 35. Even before these games, the *Scientific American* had hailed her as the most accomplished lady chess player living, based on her correspondence games and her performance at local events in her home town of Hartford, Connecticut. The claim is difficult to verify, Levy notes, because Mrs Gilbert never seems to have played against other women.

The first women's chess tournament, sponsored by the Sussex Chess Association, was held in 1884, attracting eight entrants. What might be regarded as the first national championship for women was introduced in 1887 when a Ladies Challenge Cup was donated to the Counties Chess Association, preceding the Ladies' tournament held in Hastings in 1895, erroneously reported as the first women's tournament by chess historians, Levy adds. The 1890s saw the formation of the two most durable women's chess clubs founded during the last century, in January 1894 in New York and a year later in London. Another club founded a few years earlier in London ceased to meet because 'all the female members got so speedily married that sensible mothers refused to allow their daughters to join it'. The New York club was still in existence up to 1949. The London club attracted fifty members during its first year and had over a hundred by 1897, the year in which the club sponsored the first international chess tournament for women.

This tournament excited great interest and some criticism. Adversaries of women's chess claimed that the tournament would be a farce, not merely because of the low standard of play amongst women, but also because the players would collapse with nervous strain at having to play two rounds a day for ten days. This was a well-worn jibe of Victorian male chauvinist pigs, whenever women attempted to challenge the male order of superiority. In the 1870s, Levy reports, the very same argument had been used against women sitting for university exams, on the grounds that the strain would result in a nervous breakdown. Notwithstanding the critics, the secretary of the club persevered and succeeded in attracting twenty entries, representing Canada, the US, Germany, Italy, Belgium, France, England, Ireland and Scotland. The winner was Mary Rudge (England) with 18½/19. In style careful and solid, the kind of player who waits for her opponent to make a mistake, Mary Rudge had the reputation of being the best woman player in England – though she never progressed beyond being a strong second-class player.

The organisation of the 1897 tournament was a turning point in women's chess. Women's events became an accepted part of the game, with a British Championship in 1904, a Scottish Ladies championship the next year, and a Women's Chess Congress in New York and an international women's tournament in Ostend, Belgium, the year after. The growing acceptance of women's participation in organised chess was the result of the efforts of the women themselves, Levy concludes.

A question which interests me is whether there is any sexual element in chess. Not *at* the board, but *across* the board. Why did the Victorians object to women playing serious chess? There is, naturally, some kind of feeling engendered during a chess game when the opponents are of opposite sexes, however intense the concentration on the game itself. But does it amount to anything? I have suggested that in poker when a woman appears at the table, it does alter the whole chemistry of the game (*Total Poker*, 1977). A woman is entitled to use her femininity, if she can, to throw her opponents off their game, to take advantage of her (usually lone) position as a woman. And the men, vice versa. But at chess that sort of thing could not apply – the game is silent, strictly regulated, impersonal.

But there is a rhythm in fast chess which is, one may submit, akin to the sexual excitement instanced by psychologists in relation to gambling games. There is in, say, five-minute games, a pattern of moves progressing, faster and faster, building up towards a climax, marked by a time-scramble or a checkmate, signalling a sudden release of tension. The king is mated, the flag falls, the pieces are set up again and the process repeated. This is not sexual excitement, *per se*; but the activity does have an edge of excitement to it which is emotionally very satisfying (if you win); and I suppose even if you lose, there is always the next game coming up, to get back into it, so to speak. Yes . . . it's not sex, but more of a substitute for sex, in that having experienced this intensity of excitement again and again, a player's emotions are spent, he (or she) must feel to an extent exhausted, and certainly far less motivated to pursue what one might call normal social relations. I mean, after such a chess session, who needs a routine evening of talk or drinks or TV? A long game, under tournament conditions, can also be emotionally very demanding and exhausting in its own more extended way, and frequently leads to the same kind of time scramble.

The psychoanalysts have explored the unconscious homosexual gratification provided by chess (see Chapter 7) and that has its place in helping to explain why chess exerts such a hold on people. But in this physical replication of the excitement of sex, as described above, the gender of the opponent hardly seems to matter. A man might want to beat a woman just because she's a woman, and he might be conditioned to believe it is cissy or infra dig to lose to a woman; but in terms of the excitement of the contest, the opponent's sex, or appearance, or attractiveness, does not count. 'The poets lie about orgasm,' Professor George Steiner has averred in a fulsome paean to chess. 'It is a small, chancy business, its particularities immediately effaced even from the most roseate memories, compared to the crescendo of triumph in chess, to the tide of light and release that races over mind and knotted body as the opponent's king, inert in the fatal web one has spun, falls on the board . . .'

Sexuality in chess is not a new idea, far from it. Here is a prescient example of women's lib far ahead of its time, and the perils that may attend it. It is a story of playing chess for 'love', not of a fair lady but a very attractive man. It comes from the *Boke of Duke Huon of Burdeux*, done into English by Sir John Bourchier, Lord Berners, printed in 1534, describing a challenge by King Yvoryn of Mombrant to Huon, who has boasted of his prowess, among other things, at chess.

'"Frende," quod Yvoryn . . . "I have a fayre doughter with whom I wyll thou shalt play, on ye condycion that yf she winne thou shalt lese thy hede, and yf thou canst mate her I promyse that thou shalt have her one nyghte in thy bed to do with her at thy pleasure, and a C marke of money there with.'"

Thus the episode begins. And the lady shows straight away that she has a mind of her own.

"I holde my father a fole when he thynketh that I should suffre a man to dye for wynnynge a game at chesse", she observes, but nevertheless accepts her father's bidding. 'Then she behelde Huon, whom she saw ryght fayre, and sayd to her selfe, "By Mahounde [Mahomet], for the grete beaute that I se in this yonge man, I wolde this game were at an end, so that I were in bed with hym all nyghte."' (And you thought it was just the women of today who were 'liberated', did you?) The game begins, watched by the entire court. Huon makes the prudent condition that neither the King nor anyone else shall be allowed to say a word about the game while it is in progress. The King issues an order to this effect on pain of death. However, the game does not begin too well for Huon; on losing some of his pawns, he changes colour and blushes red as a rose. The lady warns him that he is close to being mated and will lose his head. Huon replies that the game is not yet over. The Barons begin to laugh at him.

'And the lady who was surprysed with the love of Huon, for ye grete beaute that she sawe in hym, so that she nye forgate all her play to thynke of Huon, so that she lost ye game; whereof Huon was joyfull and called Ye kynge, and sayd; "Syr, now may ye se how I can play; for yf I wyll a lytell more study I wolde mate your doughter where as I lyst."'

The King was furious that she should lose to a minstrel's varlet (equivalent, I suppose, to a member of a pop group) when she had previously defeated so many great men. But Huon has a sting in the tale.

"As for the wager that I sholde wyn therby, I am content to relese it quyte; let youre doughter go in to her chambre and sporte with her damselles at her pleasure . . ." And ye lady went her way sorrowfull, and sayde to her selfe: "A false faynted hert, Mahmounde confounde the; for yf I had knowne that thou woldest thus a refused my company, I wold have mated the, and then thou haddest lost thy hed."'

I came across another vivid example of the sexuality of chess in these fine lines from one of the ancient Soviet *byliny*, the epic poems of early feudal times. In this match the lady has been mated three times in a row.

> And Katerina threw down the crystal board,
> And the chess pieces of silver she threw down,
> And took Churilo by his white hands.
> And herself said the following words:
>
> Ah, young Churilushko, son of Plenko!
> I do not know whether to play chess with you,
> I do not know whether to gaze on your beauty,
> And on your golden curls,
> And on your gilded rings.
> And my mind is confused in my stormy head,
> And my clear eyes have grown dim,
> Look at yourself, Churilo, at your beauty.

And why not? Typically, the modern American women players are cool, confident, the kind of women (dare one say) who could easily figure in an updated version of a mediaeval narrative poem. 'I've always lived with chess players,' one told me, 'except one time with a man who played backgammon. I couldn't respect a guy if I could beat him. But really, it's stupid to play chess with your partner. Every once in a while we play speed games, but not serious chess. The psychological relationship would be too difficult. Power trips, you know? Sharing power is hard enough anyway.'

There have been a number of chess marriages in the modern game. The Canadian GM Peter Biyiasis is married to the American player Ruth Haring. The first Bulgarian GM Milko Bobotsov was married to a woman master, Antonia Ivanova. Georgi Borisenko, the Soviet correspondence GM, married Valentina Belova, five times USSR woman champion. In Moscow, Boris Gulko and Anna Akhsharumova have fought a heroic battle together to be allowed to emigrate. In England, Dr Jana Miles, the Czech-born player, has married and separated from not one but two chess masters, which, to adapt Oscar Wilde, is not just a misfortune but looks like carelessness. Though none of these women, playing under tournament rules, would be able to match their husbands' abilities, at five-minute or speed games they might well win their share, and chess presumably has played a central part in such relationships. 'Thank you, darling, for learning to play chess,' Pushkin once wrote in a letter to his wife. 'It is an absolute necessity for any well organised family.'

Jana Miles now works full-time as a doctor but took time off to play top board for England in the 1982 chess olympiad where she got her women's GM title. She met her first husband, William Hartston, at a students' tournament in Prague in 1968. They married eighteen months later and Jana Hartston rapidly established herself as the best woman player in her newly adopted country. It caused a minor sensation in the closed circuit of British chess when she left him for England's first GM, Tony Miles. The first thing that outsiders knew about it was that the British woman champion suddenly appeared in press reports of chess tournaments under a different name. The affaire even reached the popular press. 'I'm one of those women who are attracted by success,' she was quoted in a gossip column. There was no ill-will in the break-up. 'We've all met at tournaments, sat around a table and talked it over,' Hartston observed at the time. 'We accept the situation.'

The 'unmentionable half' was how Jana Miles described women's chess, reporting on the Malta olympiad of 1980. Unless it was the World Champion beating one of the local GMs, no one was interested in female chess, she opined, adding ironically: 'Everyone knows that women cannot play let alone produce improvements, TNs [theoretical novelties] and interesting ideas.' On taking a closer look, the scoffers might find some interesting games after all, she suggested. As an example, she quoted the game for which she was awarded the prize for best game by a woman, which included the following no doubt deliberately 'feminine' annotation (Diagram 9).

9

Returning to her game, with what she thought was a winning position, she found her opponent had played 19 . . . Nxe4?!!

'I suppressed the immediate urge to give a shriek and run away again and fell down on my chair to try and work out what the hell was going on.' At first the situation looked grim: 20 Bxe7 Nxd2 21 Qc1 Nxf1 22 Bxf1 Rxe7 23 Nc4 Bd4+ 24 Kh1 Rxc4! 25 Bxc4 Bxb2! and Black wins, or 22 Nxf1 Rxe7 23 Bd3 Ne5 and White is getting squashed. Eventually she realised she would recapture on f1 with the king! So – 20 Bxe7 Nxd2 21 Qc1 Nxf1 22 Kxf1! protecting the bishop and neutralising any unpleasant pins, and eventually winning on move 60.

Botvinnik has offered the personal opinion that women will always play less well than men, for physiological reasons. The size of the nervous system is the same for men as for women, he says, but a woman's organism is more complicated, partly for the reason that women bear children, and therefore more organic demands are made on the female nervous system, leaving less resources, as he believes, for 'decision-making'.

Tests do show that in analytic visual-spatial ability, males tend to perform better than females, according to Arthur Jensen's *Bias in Mental Testing* (1980). Girls begin to talk a bit earlier than boys, but from then on until about age 10 or 11 there is no clear superiority of either sex in verbal ability. From that age on up to maturity, however, girls begin, on the average, to surpass boys rather consistently on a wide variety of verbal tests that were not specially devised to distinguish sex differences. In adolescence, girls average close to a quarter of a standard deviation higher (a measurement of the spread of distribution) than boys on verbal tasks. Boys begin to catch up slightly later in adolescence, but girls still remain ahead into maturity. The sex difference in verbal ability after puberty, Jensen notes, appears to be a genuine phenomenon and not just a measurement quirk.

Chess is pre-eminently a visual-spatial game. The trend of sex differences in quantitative or mathematical ability is just the opposite of verbal ability, but more exaggerated, Jensen continues (he was not of course concerned with chess but examining possible difference in ability between the sexes). Before puberty there is no sex difference. After puberty boys begin to forge ahead of girls, and the average difference by the end of high school varies from one-fifth to two-thirds of a standard deviation in various studies.

This finding that boys forge ahead of girls after puberty is a real difference, Jensen concludes, in the sense of not being a product of bias in testing. What's more, on the average, men perform better than women even on quantitative test items couched in terms of traditionally feminine activities such as reducing a cooking recipe by some fraction, or figuring out the yardage needed for a certain dress pattern, or estimating the price per ounce of two unequal-sized jars of face cream.

What does all this mean? A modest difference in the *average* of the male and female groups results in large differences in the proportions of each group that come at the *highest range*, i.e. the most gifted. Tests show a conspicuous disparity in the proportion of boys and girls with exceptional talent. (For instance, in tests of mathematical talent in all the seventh, eighth and ninth grades of school in the Greater Baltimore area in 1972, the proportion of girls who scored at or above the 95th percentile on grade level of ability was 44 per cent, but 19 per cent of the boys in this highly selected group scored higher than the *highest*-scoring girl. In another larger survey of all junior high school pupils in the Greater Baltimore area and suburbs of Washington DC who scored about the 98th percentile, 7 per cent of the boys scored above the highest girls. The highest scoring girls in this mathematical talent search had taken as much maths in school as the boys, and with apparently as much interest and motivation.) 'The mathematical superiority of males may be mainly a result of the even more clear-cut sex difference in spatial-visualisation ability, which is probably a potent mediator of mathematical aptitude,' Jensen states.

The largest and most consistently found sex difference is spatial-visualisation ability, especially on spatial tests that require analysis such as mentally breaking up a pattern into smaller units, and so on. As in the case of verbal and quantitative abilities, the sex difference in spatial ability is not established consistently until about puberty and it persists thereafter.

Jensen adds: 'The cause of the verbal versus spatial-quantitative sex difference is still an open question scientifically.' Little attention is now given to cultural or role differences, which used to be taken as the cause. 'The most plausible noncultural type of evidence to date,' he sums up, 'involves differential rates of maturation and hormonal factors that may affect different brain functions, rather than say factors that would suggest basic differences in the structure or "wiring" of male and female brains.'

That is not the view, however, of all the experts in this field. Among the latest and most original studies on the biological differences in intelligence is the work of Donna and Alan Hendrickson of the Department of Psychology at London University. The Hendricksons, working as a man and wife team, live in a dream house, with a swimming pool in the front room and his-and-hers computers in the back, in a green wood forty-five minutes from the city centre. Hendrickson takes the view that people with higher IQs achieve more in any field of activity you care to name, including sports. Their work is based on studying the physical operation of the brain. 'He'll be quite happy to explain it to you,' his wife remarked with a smile, 'because it shows that men perform better than women.'

Alan Hendrickson then proceeded to give me a brilliant exposition of the history and development of IQ tests. 'Many IQ tests show that there are no significant differences in the mean, or average, score of IQ tests between men and women,' his paper on the Biological Basis of Intelligence (1981) notes. 'There are, however, differences in the standard deviations or variability of the scores of the two sexes in many IQ tests, with men showing the greater variation.' If one takes some arbitrary lower score on a test as 'educationally sub-normal' and some equally high score as 'gifted', then there is a higher ratio of ESN males to women and likewise more gifted men than women – the swings in performance are wider, even though the average scores are the same. Why?

The brains of men and women are known to differ somewhat in size, with women having less tissue; on the other hand women have less body mass, and as the proportion of one to the other is the best index of species intelligence, this is not the explanation. Do men and women differ in terms of their likelihood of correctly receiving *incoming information signals* (termed the R parameter) either in terms of the mean or in variability? And if so, what can account for it?

Looking at the upper end of the IQ distribution, Hendrickson's paper considers what it means in terms of tests which have a very high value of recognition. The superior performance of high R people only becomes noticeable when the task length increases. In other words, we can all perform simple tasks, like crossing the road, equally well. 'People with the very highest levels of R can maintain thought processes with a time course of hours, and perhaps longer. Tasks which require these levels of concentrated mental effort are usually to be found in the realms of mathematics, science and technology of various kinds, although a case can be made to include the upper echelons of most professions. It is at these upper levels, of course,' the paper continues, 'that we find an imbalance in the sex ratios. Are there more chess grandmasters, for example, because there is a shortage of women who have the necessary level of R, or are there other explanations for the ratio difference?'

If there was a genuine superiority of the male brain, it should be manifested as a higher level of R, which in turn should show up in conventional IQ test norms. 'As we do not find this to be the case, it leads one to suspect that an additional factor must be posited to explain the shortage of women from even those activities where there seems to be little evidence to suggest social discrimination.' Hendrickson believes there is such another factor which has the effect of invalidating high levels of R in women. 'Put another way, there are probably just as many women who could concentrate on a chess problem for hours on end as there are men, but there is something that prevents them from doing so.'

To explain what this is, Hendrickson takes an analogy from computers, the 'interrupt' condition. When a computer is performing a given task, sometimes at 25 million calculations a second, it may be delayed by a peripheral unit, say a magnetic tape which has to be switched on, start to run and pass through a recording head, all of which might take a second of time. In order not to waste this valuable time, the interrupt enables the computer to perform another task. As soon as the magnetic tape comes to an end, a signal is sent to the computer to resume its first task. This kind of process is analogous to human life. Thus, the caveman is sitting in his cave, as Hendrickson graphically describes it, gnawing a hunk of meat, when he sees a sabre-toothed tiger coming toward him: he drops the bone and sets about defending himself, i.e. a higher priority interrupts his activity.

Men and women are both subject to interrupts, but not to the same extent. To take a familiar setting, a mother hears her baby cry when she is sleeping, and gets up to nurse it although the father sleeping beside her does not 'hear' the baby, or only in a muffled way senses what is going on. Women have the same physical make-up, the same IQ, the same bio-chemistry, as men; the one area in which differences exist is in the interrupts; or, in modern society, external events occur with a higher probability of causing interrupts in women than in men. The interrupts interfere with the train of thought, and take precedence over the previous activity. According to Hendrickson, this is not an acquired trait but based on genetic structure, derived from birth and sex. (This theory, interestingly enough, seems to bear out Botvinnik's intuitive explanation of the organic difference between men and women, mentioned earlier.)

'We suggest that adult women have a far larger number of interrupt conditions to attend to than men,' as the paper puts it. 'These interrupt conditions are stimuli which are attended to because there is a molecule, a repository of meaning, in the brain scanning for the condition. This particular molecule is thought to be there not as a result of learning, but comes from DNA transcription.' The biological purpose of such chemical constructs is to programme the woman to respond to such things as an infant's cry, or a possible threat from some external source. Men have the same make-up, of course; all that is suggested is that women have a much larger repertoire of events which they are biologically programmed to respond to. When some of these events occur, it may be impossible to store the original task, i.e. it overloads the memory capacity.

Take problems at chess. 'If an interrupt of sufficient magnitude occurs whilst solving a difficult chess problem, the only way that one can return to the problem is to start at the beginning. If, before you have reconstructed the point at which the interrupt occurred, another interrupt occurs, the effect can be very frustrating!' The task is effectively destroyed. 'This, we believe, is the reason for the lack of women in the professions which require long periods of concentration,' Hendrickson concludes.

I objected to all this that in playing chess a grandmaster is not looking ahead thousands of moves. On the contrary, he looks only at a very few possibilities. Hendrickson acknowledges this but says it is not the point. High IQ is essentially a matter of superior memory, a greater store of knowledge. The male has a better memory capacity, with more games imprinted in his mind, more previous positions, which he can refer to and check against the present position. 'My feeling is,' Donna Hendrickson adds in explanation, 'that this distinction in the memory capacity of the sexes is not significant at the chess master stage, of playing a game itself. It's at the stage of acquisition of knowledge, in persisting in following the plies through. Women do not get far enough into the game, in learning chess, because biologically they are less able to hold the chain of pulses in their minds, to look so far ahead.' The theory of a biological difference is a hypothesis, the Hendricksons sum up, but there is considerable independent evidence which seems to confirm it: meanwhile their research goes on.

In a variety of tests conducted by Donna Hendrickson, to test their theory of the biological basis of intelligence, she found a standard deviation of 50 for the girls and 59 for the boys. Although this ratio may not seem very significant at first sight, she noted that it has a large effect on the absolute numbers of women and men that will be found at the extreme of IQ distribution. Taking the population of the UK at 55 million, Table 2 shows how the ratio of men to women changes markedly as the IQ scale increases.

Table 2   *Number of men and women at the extreme of IQ distribution*

| IQ over | Expected number of men in pop. of 27.5m. | Expected number of women in pop. of 27.5m. |
|---|---|---|
| 100 | 13,750,000 | 13,750,000 |
| 115 | 4,833,033 | 3,713,460 |
| 130 | 858,288 | 376,680 |
| 145 | 71,463 | 12,960 |
| 160 | 2,709 | 149 |
| 175 | 47 | less than 1 |

At IQ 130, the level thought to represent the approximate mean of students undertaking post-graduate studies at university, the men outnumber women by more than 2 to 1. At IQ 145 and above, the ratio becomes 5.5 men for every woman. At IQ 160 and above, there are 18 men for every woman. Finally, there would be expected to be only one woman in 27,500,000 with an IQ of 175 or more, whereas there would be 47 men. (Note that these calculations imply more male morons than female as well as more geniuses.)

If this were to be regarded as some indication of the true differences in the distribution of intelligence in the two sexes, Dr

Hendrickson concludes, 'it would probably not be necessary to look for further reasons to explain the relative lack of women in higher occupational levels'.

Jensen pointed to differences between boys and girls in both mean and variance. By way of illustration, if the boys' mean is 0.1 SD greater than the girls' mean, then amongst players whose ability places them as 1 in 10 million, there would be 70 per cent more males than females. Even if the boys' mean was as much as 0.2 SD greater than the girls' then amongst players who are 1 in 10 million there would still be only three times more males than females. In a population like the United States of 250 million, where there are a score of grandmasters, there would be seven, or surely at least one, female as good. Where is she? Only in the pages of Walter Tevis's thriller *The Queen's Gambit*, where a plain, orphaned American girl discovers an astonishing talent in herself for chess, and progresses right up through the hierarchy of chess players to become US Champion at 18 and eventually victress over the World Champion in Moscow. What Jensen's analysis does not seem to take sufficient account of is the possibility that the variability in boys' talent is greater than that of girls, i.e. the swings are more pronounced, but the average players of both sexes perform equally well.

The only fictional account I have discovered about the emotional ups and downs of a woman chess player is *The Queen's Gambit*. As might be expected from the author of that most accomplished games-thriller, *The Hustler*, whose theme was the cut-throat rivalry among pool players, the action at the chess board is very well done. It is not easy to describe chess in a way which carries the excitement of the struggle to a non-chess-player and yet conveys an authentic sense of what is going on at the board. These descriptions of chess games, all the way up from local tournaments to a full-dress encounter with the World Champion in Moscow, are the real heart of the book, rather than the story-line or interplay of characters; nor is one in any doubt that the contender, Beth Harmon, is indeed a woman. Here she is aged thirteen, midway through her first tournament, the Kentucky State Championship:

> She seated herself and put everything out of her mind except the sixty-four squares in front of her. After a minute she saw that if she attacked on both flanks simultaneously, as Morphy did

sometimes, Goldmann would have difficulty playing it safe. She played pawn to queen rook four.

It worked. After five moves she had opened up his king a little, and after three more she was at his throat. She paid no attention to Goldmann himself or to the crowd or to the feeling in her lower abdomen or the sweat that had broken out on her brow. She played against the board only, with lines of force etched for her into its surface: the small stubborn fields for the pawns, the enormous one for the queen, the gradations in between. Just before his clock was about to run out she checkmated him . . .

She went directly to the girls' room and discovered that she had begun to menstruate.

Quite. In the end, the price of Beth's success, *Time* magazine's cover and international renown, the laurel wreath in Moscow, is despair relieved by semi-dependence on drink and pills, abandonment by her lover, isolation. But this is where *The Queen's Gambit* succeeds as a thriller so well – her victories at chess make it all seem worth it. The book ends with her stupendous endgame combination, fifteen moves deep, giving her victory over the world champion.

When she advanced the pawn to the seventh rank, she heard a soft grunt from him as though she had punched him in the stomach. It took him a long time to bring the king over to block it.

She waited a moment before letting her hand move out over the board. When she picked up the knight the sense of its power in her fingertips was exquisite. She did not look at Borgov.

When she set the knight down, there was complete silence. After a moment she heard a letting-out of breath from across the table. Borgov's hair was rumpled and there was a grim smile on his face. He spoke in English. 'It's your game.' He pushed back his chair, stood up, and then reached down and picked up the king. Instead of setting it on its side he held it across the board to her. She stared at it. 'Take it,' he said.

The applause began. She took the black king in her hand and turned to face the auditorium, letting the whole massive weight of the ovation wash over her.

People in the audience were standing, applauding louder and louder. She received it with her whole body, feeling her cheeks redden with it and then go hot and wet as the thunderous sound washed away thought.

And then Vasily Borgov was standing beside her, and a moment later to her complete astonishment he had his arms spread and then was embracing her, hugging her to him warmly.

On the practical side, what about the experience of chess trainers? Bob Wade, the former New Zealand master, echoes Botvinnik's comment about women's characteristics being based on their child-bearing role. He has found, as a coach to numerous London school children, and as captain of the English women's team which won the silver at Haifa (sans the Russians), that girls are more defensively inclined in a *crisis*. They can play a bright, sparkling, attacking game based on rules of development and mobilisation of forces. But even young boys tend to be more adventurous. 'It's a male tendency', as he put it. Women can be equally critical of games, so this is not a one-way judgement in all respects.

At primary schools, a lot of girls play and compete well. The London under-12 champion was a 10-year-old girl in 1981, for example. But there is a great waste of talents among girls after junior school. Puberty comes earlier than to boys, and competitiveness at chess is not interesting to girls in the 12–15 age range. In fact they tend to dislike the sheer brutal competitiveness of the game, Wade finds. Boys get totally bound up in sex but they do not give up sports for it.

If something happens in a game, Wade explains, which is entirely unexpected, all players are in a state of shock. They will react in certain ways: some retreat into a shell and do not look outside it; others lash out in all directions. Women tend to play a solid move, trying to return to a normal state of mind. The best plan, if something unexpected happens, is not to move at all (cf. the game of Jana Miles quoted on page 103). Wade recalls a game where he was a rook up against Korchnoi and made a careless move; Korchnoi came back with an unexpected reply and he then reacted immediately, instead of thinking it through, which would have given him at least a draw. Most players cannot handle shocks over the board in a cool, detached way. But whereas women's reaction is to retreat and defend, boys, as in boxing, feel 'if he goes for me, I'll go for him'.

Go into any chess club in the country, says Robert Bellin, coach to the English women's team in the 1982 olympiad, and what do you find? Males playing males. It is especially daunting for a girl, unlike, say, swimming. Perhaps the old Victorian idea of a club as a male preserve still prevails. Likewise at the Marshall Chess Club, 23 West Street in New York, through whose elegant swing doors have passed most of the best chess players in the US – Fischer played his radio match there in 1965 when the State Department refused him permission to travel to Havana – men outnumber women by about 200 to 1. Chess is probably less than popular with young girls, Larry Evans suggests, because they learn early on that boys have fragile egos and do not like to lose at anything which reflects on their mental abilities.

If the situation has changed at all in Britain it is because the better women players, aided by Bellin, formed a sort of pressure group with the aim of forcing the all-male British Chess Federation to make better provision for women players. It was only in the 1980s that the BCF set up a national training scheme for girls. So if this process continues, with girls being given the same opportunities and encouragement as boys, can one expect to see women players coming up as strongly as men? That, says Bellin, is *the* question.

The real point is that women chess players do not want to play against other women. They want to compete against the best players around. As Ruth Haring put the common view, 'I would prefer to become a good *chess* player, not a good *woman* chess player.' Such women play in women's teams as a kind of responsibility to chess, or to their national side, not because they believe in the idea – on the contrary. 'I study the games of Karpov, not Chiburdanidze,' her team-mate Diana Lanni pointed out.

The English women carried out a mini-coup to assert their determination to make progress when they voted out the accepted leader of the British Women's Chess Association in 1982. The deposed president, Jana Miles, may have shared the younger players' basic objective of improving women's position in chess, but took her ouster badly, complaining in an open letter to the newly elected president, Sheila Jackson, that 'the coup was not in the interests of women's chess'. In particular, she objected to the new decision to abolish the women's championship which she described as a retrograde step, taken by dictatorial methods. In reply, Sheila Jackson dismissed this 'tantrum-by-letter', citing the work done by herself and the new officers in coaching girls at grass-roots level, and pointing out how much Miles herself must have gained from being a Czech junior. The new executive's idea, Jackson continued, was to have four places for women in the British Championship itself (there had been only one entrant as of right, up to 1983), with the top woman becoming British Ladies' Champion. Other women players would take part in a one-week event, thus cutting costs and saving holiday time.

In a 'friendly' encounter, the British women players set out to prove their fitness by challenging the executive of the British Chess Federation to a match. They met at a London hotel one evening, with both sides having a lot to play for. 'The BCF was intent on proving that their administrators hadn't forgotten how to play', as the women's chess bulletin *Queen's File* reported. 'The BWCA team were out to prove that women can play chess and to do so right in the heart of the chess establishment.' The women won by just one point. More to the issue at stake, the women managed to secure (in theory) a wider entry in the men's championship, on the principle of 'positive discrimination'. Such is the catch-22 of women's chess – they can't compete against men unless they have the ratings, and they can't get the ratings unless they compete against men.

Of course, no man worth his salt wants to lose to a woman, but I fear it will become an increasingly common experience. So here is a short list of male excuses, which has been culled from the experience of women who have been so remiss as to upset male pride at the board.

1. I didn't take it seriously.
2. It's only a game.
3. I just wanted to see if she understood what it was all about.
4. Honestly, it meant a lot to her.
5. You know it's good for a woman to win once in a while.
6. One likes to enter into the spirit of the game.
7. Frankly, I felt it would be unchivalrous of me to take the draw.
8. Do you call this sort of thing chess?
9. Did you see what she looked like?

And, if all else fails, and you feel really bad,

10. Sorry, I've got a headache tonight!

Why should the strongest women players in the world come from Georgia? (Stalin's birthplace, inter alia.). Nona Gaprindashvili who held the title for sixteen years and her successor Maya Chiburdanidze are both Georgians, as is the world's next best player in the women's championships up to the 1980s, Nana Alexandria. Is it the Georgian wine? And, if so, why does it affect only the women? Georgian women have their special charm, no doubt, but that hardly correlates with chess-playing ability. No, the explanation lies elsewhere, in the very air of Tbilisi as Robert Bellin explained to me. Playing in a grandmaster tournament over there, Bellin recalls a piquant and revealing incident. It was a rest day and the players were taken on a tour of the region, stopping for lunch at a little Soviet hostelry out in the country. Nana Alexandria was among the (predominantly male) company.

As they sat in the restaurant, all of a sudden two magnums of champagne were borne aloft to the table, with a note wishing Nana good luck in the tournament. A chess fan had happened to spot her from the other side of the dining room. It was as if Nana was an opera singer or a movie star – the status and admiration accorded to chess players in Georgia is on that level. In Tbilisi there is a 'chess palace', a superbly equipped stage and theatre, entirely given over to chess. Everybody, all the boys and girls in school, learn chess, and in sampling such a large group there is obviously a much greater percentage chance of discovering new talent.

What started it off in Georgia, in the first place, was the happy accident of a woman of exceptional ability appearing, Gaprindashvili, and that set the style for others to follow. Just as, if the comparison does not seem too flip, once a really good French restaurant opens, it often encourages another one to start up in the same locality. Or in chess terms, the commanding influence of Euwe in Holland has had a permanently beneficial effect on Dutch chess. Women's chess will probably not 'take off' in the Western world until a really strong player emerges, a kind of Bobbina Fischer (perish the thought) who takes the male citadel by storm. Or at least displays true grandmasterly quality. Outside Tbilisi, the most promising woman player is probably Pia Cramling of Sweden, a slight slip of a girl, who looks more like a teenager than a 20-year-old. Cramling is a clear and resourceful player, who has several male scalps on her belt, including a draw with Korchnoi, which the latter was very lucky to get away with, as shown below. In conversation she gives the impression that chess, after all, is not everything to her and that her dedication to the game depends on what else life has to offer. She could certainly do very well in international competition if she has a mind to.

**10**

In the position shown in Diagram 10, Cramling captured the knight with 39 fxe3 when 39 . . . Qe2 + 40 Kh1 Qe1 + 41 Kh2 Qe2 + allowed her illustrious opponent a draw by perpetual. Not easy to see, especially just before the time control, how the game could be won. The answer is 39 Qxf7! Nxg4+ 40 hxg4 and Black is helpless against mate on g8 or g6.

For dedication to chess, in terms of support for her husband, Madame Rhona Petrosian deserves a footnote in the history of the modern game. She took the credit, according to Korchnoi, for making her husband World Champion, by helping him win the Candidates tournament in Curaçao back in 1962. Korchnoi claimed in his memoirs that Petrosian set up a deal with Keres and Geller to take easy draws against each other in this event, thus relieving the three of them of a vast amount of mental effort in a very long tournament, and so conserving their energies for beating the other players, Fischer included. This charge, which has never really been cleared up, bears out to the hilt Fischer's often repeated accusation of those years that the Russians were 'fixing' games. Anyway, according to Korchnoi, admittedly much embittered against Petrosian, the decisive game in the struggle between Keres and Petrosian proved to be the Benko–Keres encounter in the final cycle. It was adjourned in a position where the American GM had a slight advantage. Korchnoi claims that 'On the initiative of Petrosian's wife, a painstaking night of analysis was arranged. From whatever point of view – ethical or political – this would seem to be monstrous. But the deed was done: Benko won the game, and Petrosian the tournament,' half a point ahead of Keres and Geller. Prior to this Keres had won all his games against Benko. Madame Petrosian had been reprimanded by the controllers, Korchnoi says, for trying to prompt her husband during the tournament by telling him the press centre's opinion of his position. (Knowing what the press is usually like, that could only be a handicap!) When Petrosian met Fischer, some years later, in their Candidates' match in Buenos Aires, Korchnoi adds, she slapped Suetin's face for his poor analysis of one of her husband's games! Altogether, a lady of fighting spirit.

The role of women as non-playing supporters in tournaments is open to question, indeed Korchnoi himself has probably misjudged his own best interest. Certainly the active and highly vocal protests against the Soviet state and system made by Petra Leeuwerik, Korchnoi's companion, during the Baguio encounter were a distraction from the chess itself. In many ways, no doubt, Mrs Leeuwerik helped Korchnoi, stoking up his formidable energy and enthusiasm for the match. But in a World Championship setting, her fanatical campaign, understandable as it was for a woman who had been in a labour camp for ten years, meant that she was not helping him in what mattered most, achieving a calm state of mind to beat Karpov. Some observers even believe that Korchnoi would have won this match had it not been for her presence there. Karpov took his wife to Merano half the time, and scored about the same in each half. (He has since been divorced.) Spouses or lovers at tournaments may not tilt the balance either way, if they are content to keep away from the chess. It all depends: the wife of a British player, who thought she knew best, once wore out her husband by insisting on over-lengthy analysis of a dead drawn position: another British player actually spent his honeymoon at a chess tournament. One contemporary GM has taken a party of three to a tournament, wife, daughter and nursemaid, which might be as risky to mental stability as not taking anyone at all.

It helps, no doubt, if a wife understands chess, as a famous intervention by Sammy Reshevsky's wife once showed. In a match against Donald Byrne in 1957, the rules stipulated that it was up to the players themselves to claim any time forfeits. In the first game of the match, both players got into severe time pressure. Byrne's flag fell, but Reshevsky, intent on the game, failed to notice it, and offered a draw. Byrne accepted, whereupon referee Hans Kmoch informed Reshevsky that he could in fact have claimed the game. Thus forewarned, when the players got into a furious time scramble in the second game, and both overstepped the time limit without noticing it, Mrs Reshevsky in the front row leaped to her feet: 'I claim the game on behalf of my husband!' she shouted. Reshevsky promptly entered a claim of his own. Byrne, whose turn it was to move, saw that his opponent's flag had also fallen, and made a counter claim. As the account given in *Chess Panorama* recalls the affair, 'Pandemonium broke loose. It is hardly necessary to state Byrne's objections to Mrs Reshevsky's unprecedented intrusion into her husband's affairs, nor that he was unimpressed by the argument, advanced by some biblically minded spectator, that as man and wife are one flesh, Mrs R. was technically a participant in the game, and had acted within her rights.' In the ensuing row, Byrne temporarily resigned the match. In the end Reshevsky's claim to both the first and second games and Byrne's claim to the second were all disallowed. Play resumed and Mrs Reshevsky finally saw her husband victorious.

In our own day, the support which his mother provides for Garry Kasparov is very impressive, and possibly unique in chess, in showing how a close mother-and-son relationship may help a young player. Madame Kasparov, quite a vibrant personality in her own right, watches all her son's matches and takes a warm interest in his progress. 'Yes, I am a chess player myself and try to attend all the tournaments that Garry is playing,' she told me. 'I started chess at six and I can understand the game. [Garry began 'paying special attention' to chess at five.] I see the position on the chess-board when he is playing, but it is not the position itself which means a lot to me, it's mainly his psychological state of mind and his behaviour on the stage, that immediately makes me sense what the real situation is.' Is the responsibility of looking after such a talented boy worrying? 'Yes . . . on the other hand Garry can feel my presence in the playing hall and sometimes he confesses that before playing a move, he thinks about me, particularly if he is going to sacrifice or make an unexpected move, he will think about my reaction, and he will probably wonder if he is going to take some "hard knocks" afterwards! But in general, at important international tournaments,

I keep away from the playing hall at least for the opening of the game, and sometimes in the middle game, so that he is confident, and I can then come and control myself better.'

In the semi-final of the Candidates' in London, at the end of 1983, Madame Kasparov breached her own rule, apparently with unfortunate consequences. She sat in the front row from the start of Garry's match against Korchnoi, and was mortified to see her son lose the opening game and then struggle through a series of draws. She decided to move back to her usual place. 'I did not want Garry to see my excited face, I wanted him to see the perspective of the playing hall itself.' Things then began to go much better. She sums up: 'To have such a brilliant boy at your side all the time and to work with him is the greatest of pleasures imaginable.'

# 6

# COMPUTERS

*Chess masters as well as chess computers deserve less*
*reverence than the public accords them.*
*Eliot Hearst, Indiana University*

Cocktail time, a break from the discussions of programs, technical analysis, lectures . . . *downtime*, as the computer men call it. Whatever the machines do, the human practitioners of artificial intelligence, gathered here for a seminar at Edinburgh University, could use a drink. 'Care for a game?' inquired John McCarthy pleasantly, over the sherry. He knew, of course, that David Levy, as Scottish Champion, was a good player, a league or two above him. But as one of the world's experts in artificial intelligence whose work at Stanford was known throughout the field, McCarthy was not exactly a slouch at mental calculation either. But chess, of course, is one of those games where the difference in playing ability between even a quite good player and a master more or less rules out a serious contest, anyway for the better player, as Levy was well aware. McCarthy, as an enthusiastic amateur, was wiped out. 'Okay, okay,' he smiled, taking his defeat lightly. 'But I'll tell you something! In the next ten years there'll be a computer which will beat you very easily and beat you regularly.'

'Oh yeah,' said Levy. This was in the autumn of 1969. 'Yeah! Believe me, David, I may not know too much about chess, but I know what these machines are capable of doing!' Levy, in those days a brash and bright young man at the start of his career, more interested in chess than in maths, thought otherwise. 'Listen, I don't want to boast but I do happen to be national champion in Scotland. It just isn't conceivable that you can design a program strong enough to beat players like me.' 'We surely will,' McCarthy reiterated. He had no doubts about his own theoretical expertise to back up his claim.

Levy, fond of poker as well as chess, suggested a modest wager on the outcome. They agreed on a bet of £500 that McCarthy could not produce a machine which could beat Levy over the board, under tournament conditions, within ten years. At that time when Levy's annual salary was about £1,000 this was quite a substantial sum. They shook hands on it. And that was how the great computer wager came about. One or two other people, cognoscenti of computers, wanted a piece of the action as well. The head of the Department of Machine Intelligence and Perception at Edinburgh, Professor Donald Michie, opined that David Levy had completely misjudged the state of the art. He wanted to take half of the bet. At a seminar the following year when Levy was on the platform, Seymour Papert from MIT, the author of *Mind Storms*, began to heckle Levy from the audience. When Levy invited him to put his money where his mouth was, Papert responded by offering to reduce the period in which the new program would be written to five years. Levy retorted that that would be unfair to his challenger and gave him another £250 on the same terms. News of the wager spread around the academic community and, at a computer chess tournament in Chicago in 1971, Ed Kozdrowicki from the University of California was so sure of his ground that he bet another $1,000. Levy felt he was in far enough, so he bet £250 and another academic took the balance. He still thought his bet was safe.

The man who took Levy's side in sharing Kozdrowicki's bet was Ben Mittman of Northwestern University. So not all the experts were so convinced that their technology would prove superior to the human mind. When they happened to meet again some time later, at a party given by Mittman, Michie told him he wanted to increase his original bet. Levy thought Michie must have got sunstroke, but with the bet now due to be completed in only three years' time, he had no compunction about taking the risk. His total wager had now risen to well over his annual salary.

Levy had no special aptitude for chess as a child. After learning the game as an eight-year-old he did not become really interested in it until he was eleven. But then the bug got him. He began playing every day at school and started entering competitions. After a variety of minor successes in county championships he was selected to play for England at eighteen. Then he moved on to St Andrews University to study maths and physics. Living in Scotland he became eligible for the national team and played in the student olympiad in Romania. Chess suddenly seemed to open new vistas – foreign travel, minor celebrity, possibly financial rewards. In 1968 he became Scottish Champion and played in the olympiad in Switzerland. As a result of his standing in Scotland, though the standard was lower than in England, he was given a place in the Zonal Tournament in Portugal. He almost did not take it, having to pay his own expenses, but the trip was a chance to see a new country. And this light-hearted attitude, backed by considerable preparation in the openings, stood him in good stead: he went through the tournament unbeaten and defeated a number of players who were, in reality, better than him. This result gave him the International Master title, at the time the best performance by a British player for some years.

It was an obvious step on leaving university at St Andrews to make a career in computers. He travelled a good deal to chess tournaments, wrote a lot and played a lot. By now his bet had given him something of a reputation in academic circles and he was invited to organise several computer tournaments in the US and elsewhere. The next step was to develop a computer program to be sold commercially. He worked as a consultant to Texas Instruments and left academe behind.

The man versus machine argument began, in its modern form, in a secret establishment set up by the British War Office at Bletchley outside London, in the early days of the Second World War. The task assigned to the engineers, mathematicians and linguists gathered there was nothing less than breaking the German code. The enemy's radio signals were intercepted and the process of deciphering them was done on machines which were the fore-runners of today's electronic computers. As it happened, the team of cipher experts included the two best chess players in Britain at that time. Harry Golombek, later the arbiter at several world chess championships, and C. H. O'D. Alexander (even after the war he was never permitted to go to Moscow to play chess, because of the security risk). 'Breaking codes is a bit like playing blindfold chess with a hidden adversary,' Golombek explained to me. 'You have to find out what he is talking about. And secondly, how he is saying it. The technical processes were complicated enough. But once you understood that, it was not too difficult to handle. The whole thing was like playing chess for me. Not in the sense of a puzzle, but more like the philosophy of mathematics. It came quite easily to me, because of my training as a chess master.'

Probably the most eminent mathematician at Bletchley, according to Alex G. Bell, whose entertaining account of the origins of computer chess is contained in *The Machine Plays Chess?* (1978), was Alan Turing. Among his many interests was a fascination for automata and the game of chess. The curious thing about Turing was that despite his outstanding brilliance as a mathematician, he was quite hopeless at chess. It was this paradox which led Golombek to observe later, 'I have also known some of the world's finest brains and some of these, though passionately fond of chess, have been pretty poor players. I used to know one of the world's leading mathematicians and whenever we played chess I had to give him the odds of a Queen to make matters more equal, and even then I always won.' (This shows that while a high IQ may well be a necessary condition for playing master chess, see Chapter 5, it is demonstrably not enough in itself.) Turing's notebooks are still classified material. The point here, however, is that after the war he was given a government grant to build a general-purpose electronic computer, capable of solving a variety of problems, which led in turn to his discussing the possibility of machines being able to play an average game of chess. Turing rather pessimistically thought it would take a hundred years to settle the question.

The first recorded game between man and machine took place some time in 1952. The event was staged in Turing's office at the Royal Society Computing Laboratory and was a pretty chaotic affair – it was a 'paper' machine, a set of rules from which moves could be calculated for any legal position. Turing pored over his papers, occasionally getting muddled and back-tracking; the program's opponent, Alick Glennie, a young graduate who played chess for fun, who had been invited to take part after lunch on the spur of the moment, got a bit bored by the slowness of it all. The game took two to three hours. Turing's reaction was mixed, Glennie recalled: 'exasperation at having to keep to his rules; difficulty in actually doing so; and interest in the experiment and the disasters into which White was falling'. The program resigned 'on the advice of his trainer' on White's twenty-ninth move when its queen was about to be lost. Turing was fully aware of the weaknesses of his paper machine, ruefully describing it as a caricature of his own play, making similar oversights to his own because neither of them reliably chose the strong moves for analysis. He believed it quite possible that a computer would be able to beat him and began to programme the Manchester University computer as a spare-time occupation. He died in 1954 before this aspect of his work could be carried much further.

It was an American, Claud Elwood Shannon (who like Turing had also worked on code breaking) who gave the first account, in 1949, of how an electronic computer could be instructed to play chess using a mini-max procedure, i.e. by looking ahead about three moves and backing up the best line on the basis of a simple evaluation function. He defended the idea of a chess machine, Bell notes, because 'although of no practical importance, the question is of theoretical interest . . . chess is generally considered to require "thinking" for skilful play; a solution of this problem will force us either to further restrict our concept of "thinking" or to admit the possibility of mechanised thought'.

From here on the United States took the lead in this field, though the first chess program run on general purpose computers was at Manchester University in 1951. It did not play any games but was used to solve simple chess problems – the first one (Diagram 11, White to play) took about fifteen minutes. Most chess players could do it faster than that, though I must admit it took me several minutes of laborious trial and error. As Bell points out, this was a whole generation ago, and nowadays a modern machine can solve mate-in-two problems in about a quarter of a second. To test your time, I give the solution at the foot of the next page.*

Shannon built the first chess machine soon after his historic paper. It was a metal cabinet about the size of a tea table and

**11**

included some 250 relay switches; it was named Caissac after Caissa the goddess of chess (an eighteenth-century incarnation). The next step forward took place at Los Alamos, New Mexico – yes, *that* place. The link between the early development of the atomic bomb and the games people play seems rather extraordinary. President Truman spent most of his leisure time before the first detonation of the atomic bomb over Hiroshima playing poker with the pressmen aboard the presidential cruiser, as I related in *Total Poker*, as a way of relieving the tension. Poker is more popular than chess, but like chess requires continuous concentration. Research and experiments in producing the first atomic bomb lie behind the development of the modern electronic computer as used in chess; a number of electro-mechanical computers were brought in to Los Alamos, which the physicists became interested in and began to play around with in their spare time. In the early fifties when the new fully electronic computer came in, a group of scientists, including Stanislaw Ulam, the man who played a key part in making the hydrogen bomb small enough to carry in a bomber, began to make 'some experiments performed on a fast computing machine on the coding of computers to play the game of chess'. They used a simple but recognisable version of chess on a 6 × 6 board. And in the machine's third and final game a young woman who had no knowledge of chess, but was specially coached for a week, was chosen for its opponent. She got well beaten, the first human to lose to a machine. At this stage of the computer game, the verdict of the experts – given the immense complexity of looking ahead more than four or six plies (two or three moves for each player) – was that it was impractical to expect that a machine could be designed to beat a competent chess player. The first program to play real chess was written by Alex Bernstein of MIT for the IBM 104 in 1957. It worked by selecting the seven best moves, examining the seven best replies to these moves, then the seven best replies to these replies, and finally the seven best replies to each of these replies. This produced a tree of variations which culminated in $7^4$ or 2,401 positions. These positions were evaluated using a numerical function of various chess elements such as material and mobility, and a 'path' through these was selected which represented best play of both sides. The program took

* R-h6!

eight minutes per move and played at the level of a weak club player.

It was not for another decade, according to Bell, that computers which could play chess made a significant advance, thanks to the introduction of the alpha-beta principle. This involves lopping off branches of the tree which show that the opponent can benefit more than the best line analysed so far, thus reducing the search by an enormous factor. In the late sixties at least eight new programs appeared in the United States and in the autumn of 1970 there took place in New York the first United States Computer Chess Championship. It was won by a program written by David Slate, Larry Atkin and Keith Gorlen of Northwestern University. Their program, CHESS 3.0, won all its three games. The next year's tournament in Chicago was also won by CHESS 3.5 (the higher number indicating how its capabilities were refined a bit each year) and again in 1972 by CHESS 3.6. Commenting on one of CHESS 3.6's games in this championship, Reshevsky was highly complimentary, while noting that computers still had a long way to go before they could attain the level of grandmasters. Fischer, characteristically, observed: 'Up till now they've only had computer scientists developing such programs, and they won't get anywhere until they actually involve some good chess players.' The fourth Association of Computer Machinery tournament took place in Atlanta in 1973 and, as usual, the winner was CHESS 4.0. But in the following year, when it entered the first World Computer Chess Championship in Stockholm, the program got a nasty surprise . . . it was beaten into second place by KAISSA, the solitary entrant from Russia.

During this tournament a move was acclaimed as the 'finest ever made by a computer'. It was produced by CHAOS, another American entry, against CHESS 4.0. In the position shown in Diagram 12, CHAOS played – well, what would you have played?

White evaluates its domination of open lines as compensation for a piece, a judgement that is absolutely correct. 16 Nxe6!! Of course the piece is not sacrificed entirely. 16 . . . fxe6 17 Qxe6 + Be7 18 Re1 and CHAOS rapidly put on the pressure.

Before the birth of KAISSA, only one Soviet chess program had been heard of. As Levy picks up the story (*Chess and Computers*, 1976), it played very weakly and was annihilated in a game played against the readers of the newspaper *The Ural Worker*. Each week the program's move would be published in the paper and readers

**12**

were invited to send in their suggestions for a move in reply. The move that received most votes was played. In his notes Polugayevsky calls the computer program 'he' instead of 'it'. KAISSA made its public début against the newspaper *Komsomolskaya Pravda* in 1972, drawing one game and losing one. The previous year Spassky had played a couple of games against it and found KAISSA was no rabbit. (Some indication of the range of search involved occurred in the first game when after e4 c5, the standard Sicilian opening, KAISSA thought for forty minutes and examined over half a million positions before playing, correctly, Nf3.) When the newspaper game ended, the team at the Institute of Control Science continued to work on the program. Altogether about ten people were involved, including Dr Mikhail Donskoy who told Levy that its evaluation function was so complex, 'I don't even remember what is in it.' It ran on a British built ICL 4/70 (an IBM would have been faster but there wasn't one in the Soviet Union).

KAISSA's appearance at the 1974 championship was the first occasion it had played outside the Soviet Union. It won two of its games very convincingly, was temporarily in trouble in a third, and was totally lost for much of the final round, but in the end won all four games and with them the title of World Champion. This result was quite a surprise. No one knew anything about the Russians; and it marked the start of a long and sporting participation by the Russian programers, Dr V. Arlazarov and Dr M. Donskoy, in the world computer championships. In the next event KAISSA came a respectable third but by 1980 it was scoring only 50 per cent and was well down the field. Over the years it seemed that the Russian program had not made the same advances as its American and other rivals, possibly due to lack of official support, possibly lack of computer time (besides which, the Russians are far behind the West in computer technology). In any case, the Soviet presence in the inner circle of chess computer enthusiasts has certainly contributed to the gaiety of nations.

As might be expected, the father of computer chess programs in the Soviet Union has been Botvinnik. 'Will the computer in the future be able to play chess better than men?' he was asked by Euwe, back in 1958. '"Yes," I replied immediately.' When he was in Montreal, nearly twenty years later, he recalls how someone expressed doubts about the possibilities of artificial intelligence. Monroe Newborn, who had organised the first computer championship in 1970, reacted in furious fashion: 'By the year 2000,' he declared, 'a computer will write such novels that the readers will weep.' Botvinnik himself has played a seminal role in bringing the science of computer chess to a wider audience, by his writing on the subject, without ever quite being able to crack the problem in the way he had hoped. In his essay *The Tale of a Small Tree*, developing an earlier lecture long before he had come across Shannon's paper, he set out the central dilemma. '. . . we will consider the thinking process of a chess player. Everyone knows that a player never works out all the possible variations, and does not look at all the possible moves on the board . . . during a game when considering a certain position, a player examines roughly two to four moves; he selects these moves intuitively, on the basis of experience, etc. If it is taken into account that on average a game lasts forty moves, during a game a player must analyse approximately 100 first moves . . . Of course, in his calculations a player does not examine a total of 100 moves during a game, but analyses far more. If on average a variation is examined some 2–3 moves deep, even then the number of analysed moves becomes quite imposing.' In sum, when a player is calculating variations, he 'sees' only some of the pieces and a part of the board; variations contain only a small number of moves; and a player operates by a method of 'successive approximations'. But in the mathematical 'tree' of chess, it is reckoned that the full search, though finite, contains approximately $10^{120}$ positions! That is 'brute force' versus 'selective search'.

One curious little fact is that Botvinnik's own computer program missed something which he himself had previously overlooked in one of his most famous games, his victory over Capablanca at the Avro tournament in 1938 (Diagram 13a).

**13a**

Botvinnik's winning idea, which involved a combination 15 moves deep, was correct. 30 Ba3! Qxa3 31 Nh5+ gxh5 32 Qg5+ Kf8 33 Qxf6+ Kg8 34 e7 Qc1+ 35 Kf2 Qc2+ 36 Kg3 Qd3+ 37 Kh4 Qe4+ 38 Kxh5 Qe2+ 39 Kh4 Qe4+ 40 g4 Qe1+ 41 Kh5 1:0. But later analysis showed that he could have won even earlier with the most accurate play. His own program, according to David Levy, also missed the quicker win, 34 g3! Is this a case of the mind of the master in the machine? (Diagram 13b).

**13b**

In those days machines sometimes did very funny things. Ed Kozdrowicki had made his $1,000 bet with Levy at breakfast time.

That same afternoon his own program reached a position in a game where after making an adroit sacrifice (Diagram 14) it could give mate in one move. After 120 seconds calculation COKO offered a sacrificial pawn to pull the Black king out further (notes by Bell).

**14**

**28 c5+ Kxc5**

In fact COKO had looked ahead 8½ moves (a full move is a move by each side) and seen the following mating sequence which it now played very quickly.

**29 Qd4+ Kb5**

This move took three seconds and COKO, because of Black's Kxc5, had already announced the mate. The next eight moves of COKO took less than a second to be retrieved from its memory. 30 Kd1+ Ka5 31 b4+ Ka4 32 Qc3 Red8+ 33 Kc2 Rd2+ 34 Kxd2 Rd8+ 35 Kc2 Rd2+ 36 Qxd2 Ka3 37 Qc3+

At this point GENIE had thrown away two rooks to delay the inevitable. No further delays were possible.

**37 ... Kxa2**

As Reshevsky said, good computers fight to the bitter end, and here's the reason why: 38 Kc1 f5 39 Kc2 f4 40 Kc1 g4 41 Kc2 f3 42 Kc1 fxg 43 Kc2 fxh1=Q.

Do it now!? COKO proved that it had a mind of its own. 44 Kc1 and GENIE plods firmly back into the game . . . After losing the white bishop and suffering a few more checks COKO's authors could stand it no longer and the program was resigned. Judging from COKO's performance, the game was subjectively drawn at that point. GENIE would have queened its g-pawn and then probably spent the next hundred moves or so making irrelevant checks. Kozdrowicki was heard to mutter darkly that he'd made a dam' fool bet that morning at breakfast . . .

I ought to explain at this point that it is rare for computers to be present in the tournament hall. Most are much too large, too sensitive and too valuable to be transported hundreds of miles. The usual way of communicating is by telephone. As Levy describes it, 'A normal telephone handset is clipped into a device called a modem which transforms the sounds that come through the telephone into impulses that can be decoded by a teletype or some other device. When the computer wants to communicate its move to the programmer, it sends a signal along the telephone line (via another modem situated in the computer room) and the signal appears as a move typed out in the tournament hall. Occasionally there is too much interference on the telephone line and the programmers are reduced to speech communication – they receive the moves from an operator in the computer room and give back the reply moves to the operator who types them in on the computer's console.' The time limit is usually 40 moves in two hours and 10 moves in every subsequent half-hour, plus up to three twenty-minute breaks during a game if there is technical trouble. A lot of things can go wrong, and usually do. The other distinctive aspect of computer tournaments, in the starkest possible contrast from ordinary play, is that such events are very, very noisy. Everyone is talking, analysing the game, discussing possible moves this way and that, while the software is humming away in the background, doing its own thing.

There is a science-fiction fascination about computer chess which goes back to the very first machine which played chess, the celebrated contraption known as 'the Turk'. Like many fairground attractions, the Turk was a bit of a fraud. In 1769, an ingenious engineer built a life-size figure dressed in Turkish costume – a bearded face under a turban – sitting behind a kind of elegant writing desk, well filled with drawers, bearing a chess board. Designed for the entertainment of the Viennese court, this Turkish figure – as I say, life-size – played chess against all comers, moving the pieces with its left hand. The public were enthralled by it. Few people, it appears, were taken in; the fascination lay in trying to detect how the figure was operated, and won so many of its games. Was there a little boy hidden in one of the drawers of the desk, which were opened up before the game started – a variation of the conjuror's patter, 'Look, nothing up my sleeve' – and if so how did he follow the game? How was the Turk's arm moved? The designer, Wolfgang von Kempelen, had intended to demonstrate a telechiric or 'distant hand' device; but to his dismay, according to Bell, his trick became a popular attraction, and its fame spread far beyond the court, while eclipsing his many serious contributions to engineering.

The machine was exhibited widely abroad. When seen in London in 1784, the audience paid a price for admission equivalent to a good seat at the opera nowadays. First the audience was allowed to see how the machine worked – the different doors in the desk were opened and shut, a candle was passed behind it; then, as the Turk won game after game, more and more doors were left open, so that finally it was difficult to imagine how a human being could be inside the machine, even a small boy. Later the Turk was sold to a Bavarian musician, who succeeded in staging a performance against Napoleon himself, in Vienna in 1809. According to popular report, Napoleon made an illegal move to test the machine, whereupon the Turk shook its head, and replaced the piece. On the third illegal move the automaton swept all the pieces off the board and refused to continue. Pure fantasy, suggests Bell, because no one would have dared to treat the Emperor in such a way. It seems more likely that Napoleon, no doubt flattered into a wholly false estimation of his own ability at the game of war, himself swept the pieces to the floor. What is certain is that he did play the machine on three occasions and lost each time. In America, the Turk made headlines whenever it appeared. Its owner employed a regular player named William Schlumberger to assist him, and it was noted by Edgar Allen Poe among others that this character, though on the scene before the games started, and quickly in evidence afterwards, was nowhere to be seen while the games were actually in progress. Poe thought he was hidden in the figure of the Turk. Napoleon on the same theory had on one occasion wrapped a shawl around the Turk's face and body. Or was it all done by magnets, so that a figure inside the desk could detect what was going on above, on the upper face of the board?

The mystery has never been completely cleared up. Levy is quite sure a figure was concealed inside the Turk. Bell suggests a double bluff. While the audience was looking for a figure in the drawers of the chest, in fact the showman was passing signals to an accomplice, a strong chess player, somewhere else in the room; he passed the next move back – all quite easy by hand or other signals – and a small boy, perhaps, within the machine adjusted the pieces by magnets, or by operating the arm itself. Not so difficult when the audience is looking in another direction altogether. Unfortunately the answer will never be known for certain because the Turk, after passing through different ownership, was retired to a glass case in the Chinese Museum in Philadelphia where it perished, unbowed, in a fire in 1854.

The idea of a machine which can out-think man seems to touch a mystical, anyway an irrational, chord in people. But computers are, in practical terms, limited because chess is not a finite game. In theory it is because there is a limit to the number of moves that can be made in any position. But the number of possible chess games is approximately $321^{6300}$ which is roughly $10^{15790}$. To illustrate how big that number is, consider that less than $10^{18}$ seconds have elapsed since the Earth was formed some 4.6 billion years ago. 'Even if one considers a reasonable statistic, such as all games last 40 moves, then assuming an average choice of 30 moves per position, the number of games is $10^{120}$ which is far more than the number of atoms in the universe,' observes Levy. 'This fact leads us rapidly to the conclusion that if all these computers worked together then they would still not be able to play the first move in the perfect game of chess in anything less than millions of years, by which time all the computers would have died of old age . . .'

Spectacular moves leading to a forced mate, which look so marvellous to the spectators, are in reality the easiest thing for computers to do. They have the capacity to calculate deeply and accurately. What is very difficult for a program, Levy explains, is to make a really good, subtle, strategic move, because that involves long-range planning and a kind of indefinable sixth sense for what is right in the position. This sixth sense, or instinct, according to Levy, is what really sorts out the men from the boys on the chess board. He recalls an example from a game by Mikhail Tal. In a certain position his king was in check on g8, and he had a choice between moving it to the corner or moving it nearer to the centre of the board. Most players, without much hesitation, would immediately put the king in the corner, because it's safer there. But he rejected the move. 'I thought that *when we reached the sort of end game which I antici-pated*, it would be important to have my king near the centre of the board.' When the endgame was reached, Tal won it by one move, because his king was one square nearer the vital part of the board than his opponent's. This was something he *couldn't* have seen through blockbusting analysis, by looking ten or twenty moves ahead. It was just 'feel'.

Computers do have certain advantages over human chess players. If no technical problems occur during a game, the best constructed programs will never commit simple blunders, such as leaving a piece to be taken for nothing, or overlook a checkmate in one or two moves. The computer will never fall victim to fatigue or inattention, and it will store and retrieve thousands of specific opening variations better than a human. Most other differences between human and computer players, notes Professor Eliot Hearst (a US senior master himself) in his contribution to *Chess Skill in Man and Machine*, strongly favour the human. The differences are not so much in general processes of learning or thinking, he argues, as in weighting of various specific criteria for move selection, that is in evaluative functions. It comes down to massive tree search versus focused or restricted search. Computer programs generate all possible first moves, prune some of these to retain the most plausible alternatives (a step which often eliminates sacrifices or other uncommon first moves) and then continue the analysis for four or five half-moves. The search ends and a move is selected, after tens or hundreds of thousands of terminal positions have been evaluated and certain specific algorithms applied. In contrast a human player considers very few first moves, sometimes only one. The difference between computer and human in 'learning capacity' is perhaps the hardest of all for computer programmers to take into account, notably the relatively strict depth limitations versus flexible depth analysis. Perception, as Neil Charness summed it up in another contribution, operates in two main areas: generating plausible moves and stati-cally evaluating terminal positions. Not only will a plausible move be generated more quickly by the master, but his long experience with many patterns on the board (50,000 or more) translates into the advantage of being able to evaluate the resulting position more readily.

It was David Slate, one of the programmers of CHESS 4.6, who devoted some six months' work to the program being prepared at Northwestern University to challenge Levy. The predecessor of this machine, CHESS 4.5, was good enough to beat a number of masters, including Levy, at blitz chess, a game where the moves are played fast, like five-minute games, or each player having to make a move every five seconds. As Botvinnik had noted, in lightning chess the strength of a master is considerably reduced, but that of the computer only marginally so, because a reduction in the computer's *breadth* of performance in examining its millions of positions reduces only slightly the *depth* of moves in its search. The new Northwestern program CHESS 4.7 (CHESS 5.0 was not ready), run on a powerful Control Data Corporation Cyber 176 computer, the fastest available commercially, represented a further advance on its predecessors and was stronger, so Levy declared, than 99.5 per cent of all the world's chess players.

As a poker player, Levy was not averse to covering his bet. Interest in the match had spread so widely through articles in the press and so on, that the Canadian National Exhibition offered to sponsor him in playing the event in Toronto. Financial considerations apart, it was highly advantageous to Levy's burgeoning career to play the match in a blaze of publicity. And sceptical as he was about the scientists' claims, he was surprised by the advances which chess programs had made before the bet fell due. For instance, by 'thinking' in its opponent's time, so that it could examine more variations, and running on more powerful computers, a machine could look at three million positions before making each move. Programs do not of course 'think': they perform a set of instructions. The principles on which they operate give them a different and distinctive style of play, with its own strengths and weaknesses. It was this fact, in effect a psychological observation, that was at the core of Levy's confidence. Levy intended to play in a style which exploited the machine's weaknesses – poker again. Computer programs don't have feelings, but their programmers and their opponents do tend to regard them as having almost human moods. That is why they refer to them sometimes as 'he'. And certain tendencies repeat themselves – for instance, Levy had noted that in the standard version of the Sicilian where White has a knight on d4 and Black a knight at c6, whereas a master does not go for the exchange because Black can counter-attack along the b-file, the Northwestern program usually did, because in doing so Black is left with an isolated a-pawn which it 'knows' is a bad thing. What it did not know was that in the Sicilian, Black's isolated rook's pawn does not matter, but having a pawn majority in the centre does. Levy, by making an inferior move in the opening, could tempt the computer to make this exchange, giving him the kind of position he wanted.

Playing the 'man' rather than the board? Yes, he treated the computer like a human opponent who was rigid in certain respects. Human is not quite the right word; as Levy describes it, it was more like a dog or a cat. 'Look at this move it played, such a nice move! What a clever boy!' The responses from the machine, some of which send out messages saying 'Be careful' or 'That was easy', do create a sort of empathy. Some players, even good ones, become very nervous; the machine, however, does not suffer from nerves. Chess can be divided into strategy and tactics. The best programs are excellent tacticians. Their calculating ability gives them an obvious superiority over most humans. They are less adept at evaluating positions and according to Levy do not plan at all. His own tactic, therefore, was to avoid tactics. 'Thus the strategy I adopt is to do nothing. But I do it very carefully. Sooner or later the program will dig its own grave.' So far as tactics were concerned, Levy favoured making a bizarre early move to 'confuse' the program and take it out of the book openings programmed into it. Subtle stuff! In other words, as George Steiner put it in *White Knights of Reykjavik*, the interactions between immediate perception and stored knowledge are themselves complex and inventive beyond anything reproducible in computers, with their yes–no logic and essentially static memory banks. 'Such key concepts as "advantage", "sound sacrifice", and "simplification by exchange", on which the choice of moves will depend, are far too indeterminate, far too subjective and historically fluid to be rigorously defined and formalized. The idea of "the one optimal move" is, in all but the most elementary or nearly final positions, a crude simplification.' Many celebrated positions and decisions in the history of master play remain disputed and unfathomed to this day, he avers. 'The vital parameters of psychological bluff, of time pressure, of positional "feel", of tactics based on a reading of the opponent's personality largely elude formal notation and judgement. They belong to the unbounded exactitudes of art.'

To add to the drama of the occasion, Levy wore a dinner jacket for the match, sitting in a glass booth under television cameras. The program was run from its computer in Minnesota via an open telephone line. A specially designed electronic board registered Levy's moves by means of a number of magnetic-sensitive switches located between the squares. When CHESS 4.7 was ready to reply it would switch on the lights on the 'from' square and the 'to' square to show the path of the moving piece.

In the opening game, Levy got into serious time trouble. He underestimated a knight sacrifice, which gave the program the opportunity of developing a very strong attack. As mentioned earlier, sacrifices are the hardest concepts for programs to carry out successfully, because the advantage gained, instead of being in the form of material, is usually positional. Levy saw the sacrifice but thought it was completely unsound and accepted the offer. But the program replied with a crushing blow and then sent him the laconic message, 'That was easy.' At this point the program was in a commanding position. 'My God, this thing is beating me!' Levy thought (Diagram 15).

15

| 12 | ... | Nxe3!! |
|----|-----|--------|
| 13 | fxe3 | Qg5 |
| 14 | g4 | |

Realising he was busted, Levy thought his only hope was to sacrifice the exchange to get the Queens off. So:

| 14 | ... | Qxe3+ |
|----|-----|-------|
| 15 | Rf2 | Bg3 |
| 16 | Qe2 | Qxf2+ |

Of course it would be crushing to take with the bishop and keep the queens on the board, so that the White king would die of exposure. But the program, Levy noted, knew it should trade down when materially ahead.

| 17 | Qxf2 | Bxf2+ |
|----|------|-------|
| 18 | Kxf2 | f5! |
| 19 | gxf5 | Ne7 |
| 20 | c4 | Rxf5+ |
| 21 | Kg1 | c6 |
| 22 | Nc3 | Rh5 |
| 23 | Kh2 | Rf8 |
| 24 | Nd1 | Ng6 |
| 25 | Rc1 | Bxh3! |

Levy had seen this coming but was powerless to prevent it.

| 26 | Bxh3 | Rf1 |
|----|------|-------|
| 27 | Ng2 | Rf3 |
| 28 | cxd5 | Rhxh3+ |
| 29 | Kg1 | cxd5 |

At this stage, three pawns down for his minor piece and his king naked to the winds, White somewhat resembled King Lear on the blasted heath, if that is not putting it too tragically. However, Levy kept his nerve. He managed to finagle back a pawn, then a second one; his position improved from being totally lost to merely hopeless; then he got a third pawn. By move 54 White had re-achieved, at long last, what he started out with on move 1, material equality (Diagram 16).

Levy had just played 55 b7! at which critical point in the proceedings the computer had a malfunction and its medical advisers were

**16**

called in. Twenty-five minutes later, with the program still having plenty of time on its clock it played 55 . . . Nxe7! – in Levy's judgement, 'a brilliant decision'. It is probably the only way for Black to draw.

56 dxe7 Rh8! (on . . . 56 Re8 57 Ba5 White wins) 57 Bd6 Kf6 58 b8=Q Rxb8 59 Bxb8 Kxe7 60 Bf4 Kf6 61 Bd2 Kg6 62 Be1 Kg5 63 Bf2 Kh5 64 Be1. And David Slate on behalf of the program offered a draw. A remarkable and exciting game and one in which the computer found several moves far beyond the present author's capability, if not the reader's.

The next day saw game two of the match. And here Levy as Black contrived to set the program more difficult problems in the opening by going out of the book and then tempting it to exchange knights on move 8 in the Sicilian, in the unstrategic way described earlier. After making this error the year before, the program had been modified in an attempt to prevent it exchanging in such a situation. But the basic tendency evidently remained in the works. By move 18 Levy had an easily won game. Came the third game when Levy chose the English and managed to go out of the book on move 2. Again, the program made an unwise knight swop, which, for the apparent gain of isolating its opponent's a-pawn, lost it the central pawn majority. It was comparatively easy for Levy to transpose quite early into the ending, confident that the program's weakened pawn structure compromised its position. He secured a passed pawn and marched to victory with some ease.

So, leading by 2½ to ½, humankind's gallant representative only needed a half point from the remaining three games to win his bet.

But the match was not over yet. Having demonstrated that his do-nothing strategy worked, Levy decided to experiment in game four by taking on the program at its own game, playing sharp, tactical chess, and trying to out-analyse it.

As Black, he played the risky Latvian Counter-Gambit which gave the program a pawn, followed by an early exchange of queens and a cut-and-thrust middle game. Levy conjured up a fast attack with doubled rooks down the h-file, but failed to spot all the defensive resources open to the program. It neatly repulsed the attack and then built up a pawn roller on the king's side. Levy seemed once or twice to be on the verge of achieving a winning position, or at least to have convinced himself he could hold the draw. Then he blundered by the kind of mistake which humans under pressure tend to make (Diagram 17).

**17**

Position after 47 Rd4–d8+ Kf8–e7??

'The final blunder. I had still not noticed White's next move and assumed that the program was going to play 48 Bxc5+, when either 48 . . . bxc5 or 48 . . . Kxd8 49 Bd4 (of course Bxb6 is also possible, but the program would be expected to go after the g-pawn in order to add to its passed pawns) 49 . . . Rxa2 50 Bxg7 would produce the unbalanced type of endgame at which the program fares less well due to its inferior understanding of passed pawns.

After 47 . . . Kf7 I don't think the program could have won.'

But 48 Bh4+! settled it. 48 . . . Kf7 49 g5 g6 50 Rd7+ Kf8 51 fxg6 Rxa2 52 f5 Ra3+ 53 Kg4 Ra4+ 55 Kh5 Rd4 56 Rc7 Be7 and Black resigned. This was the first occasion on which a computer program defeated a master in a serious game, though it must be admitted that Levy's performance was below par for a player of his rank.

In the fifth game, Levy reverted to his no-nonsense approach. Again he went out of the book very early, playing an English opening, tempted the program to exchange a centre pawn for a wing pawn, and rapidly achieved a strategically won game. The computer broke down again, but despite leaving itself only twenty minutes for thirteen moves to the time control, managed to find the best defensive moves, in an inferior position. Levy had no trouble in transposing into an easily won end game, when CHESS 4.7 had yet another breakdown (psychosomatic?). It was all over. David Slate decided to resign the game and with it the match. In settlement of their bet, McCarthy sent Levy a cheque post-haste from Japan, as soon as he learned of the result. Michie came up with his wager in cash. They had seen defeat coming, of course. The science had not advanced as fast as they had expected. But Kozdrowicki has not yet paid, claiming he needed the money to buy a house . . . This illustrates a precept of gambling which I learned from the pros in Las Vegas, which runs as follows: 'Winning is one thing and getting paid is another.' One of the curious aspects of the computer bet story was the confidence, the absolute faith, expressed by the scientists concerned that they would win their bets. They were so sure of their technological superiority, their confidence went further than the natural inclination to back your own side. The explanation, looking back, seems to be that they *had* to believe in their own branch of knowledge, and this conviction – rather unscientifically – went beyond the facts of the case. Levy knew more about *chess* than they did and therefore had better reason for believing he would win, given the state of chess programming at the time. 'They had to be confident that in a relatively small number of years, machine intelligence would make such advances that there would be computer programs which would play chess like a world champion, translate natural languages like a bilingual person, prove theorems in calculus or geometry with great speed, and so on and so forth. Their optimism was, in a way, just as realistic from *their* point of view as my confidence that I couldn't possibly be beaten was from my point of view.' Levy added generously enough: 'The really interesting thing is that progress in the field since I made the bet has shown they were more on target than I was.' Was it all just a matter of timing?

The match did not 'prove' anything, except that a chess master with a rather devious approach to strategy, an approach which would *not* triumph against another chess master – with the same rating – could beat a computer program which was lacking in long-range positional grasp. This particular program had not been instructed to take sufficient account of the significance of passed pawns in the endings. No doubt such a deficiency could be partly made up in time. The program did show, nonetheless, a very acute and wide-ranging ability in its chess play, producing numerous moves, both in attack and in defensive resources, beyond the powers of most chess players; and in tactical play, as expected, it proved sharper than its opponent. The plain fact is, according to Bell, that there is no simple way to reach human master level; no trick in maths, programming or knowledge of psychology that can replace the years of hard concentration that players like Levy have spent in order to play as well as they do. Could a machine ever think like a human player? Can it ever appear 'intelligent' to chess players? A test to decide the 'human' quality of machines was devised by Alan Turing, as follows. If a person is in a room communicating along two separate lines with a human being on the one hand and a computer program on the other, and if the person cannot tell which is the human being and which is the computer program, then the program can be said to be intelligent. The best computer programs have now passed the Turing test as far as chess is concerned.

And if this can be done for chess, the most difficult of intellectual games, it supports the belief that machines can be designed to undertake other socially more useful tasks, such as economic planning or strategic analysis.

Computers playing to a depth of, say, 15 ply will give masters a hard game, they may even get to an objectively won game; but they will not beat a master because, says Bell, they will not know what they are doing, they possess too much useless knowledge which slows down the deep tree search, and very aptly he cites Swift. How brilliantly this dilemma of modern computers was anticipated in Gulliver's visit to the Academy of Lagado!

The first professor I saw was in a very large room with forty pupils about him. After salutation, observing me to look earnestly upon a frame, which took up the greatest part of both the length and breadth of the room, he said perhaps I might wonder to see him employed in a project for improving speculative knowledge by practical and mechanical operations . . .

He then led me to the frame, about the sides whereof all his pupils stood in ranks. It was twenty foot square, placed in the middle of the room. The superficies was composed of several bits of wood, about the bigness of a die, but some larger than others. They were all linked together by slender wires. These bits of wood were covered on every square with papers pasted on them, and on these papers were written all the words of their language in their several moods, tenses and declensions, but without any order. The professor then desired me to observe, for he was going to set his engine at work. The pupils at his command took each of them hold of an iron handle, whereof there were forty fixed round the edges of the frame, and giving them a sudden turn, the whole disposition of the words was entirely changed. He then commanded six and thirty of the lads to read the several lines softly as they appeared upon the frame; and where they found three or four words together that might make part of a sentence, they dictated to the four remaining boys who were scribes. This work was repeated three of four times, and at every turn the engine was so contrived, that the words shifted into new places, as the square bits of wood moved upside down.

Six hours a day the young students were employed in this labour, and the professor showed me several volumes in large folio already collected of broken sentences, which he intended to piece together, and out of those rich materials to give the world a complete body of all arts and sciences; which however might still be improved, and much expedited, if the public would raise a fund for making and employing five hundred such frames in Lagado, and oblige the managers to contribute in common their several collections.

'One often hears criticism of the large investments in time and money which have gone into the computer chess tournaments,' noted Ben Mittman, reviewing the history of such events in *Chess Skill in Man and Machine*. Why should sponsors promote tournaments where the quality of the chess was, at best, class B or C? What possible benefits could accrue from chess programs playing other programs? 'To answer these questions one only has to experience the enthusiasm which is generated by these events. For the participants, the tournaments and panel discussions have been a unique forum for comparing notes and testing new ideas. Even though a master-level program may still be far in the future, the annual tournaments have shown that improvements can still be made in a steady incremental fashion. This may be too slow for some, but nevertheless, progress is progress . . . Writing a chess program is fun and challenging. No other justification is needed.'

Considering computer prospects some years after his paper *The Tale of a Small Tree* had appeared, Botvinnik still sounded optimistic, without evoking quite the same enthusiasm that marked his first comments on the subject. Could a program ever be written which embodied all the concepts of chess? he was asked. 'It should be reasonably soon though I cannot tell you any specific time,' he said. 'At the moment a human brain has very few resources compared with a computer. Mathematically a computer can perform so many equations. If it were possible to program a computer with everything necessary for the game of chess, it would certainly beat a human being. If it could be programmed to make only the most sensible moves, no human being could touch it.'

If you are going to play a computer, there is no reason to be scared, according to Professor Hearst. He proffers four simple rules to human players. 1. Play positionally and avoid tactical scrambles. 2. Examine all checks and captures that the machine can conceivably make in the next two or three moves, since these are the possibilities it will be concentrating on. 3. *Gradually* mobilise the pieces towards achievement of a long-term plan. Take advantage of the program's limited horizon by developing threats slowly. 4. Play for the endgame, where the machine is likely to be ignorant of the niceties of timing and position in pushing pawns and activating the king. He also adds: inspect *Modern Chess Openings* for technical or typographical errors – then manoeuvre the machine into one of these unsound variations!

In 1980 the International Computer Chess Association newsletter published by Mittman and his colleagues celebrated the arrival of a new world champion at Linz, Austria: BELLE, written and built by Kenneth Thompson and Joseph Condon of Bell Telephone Labs in Murray Hill, New Jersey. BELLE won the tournament in an exciting play-off against CHAOS. The two former world champions, CHESS 4.9 of Northwestern University (1977) and KAISSA of the Institute for System Science in Moscow (1974) scored only 2½ and 2 points respectively. The prize for the winner consisted of an aluminium cube, its top surface made up of a three-dimensional chess board of 64 moveable aluminium blocks formed in relief; the interior of the cube housed an electronic control system causing the individual blocks to move up and down. 'This computer chess prize is intended to symbolise the tremendous possibilities of the game as well as those of the computer,' the report explained. 'It is programmed so as not to repeat any single pattern during the coming 1.169 trillion years, provided the apparatus doesn't stop working before reaching that age.' Such are the games scientists play.

# 7

# MADNESS

*Madness is the professional disease of genius.*
*Hans Binder*

Does chess make players who spend their lives on the game go mad? Are they all mad, at the highest level . . . or only half of them? Or is it perhaps that all the top players are mad half the time? Eccentric seems too mild a term.

Certainly it is a serious question if you take as the starting point the fact that of the first nine world champions, two were without doubt clinical cases – Paul Morphy and Wilhelm Steinitz; one was probably unbalanced – Alexander Alekhine; and one seems to live rather oddly, to say the least – Bobby Fischer. Moreover, the two most imaginative stories about chess, Stefan Zweig's *The Royal Game* (1944) and Vladimir Nabokov's *The Defence* (1964), deal with players who have gone mad.

It helps, to begin with, to make a distinction between psychosis and neurosis. The latter is a minor disorder, like ritual or over-zealous washing of hands, or fear of the banal, such as certain ways of crossing or not crossing the street, which exists within everyday life. What happens in these cases is that energies are being wasted. (I follow here the comments of Dr Paul Matussek, professor of neurology and psychology at Munich University, in a round-table discussion on chess, genius and madness in *Schachweltmeister* edited by Werner Harenberg, published by Spiegel-Buch in 1981.) Psychosis, on the other hand, is a more incapacitating withdrawal from day-to-day reality, as in manic depression or schizophrenia. Most people, to the extent that none of us are wholly rational beings, display some neurotic tendencies – in chess as in life – such as sitting in a certain chair, or a particular position, or wearing a certain scarf or tie for 'luck', or having a favourite pen or coin or some other talisman to bring us success, like football teams with their mascots. No harm in any of that, within limits.

Morphy's problem was that he isolated himself from the world, broke off all contacts, after Staunton evaded his challenge for what was in effect the title of world champion. In a famous case history of Morphy, Ernest Jones, one of the first followers of Freud in England, suggested (1930) that 'the unconscious motive activating the players is not the mere love of pugnacity characteristic of all competitive games but the grimmer one of father murder'. The point is that the king is of crucial importance in chess – with the ambivalent quality of being both the most vulnerable piece on the board and at the same time the most important. 'The sense of overwhelming mastery on the one side matches that of inescapable helplessness on the other. It is doubtless this anal-sadistic feature that makes the game so well adapted to gratify at the same time both the homosexual and the antagonistic aspects of the father–son contest.'

The king symbolises the father, as in fairy tales depicting rites of family life. The theory is that in seeking to defeat Staunton, Morphy was in his unconscious mind wanting to kill his father and wreak a sexual assault on him – in short to mate him in both senses of the word. The very expression 'check-mate' is an unconscious replication of this process, from the Persian *shah-mat* meaning 'the king is dead'. Jones argued that before Morphy's trip to Europe, chess had served to sublimate these (entirely natural to all sons) destructive impulses, but that when Staunton eluded him, Morphy's mental and moral stability was shattered and broke down.

Wilhelm Steinitz's career, by contrast, was distinguished by the fact that he went on playing right through to old age, and playing very well. But he suffered from various delusions in his latter years, such as that he could speak by telephone without using an instrument and that he could radiate electric current through his finger tips to move the pieces on the board; and – this is so far-fetched that only a genius could imagine it – that he could challenge God to a game of chess giving Him a pawn. Such delusions did not take over his life as a whole, but were intermittent: and he could write from a psychiatric clinic in Moscow, during the breakdown he suffered after his final defeat by Lasker, 'Like all fools, I imagine the doctors are crazier than I am'. Modern psychiatrists would certainly see in Steinitz's behaviour borderline traces of schizophrenia. But rather than being induced by chess it seems equally plausible that chess, for long periods, kept such destructive impulses in check.

Alexander Alekhine was a wholly different type again. According to accounts of his play, he was always in a kind of nervous state, which sometimes exploded with uncontrollable force. He turned his back on his family and on Russia, his homeland; he was consumed with ambition, he loved fighting; he was also self-destructive in his addiction to alcohol, so much so that he drank himself out of his world championship; but he had the self-discipline to go off the bottle and win the title back from Max Euwe, the epitome of sobriety, two years later in 1937. His passion for chess was so intense that wherever he was – in a train or a restaurant or even a theatre – he would be engrossed over his pocket chess set. Married three or four times – the legal status of his relationships is not absolutely clear – his fondness for older women seems to indicate insecurity or search for a mother figure. His collaboration with the Nazis during the occupation of France may have stemmed from the same kind of opportunism – the feeling that in any situation he could find 'a saving combination' (Bernard Cafferty) which led him to exploit, in different ways, the women in his life.

One cannot but see in Alekhine's life the symptoms of a highly unstable character, though Golombek insists: 'I knew Alekhine very well and he was perfectly sane; there is not a scrap of evidence that he was anything other than a chess genius who was perfectly sane either over the board or away from it.' Alekhine's posthumous rehabilitation by the Russians was not justified by new evidence putting his war record in a better light: it arose simply and solely from the desire to reclaim, as one of their own, a most original and artistic player, prefiguring the Soviet school of chess. Alekhine's case, in the contemporary psychoanalytic view, was not on the borderline, leading to the psychosis of a Morphy or a Steinitz; his conduct was a barrier to such a transition.

Even at seventeen Bobby Fischer wanted to avoid contact with the world. Up to the point when he withdrew from the world chess championship his conduct was not irrational, in the opinion of Dr Helmut Pfleger, the West German grandmaster and himself a psychoanalytic therapist, even though he may have done some pretty peculiar things. According to Pfleger, in the same round-table discussion, Fischer's only aim in his life had been to win the world title, although he thought for a long time that he was never going to have the opportunity to win it. When he did, his self-esteem rose to the level of a god; and all of a sudden, as Pfleger puts it, he had such 'panic-fright' of what he had achieved that he just could not cope with it. But this is not 'mental illness', Matussek explains. In order to become world champion a player has to concentrate to the exclusion of anything else on this particular game; isolation is to some extent mandatory; and a person who ascends such rarefied heights is likely to be very lonely; in order to return to the world of ordinary mortals, a player needs 'happy circumstances', the most important of which is understanding friends. In Fischer's case (unmarried, without girl friends), this condition was signally wanting; he saw only enemies around him. Was he trying to copy Morphy? There is a resemblance in their conduct (assuming Fischer never plays serious chess again) but their social and psychological backgrounds are so different that such a comparison can only be on the surface. Who knows what Fischer was trying to escape from? His mother, a prominent campaigner for revolutionary socialism, had left him for East Germany when he was still in his teens. She was obviously the decisive influence on his life. Without presuming to pry into this relationship, it is easy to see how chess could serve as a refuge.

Fischer obviously still felt, Karpov notwithstanding, that he was World Champion (unlike a deranged person who might think he was Napoleon, he had good reasons for this conviction) and still thought so, judging from his abortive negotiations on playing a match (see Chapter 4) seven years later. Isolation can be a condition of creative talent and is not necessarily coupled with psychosis. The point Matussek emphasises is that psychological help must come 'at the right moment' for the person in trouble. If such a person has soared so high, it is hard to get back down; instead of castles in the air he needs comfortable accommodation on earth.

Living in a private inner world, a world of illusion overlying the real world, points up another potentially dangerous aspect of chess, termed in psychoanalysis the narcissistic element. The pleasure of being all-powerful, of controlling the game and through it his fate (even giving a pawn to God); with the knowledge too that his constructions in this self-created world of his will be displayed, analysed and admired around the world – all this can foster delusions of omnipotence which are correspondingly shattering when broken. Capablanca was surely the prime example of the narcissistic type of player. Everything came easily to him, from the age of four when he learned chess simply from watching his father play; he found moves and combinations and pursued strategies through into the end game, as it were without effort, smoothly, easily, intuitively. He himself boasted how he had never bothered to study openings, never had to labour at the game. In his public life he was an immensely attractive figure, a ladies' man, a star . . . Chess, for him, served his inner needs ideally well.

The Freudian view of chess, as advanced by Ernest Jones, is persuasive, up to a point, certainly in offering an explanation or Morphy's strange conduct and tragic withdrawal from the world of chess. (Another factor stressed in later studies was the refusal of his home town, New Orleans, to take him seriously as a lawyer on his return from Europe.) But as with all Freudian theory goes only so far; to the extent that it is valid, it is valid for the single individual concerned; it seems to need a grain or two of common sense, in applying it to chess as a whole. Yes, chess involves playing out the family drama, in a symbolic representation of the oedipal and other conflicts that exist in all of us; but not all chess players are working through this experience in a traumatic way. Moreover, the king is the father, but there happens to be *two* kings on the board. As Robert Hübner, one of the best three or four players in the world at the start of the 1980s, and himself a somewhat highly-strung competitor – he has walked out of more than one crucial match – pointed out in the same discussion, a player takes an ambivalent attitude to the two kings, his own and his opponent's. It is not so much ambivalence, as an emotional split attributing some aspects of feeling on to the one, some on to the other object. A player may indeed be confronting his father, but does he need chess to do that? Any number of activities, without a king symbolising the father, would serve as well.

Here Drs Pfleger and Matussek, in a revealing little exchange, disagree:

Pfleger: You have to checkmate one king and therefore you can play the role of murdering your own father. The other king gives you the possibility of identification with the all-powerful father.

Matussek: But what happens if a chess player does not have any ambivalent feelings for his father?

Pfleger: There is no one like that, such a person does not exist.

Matussek: So therefore if there is ambivalence always and everywhere, you can't use it to explain psychological phenomena which are only explicable in individual situations.

Citing what he calls empiric evidence, Pfleger goes on to note that 'many of the top players either had conflicts with their fathers or grew up without a father'. Well, it's hardly practical, even if it were possible, to 'psychoanalyse' all the world champions. So I present Table 3 simply as a rough and ready guide to show how the top players' or world champions' family upbringing compared, one with another. Where I do think the oedipal analogy is rather suggestive is in the father–son conflict represented by the successive generations of sons who rise up to take over mastery of the game from their fathers, the older generation. Each of the world champions from Steinitz on was defeating an older man (apart from the decade of the 1960s when the new breed of Soviet champions were in effect interchangeable as brothers) and must have seen himself, more or less consciously, as defeating his father. Though experience in chess counts for more than in any other game, in the end, age pays its toll.

Another issue is the role of the queen. Before the eleventh or early twelfth centuries the queen, as such, did not exist; she is a European innovation, not only a woman in a man's world, but the most powerful piece on the board. Adapted from the mediaeval *firz*, meaning an advisor (vizier), when the game first came to Europe the piece was restricted to moving three squares in any direction on the first move, and then one square diagonally at a time; it was, as befits an advisor to the king, close to the king. It is not known exactly how or when the *firz* changed sex and turned into the queen.

Was it a linguistic confusion between *fierge* (French for the Arabian *firz*) and *vierge*, a maiden? Only a pretty guess, according to Murray. Or is the explanation to be found in the psychoanalytic approach, namely that the introduction of the queen, wife to the king, shows how an adult game may be adapted to serve the oedipal conflict? In the late fifteenth century the queen's mobility was enhanced, to become the most valuable piece (mother-like) radiating power across the board. Again the how and the why are not known: obviously this change speeded up and opened up the game and in that sense reflected the quicker pace of the martial arts in Europe. It was an age of strong women, Isabella of Spain (1451–1504) and Lucrezia Borgia (1480–1523) to name but two: and perhaps the best model, considering this aggrandisement of the queen probably took place in Italy, Caterina Sforza (1462–1509), 'the warrier-countess of Forli' who wore men's armour, carried a sword, led troops into battle on horseback and ruled the Italian city-state of Romagna because her husband, the rightful king, was too weak to do so. This suggestion comes from a light-hearted psychoanalytic speculation about the arrival of the queen in chess by K. M. Colby. He argues that out of a man's ambivalent conflict between a desire to be allied with a virago and a hatred of her domination the queen was empowered. 'The changed game then represented a compromise formulation in which both elements of this conflict gained expression.' ('Gentlemen, the Queen!' *Psychoanalytic Review*, 1953). Golombek has pointed out in his *History of Chess* (1976) that since, in a mediaeval court, the queen was seated next to the king, it was entirely natural, when mediaeval Europe received the game from the East, to take the chess piece that was both as large as the king and sat next to it, as the queen.

However, let's suppose, leaving aside the question whether the queen arrived as a reflection of psychological needs or of cultural patterns or both, that the power of the king and the queen had been *exchanged* in chess – so that the king was the most powerful piece on the board, and the queen had been the most vulnerable in terms of protecting her against checkmate. Would the oedipal theory hold in that case? Or would a totally different group of people have emerged – women perhaps! – as world champions? People not seeking to kill their father, in a replay of the oedipal conflict, but people seeking to kill their mother . . . Thus Norman Reider, in his scholarly analysis of chess legends: 'It may even be argued that the fact that women in general find no fascination in chess is explained in the psychological event that they have no need for father-murder' ('Chess, Oedipus and the Mater Dolorosa', *International Journal of Psychology*, 1958). Merely to raise questions in this extreme form makes the point that one should not press oedipal theories too far.

More likely, as modern psychoanalysis would put it, the king stands for different aspects of the player's internal world, not necessarily the father. The king in this sense reflects a powerful person – it could be the brother, or the mother herself, the mother–son conflict being displaced on to the father. The opponent's king is a figure whom the player wants to destroy, while his own king represents a loved figure whom he wants to preserve. The split is not only between feelings of love and hate; the object or significant

Table 3

*Family background of the Champions*

| *Name* | *Date of birth* | *Place of birth* | *Family background* | *Marital status* |
|---|---|---|---|---|
| STAUNTON | 1810 | Westmorland | parentage unknown; father either died or deserted mother; learned chess late | married a widow |
| ANDERSSEN | 1818 | Breslau | learned chess from father at 9; lived with widowed mother and sister | bachelor |
| MORPHY | 1837 | New Orleans | well-to-do family; watched father play as a child | affianced but unmarried |
| STEINITZ | 1836 | Prague | large Jewish family; learned chess from a schoolfriend at 12 | first wife died; young second wife |
| LASKER | 1868 | Berlinchen | learned from father at 10 or 12 | married a widow with grandchildren |
| CAPABLANCA | 1888 | Havana | father cavalry captain; watched him play at 4, self-taught | married twice |
| ALEKHINE | 1892 | Moscow | aristocratic landowning background; learned from mother or older brother at 7 | married four times, attracted to older women |

| | | | | |
|---|---|---|---|---|
| EUWE | 1901 | Amsterdam | learned from mother at 4 | family man |
| BOTVINNIK | 1911 | St Petersburg | mother and father separated when he was 9, learned at 12, mother opposed to chess | family man |
| SMYSLOV | 1921 | Moscow | learned from father at 6; musical | family man |
| TAL | 1936 | Riga | learned from father at 8; enrolled in chess club at 10 | married twice |
| PETROSIAN | 1921 | Tbilisi | parents died when young | wife active in chess scene |
| SPASSKY | 1937 | Leningrad | parents divorced at 7, learned at 5 | married three times, lives abroad |
| FISCHER | 1943 | Chicago | parents divorced; learned with sister at 6, child prodigy; mother left USA when he was 17 | bachelor |
| KARPOV | 1951 | Southern Urals | learned at 4½ in the family | divorced 1983 |
| KASPAROV | 1964 | Baku | father died at 7, self-taught at 6; child prodigy | |

member of the family is also split. In this way the game serves players' unconscious feelings, for while we may not always be aware of it, the inner world is just as real for most of us as the outer world. But the unconscious forces in the thirteenth or fourteenth centuries, in an age when so many people died so young, when there was a preoccupation with death, may have been quite different from the Renaissance; and that period no doubt different in turn from our own, with the rise (among other things) of militant feminism. So people read into chess in each age what they want to read.

The players at the top obviously differ from ordinary chess players in the intensity of their psychological involvement in the game. Is it a further source of strain, heightening introverted tendencies, that in championship chess the players have to do all their planning internally, that they cannot speak or touch the pieces except when making a move, almost like religious ascetics, bound to silence? It means that they are living in a totally inner world (even though, of course, they may move around and talk outside the immediate physical space of their game); and can it then happen that a player, under particular strain, equates the chess world – with its intensity, its silent argument, its order – with the 'real' world outside, where people do not behave like chess pieces and make moves which are not in the game? Such strains could well be accentuated by the fact that the competition itself, the struggle to win, is very aggressive. But a chess player must keep quiet, he can't give vent to these aggressions (like a tennis player cursing on court or violence in football). It is all internalised.

In modern chess, it is rather the other way round – that players themselves recognise the need for psychological help of one kind or another. Karpov, in the entourage which supports and surrounds the World Champion, has in the past included a psychologist: though what the role of Dr Vladimir Zoukhar really was at Baguio was never quite clear. Throughout the first part of the match he sat in the front row of the audience, staring with an unblinking 'hypnotic' gaze at Korchnoi. And he certainly had a highly unsettling effect on the challenger, who claimed that Zoukhar was a 'para-psychologist' whose sole aim was to put him off. But was this achievement due to Korchnoi's formidable capacity for auto-suggestion rather than mysterious para-psychological forces? Later, after much wrangling, and the rapid loss by Korchnoi of three games on the trot, Dr Zoukhar removed himself to the back of the hall, at which longer range his 'evil eye' was presumably weakened. Korchnoi himself, in seeking psychological assistance, turned to the rather weird Amanda Darga sect, whose reputation was extremely unsavoury. In the next series of Candidates' matches when Spassky wore a green eyeshade and deliberately sat apart from the chess table, was it to thwart the 'rays' which Spassky claimed Korchnoi was projecting – or simply a cheap ploy to put his opponent off? Secret mind-bending rays! Isn't this the world of boys' comics, of superman? Or does the fantasy world which tends to colour and distort the vision of chess players sometimes spill over into the real world? These sort of antics began with Fischer at Reykjavik, but in Fischer's case the bad behaviour – turning up late, insulting his hosts, making more and more outrageous demands – seemed to be a product of his frenzied commitment to chess, not a calculated manoeuvre to upset Spassky, though no doubt his conduct had that effect. So much so indeed that the Russians, in retaliation, came up with the science-fiction accusation that Spassky's special swivel chair had some sort of hex put on it by the Americans. The chair was actually stripped down to its bits and pieces, but revealed only the sum of its parts. The incident showed that under provocation even the well-grooved Soviet school of chess could, shall we say, flip its lid. Hübner had a psychologist, Dr Lorezetto, to help him against Korchnoi: his role was the sensible and unexciting one of advising Hübner on his overall physical preparation. His presence, however, did not prevent Hübner from committing a gross blunder in a crucial game of the match and, shortly after, abandoning the whole contest. Why he gave up, when he might very well have won, is not really clear: according to Hübner it was not any one reason but a sort of generalised distaste for the tactics and publicity of the event. Korchnoi qualified but it was probably in this match that the first signs showed of a weakening of his game.

The thoroughness of Soviet preparation may be gauged by the visit made by an advance party, including Karpov, to Merano several weeks before the match with Korchnoi. They analysed the drinking water of the area, the level of radioactivity in the playing hall and elsewhere, checked noise levels and asked about seventy questions on the political situation in Merano and the South Tyrol region, the climate, the ownership and political line of the local press, and the professions, competence and standing of the members of the organising committee. (Interview with the president of the organising committee given to the Swiss *Chess Press*.) The total budget for the match, to be recouped by TV rights, gate money and other promotion, was 2.8m Swiss francs.

Hübner has offered an interesting explanation for the superstitious attitudes of some chess players. It could be that players from the Soviet Union are more prone to these kinds of fears and suspicions, because in the Soviet Union, and probably in the Eastern bloc as a whole, things very often happen which are difficult to give reasons for afterwards, because of the political set-up. People often don't know what is going to happen to them – whether they will get a visa, catch the plane they are booked on, be recalled to face some interrogation. It's not like the Stalin era, of course, but a climate of uncertainty can induce a sense, if not exactly of superstition, then of the uncontrollability of things. It's a pity there is no word in the language, as it were the obverse of paranoia, for a sense of being persecuted which a person cannot explain, cannot express!

One might sum up, following the useful analysis of London psychotherapist Dr Joseph Berke (fond of chess but with no clinical experience of cases involving chess), that chess does not itself drive people mad: it seems much more likely, on the contrary, that chess may protect these people who are unbalanced in the first place from their own madness. But there are ways in which this protection can break down. Chess can become too concrete or literal, it loses its symbolic quality. In other words, players begin to hate things concretely (the Russians, their opponent) rather than the symbolic representation of the pieces. They may feel threatened by the rivalry and competitiveness involved in chess. Having reached the top they try to stay there: but there are numbers of people (in Freudian terms, hordes of vengeful sons or brothers) seeking to bring them down. From the pinnacle of achievement, loss of rank or self-esteem (diminution of the narcissistic element) leads to a loss of self, and some players may not cope. The rules of chess belong only to the game itself: it is a narrow world: and after having lived as a god, coping with mundane human relationships (when other people stop behaving like chess pieces) may prove too difficult. All these underlying forces are essentially persecutory in nature. They lead to anxiety and depression and may, in emotionally immature people, provoke psychotic mechanisms to deal with them. If the same people have the necessary emotional maturity, they will cope –

some people grow up in the course of their lives, some people use chess.

> It hath not done with me when I have done with it.
> Letter from a Minister of Religion to his Friend, 1680

It is infuriating, isn't it, to lose to someone who in every other cultural accomplishment is obviously lacking? The classic instance is Mirko Czentovic in Stefan Zweig's *The Royal Game.*

This portrait of a chess player who, one step away from the board itself, is a crass uncultivated oaf, a man in whom all normal human feeling has been submerged under a brute-force mania for winning, is what has made Zweig's story so renowned. Czentovic has burst into the magic circle of chess, a peasant prodigy, a blockhead without any redeeming feature whatsoever, except for his genius for chess lying in his inert mind 'like a single vein of gold in a hundred-weight of dead rock!' Don't we know the type? Well, yes and no. A curious limitation, Zweig explains, of Czentovic's style of play was that he never managed, even for a single game, to play from memory, as it were blindfold. He completely lacked the ability to visualise the board in imagination, always had to have the 64 squares and 32 pieces physically in front of him. This limitation (like a pianist unable to play without a written score) is deliberately contrasted with the imaginative capacity of the other chess player in the story, the man of feeling and civilised values, Dr B. He indeed has survived solitary confinement by the Nazis solely thanks to his extraordinary feat of playing chess entirely in the mind. But Czentovic's inability to visualise the board in no way slowed down his progress . . . 'From the moment he won the world championship he thought he was the most important man in the world; and the knowledge that he had beaten all those clever, intellectual, brilliant speakers and writers in their own field, and above all, the plain fact that he had earned more money than they had, turned his initial insecurity into a cold and tactless display of pride.' Yes, the quest for money that Czentovic displays so crudely, as the only measure of his worth, is alarmingly familiar. '. . . he had contractual obligations to his agent which expressly forbade him to play on the whole trip without payment of a fee. His minimum is 250 dollars . . .' (and this is 1940 dollars). Provided the money is up front, though, Czentovic will play chess with anyone . . . apparently with no other interest in the game. Could it be that a former world champion might have seen a moral in this cautionary tale?

At a more profound level, the story explores another theme, the relation between chess and madness. Who has not felt, at some moment, that chess opens a bright-dark doorway in the mind leading to a kind of hallucinatory state from which, if the door ever closed behind one, it might be impossible to find the way back? In the mental anguish of his incarceration, Dr B. saves his sanity by the discovery of a book of master games, which he plays through and learns by rote and which overwhelms his imagination to the point that his entire being is consumed by chess. Zweig has a quaint name for this obsession: 'chess poisoning'. The prisoner plays against himself in space, in imagination, as if there were two minds in one self. 'My White ego had scarcely made a move before my Black ego feverishly pushed itself forward. Scarcely was one game finished before I was challenging myself to the next, because every time one of my chess egos was, of course, beaten by the other, it wanted a return game. I couldn't even tell you, even approximately, how many games I played against myself in my cell as a result of this insatiable madness – a thousand, perhaps, possibly more. It was an obsession I couldn't resist. From morning to night I thought of nothing else except Bishops and pawns, Rooks and Kings, ranks and files, and Castling and Mate. My entire being and senses were concentrated on the chequered board. Playing for fun turned into enthusiasm, which became a compulsion, a mania, a frenetic madness that gradually invaded not only my waking hours but my sleep, too. I could think only in terms of chess, chess moves, chess problems . . .' Dr B. becomes delirious and breaks down and awakes in hospital. There he slowly regains his sanity.

The climax of the story is the meeting over the board between Czentovic and the man who suffered from chess poisoning, when they are brought together in the challenge arranged by the passengers on board a cruise liner. It is a frightening experience for the former prisoner now restored to liberty and, so he hopes, mental health. '. . . the doctor warned me, expressly: the victim of any mania is always in danger. With chess-poisoning – even if you are cured – it's better not to go near a chessboard.'

And so it proves. Dr B., in a long, hard-fought game, defeats the world champion and the exhilaration of the struggle seems to bring on the fever of his madness again. He paces the saloon, faster and faster, unconsciously retracing the steps of his former cell, the glowing light of madness in his staring eyes. A return game is started. Czentovic, deliberately seeking to provoke his opponent, takes longer and longer over his moves. He sits there stubbornly, like a block of stone. And from one interval to the next, the challenger's behaviour grows stranger. 'It seemed as though he was no longer interested in the game but was occupied with something quite different. He stopped walking up and down and remained motionless on his chair. He had a fixed and almost crazed expression as he stared into space, ceaselessly muttering unintelligible words to himself. Either he was lost in endless combinations or . . . he was working through completely different games.' Dr B.'s feverish concentration finally explodes. He makes a move which evidently referred to some other game altogether. Acutely concerned for the balance of his mind, the anxious narrator of the story, watching the game, intervenes, to save Dr B. from himself, grabbing him fiercely by the arm so tightly that even in his fevered and confused state the man felt the hold upon him.

'Remember!'
'For God's sake . . . Has it really happened again?'
'No . . . But you must stop playing at once . . . Remember what the doctor told you!'

Dr B. stands up, manages to stammer an apology and leaves. 'That's the last time I shall try my hand at chess.' Czentovic shows a glimmer of human feeling at long last. 'Pity . . . The attack was quite well conceived . . . For an amateur.'

The original of Dr B. may have been an Icelander, Bjorn Palsson Kalman. His addiction to chess, it turns out, possibly served as a model for Zweig's story. As a schoolboy, Bjorn beat all opponents, including at the turn of the century the English champion Napier, when he visited Iceland. News of the talent of the young student spread, leading to an invitation to enrol at Harvard. During the voyage across the Atlantic, Bjorn was very seasick and spent most of his time in his cabin. But there were two chess masters on board who used to play in the passengers' lounge, defeating all comers. It was not until the ship sailed into St Lawrence Bay that Bjorn emerged; challenged to a game, he beat them repeatedly, finally defeating them simultaneously in blindfold play. But on arrival at Harvard, Bjorn found he could not play in the chess team until he had been in residence for a year, which was a great disappointment. He studied chess intensively and could not forget a single game, playing them over and over in his mind. In this obsessive state he was unable to sleep and feared he was going mad. His passion for chess went so far that he abandoned university life. Next heard of, he was living in Winnipeg, working as a bricklayer, having resolved to give up chess.

Now comes the most striking parallel with Zweig's story. Some time later Frank Marshall, the American master, came to Winnipeg to play a simul. A friend took Bjorn to watch and he was induced to play, much against his will. In the display, Marshall lost only one game: the story goes that after a few moves Marshall, who played very fast, slowed his pace and looked in astonishment at his opponent. 'Why didn't you warn me there was such a strong player in the group!' On losing, Marshall wanted revenge, but, fearing for his sanity, Bjorn declined the challenge. He walked away, vowing never to play again.

Recounting this little story, Gudmundur Thorarinsson (*Olympiad tournament magazine*, No. 10, 1982) points to several similarities with *The Royal Game*. Zweig had visited Harvard at a time when the story of the strange Icelander was current; he used the same initial B.; part of the story takes place on an ocean liner; Bjorn's passion for chess is close to insanity; and finally, like Dr B. when he beats Czentovic, Bjorn stands up and abjures chess for life. Whatever its origins may have been, *The Royal Game* works as a tale of macabre imagination, and has become a part of chess lore.

Madness is the theme of Vladimir Nabokov's *The Defence*. Or rather, one of the themes. As a highly wrought work of art, its meaning, its secrets, cannot simply be wrenched out of its poetry. On the cover of my copy, Nabokov's face, subtly, silently, peers out, as if to warn against trespassing on his text. Nabokov was a chess problemist of some distinction, who published a number of studies. And part of the originality of his story of Luzhin – fated as a child with the genius of chess, the genius of chess itself fating him in life – was actually to construct the story in terms of a chess problem. Thus, explaining his key, the author discloses that in an early chapter (4), he makes an unexpected move in the corner of the board, placing his young boy in a future scene in manhood, talking to a woman whose identity is not discovered till two chapters later; the retrospective theme shading in the intervening chapter into the image of Luzhin's father, recalling his son's early chess career. 'The entire sequence of moves in these three control chapters reminds one – or should remind one – of a certain type of chess problem where the point is not merely the finding of a mate in so many moves, but what is termed "retrograde analysis", the solver being required to prove from a back-cast study of the diagram position that Black's last move *could not* have been castling or *must* have been the capture of a white Pawn en passant.' This is typical of Nabokov's ingenuity: and there are many other chess-like themes and images in the skein of the narrative which give the story an extra dimension, which makes its composition a kind of chess struggle in itself.

Luzhin rhymes with 'illusion', the author points out, and in the original Russian title, the novel was called *The Luzhin Defence*. I wonder if it occurred to Nabokov that the name rhymes even more easily, in the English translation, with 'losing' and how appropriate that is. For Luzhin is fated, somehow. As a small boy, a ten-year-old quietly passing a summer in the country, not far from St Petersburg, before being sent off to school for the first time, a boy who did not run about with other boys . . . a listless child, always sitting in a heap, he was, in a word, undistinguished . . . until that inevitable day came . . . 'when the whole world suddenly went dark, as if someone had thrown a switch, and in the darkness only one thing remained brilliantly lit, a newborn wonder, a dazzling islet on which his whole life was destined to be concentrated'. The child's dis-covery of a passion for chess, secret at first, connived at by his adulterous cousin, encouraged, when at last discovered by his father, her lover, leads Luzhin on: he is destined to become a great player. While remaining himself undistinguished – as the author terms it, uncouth, unwashed, uncomely, but with something in him that transcends the coarseness of his grey flesh and the sterility of his recondite genius – Luzhin becomes internationally famous.

Nabokov evidently saw chess genius, or in the central figure of his story saw it, as a natural gift, an inborn quirk of the mind over which its owner has virtually no control. Luzhin of course reads chess books, he trains his talent, but still, his overwhelming ability takes hold of his life, not so much against his will but as if he had no other life. One of the magical effects of the book is to turn real life into a dream and chess into reality. 'He was wide-awake and his mind worked clearly, purged of all dross and aware that everything apart from chess was only an enchanting dream . . . Real life, chess life, was orderly, clear cut . . . how easy it was for him to reign in this life.'

Luzhin is a sort of white-squared opposite to Zweig's black-hearted champion. Czentovic was a terrible boor, who deliberately exploited his talent for chess to hurt and humiliate those around him, to avenge his sense of being culturally inadequate; he exploited this gift with the utmost crudity. Luzhin is no less a victim of the game, but despite himself; he has no inkling really of the other world around him, which is a dream to him, insubstantial or disordered; and he is, in his lost way, lovable. A gentle young woman comes to love him. And the central event of the story, like a transition from middle to endgame, is Luzhin's mental black-out and breakdown while playing at a great tournament in Berlin, and her attempt to save him so that he can, somehow, while putting chess out of his being entirely, make a new life with the aid of so devoted a wife. In chess terms it is not quite clear why Luzhin does break down, because he is highly successful, his games at the Berlin tournament, as elsewhere, are regarded as classic examples of the art, even immortal. By contrast, Dr B.'s madness arose from the mental strain of imprisonment in which he was driven to throw his whole self into chess, as the only way to hold on to his sanity.

There is one player, however, whom Luzhin cannot beat or finds it very hard to beat, an Italian named Turati. We are not told very much about Turati – he figures in the drama only as an ancillary character, off-stage – but apparently his challenge to Luzhin – they are joint leaders in the tournament and their own encounter at the board is poised, quivering, never finished – precipitates the break-down. Luzhin possibly suffers from the fate of the avant-garde artist who finds his ideas taken up, repeated and overtaken, so that imperceptibly a new generation arrives which, having assimilated his creative advances, leaves that phase behind, leaving the origina-tor looking slightly out of date, even old-fashioned. Turati, a representative of the then latest fashion in chess, 'opened the game by moving up on the flanks, leaving the middle of the board unoccupied by Pawns but exercising a most dangerous influence on the centre from the sides'. Luzhin, aware of his latter-day reputation as a cautious, impenetrable, prosaic player, so much at variance with his inner spirit and feeling for the game marked by boldness and disregard for the basic rules, resolves 'with gloomy passion' to enter new calculations, seeking a dazzling defence to counter Turati's brilliance. In their fateful game, though, a strange thing happened. Turati, despite having White, did not launch his famous opening! So the defence Luzhin had worked out proved an utter waste – and I suppose Nabokov here was pointing up in this crucial game a parallel with the experience of Luzhin in his life as a whole: no defence.

I quote here an extended passage from the game because, with its analogy with music, another recurrent motif in the story, it is perhaps the most beautiful description of chess in English (I can't vouch for the Russian version of 1930).

At first it went, softly, softly, like muted violins. The players occupied their positions cautiously, moving this and that up but doing it politely, without the slightest sign of a threat – and if there was any threat it was entirely conventional – more like a hint to one's opponent that over there he would do well to build a cover, and the opponent would smile, as if all this were an insignificant joke, and strengthen the proper place and himself move forward a fraction. Then, without the least warning, a chord sang out tenderly. This was one of Turati's forces occupying a diagonal line. But forthwith a trace of melody very softly manifested itself on Luzhin's side also. For a moment mysterious possibilities were quivering, and then all was quiet again: Turati retreated, drew in. And once more for a while both opponents, as if having no intention of advancing, occupied themselves with sprucing up their own squares – nursing, shifting, smoothing things down at home – and then there was another sudden flare-up, a swift combination of sounds: two small forces collided and both were immediately swept away: a momentary, masterly motion of the fingers and Luzhin removed and placed on the table beside him what was no longer an incorporeal force but a heavy, yellow Pawn: Turati's fingers flashed in the air and an inert, black Pawn with a gleam of light on its head was in turn lowered onto the table. And having got rid of these two chess quantities that had so suddenly turned into wood the players seemed to calm down and forget the momentary flare-up; the vibration in this part of the board, however, had not yet quite died down, something was still endeavouring to take shape . . . But these sounds did not succeed in establishing the desired relationship – some other deep dark note chimed elsewhere and both players abandoned the still quivering square and became interested in another part of the board. But here too everything ended abortively. The weightiest elements on the board called to one another several times with trumpet voices and again there was an exchange, and again two chess forces were transformed into carved, brightly lacquered dummies. And then there was a long, long interval of thought, during which Luzhin bred from one spot on the board and lost a dozen illusionary games in succession, and then his fingers groped for and found a bewitching, brittle, crystalline combination – which with a gentle tinkle disintegrated at Turati's first reply. But neither was Turati able to do anything after that and playing for time (time is merciless in the universe of chess), both opponents repeated the same two moves, threat and defense, threat and defense – but meanwhile both kept thinking of a most tricky conceit that had nothing in common with these mechanical moves. And Turati finally decided on this combination – and immediately a kind of musical tempest overwhelmed the board and Luzhin searched stubbornly in it for the tiny, clear note that he needed in order in his turn to swell it out into a thunderous harmony. Now everything on the board breathed with life, everything was concentrated on a single idea, was rolled up tighter and tighter; for a moment the disappearance of two pieces eased the situation and then again – *agitato*. Luzhin's thought roamed through entrancing and terrible labyrinths, meeting there now and then the anxious thought of Turati, who sought the same thing as he. Both realized simultaneously that White was not destined to develop his scheme any further, that he was on the brink of losing rhythm. Turati hastened to propose an exchange and the number of forces on the board was again reduced. New possibilities appeared, but still no one could say which side had the advantage. Luzhin, preparing an attack for which it was first necessary to explore a maze of variations, where his every step aroused a perilous echo, began a long meditation: he needed, it seemed, to make one last prodigious effort and he would find the secret move leading to victory. Suddenly, something occurred outside his being, a scorching pain – and he let out a loud cry,

shaking his hand stung by the flame of a match, which he had lit
and forgotten to apply to his cigarette. The pain immediately
passed, but in the fiery gap he had seen something unbearably
awesome, the full horror of the abysmal depths of chess.

The game is adjourned. Luzhin suffers some kind of collapse. He
is taken to hospital. The game remains an enigma, unfinished. The
remainder of the story itself, the endgame, pursues a different,
contrary theme to what had passed before: the inner and external
struggle of Luzhin, aided by the charming, warm-hearted (but
completely unchessy) young woman who becomes his wife, to
suppress his monomania, to excise it from his mind entirely like a
malignant tumour. 'I shall stop loving you,' she had told him, 'if you
start thinking about chess.' But why did Luzhin have to take such a
radical step of self-censorship? Was he losing his reason in playing
chess? The psychiatrist (one must note in passing that Nabokov was
almost pathological in his ridicule of the Freudian approach)
diagnosed prolonged strain, prescribed care, attention and diversion; and predicted a complete recovery.

But the problem in Luzhin's case went far deeper. He was an
utterly helpless victim of Dr B.'s chess poisoning. The game's
possession of him allowed no 'cure', no way out: he was only dimly
aware of what he was trying to do, so tenuous was his grasp of the
'real' world about him. Yet he manages to half-perceive that *life
itself*, the course of his days since childhood in the country, through
his boyhood, to growing up and becoming a master of the game,
was in some inexplicable way *playing a combination against him*
whose point, whose purpose, he could not define. 'Just as some combination, known from chess problems, can be indistinctly repeated
on the board in actual play – so now the consecutive repetition
of a familiar pattern was becoming noticeable in his present life.'

As presented in *The Defence* Luzhin is fated. I am not quite sure
why he had in the end 'to stop the clock of life', to perish, sui-mate,
except to say that that *is* the story of Luzhin. It is rendered by
Nabokov in such flighted language, with such intricacy in turning
chess-into-life and life-into-chess, that in its own terms the story
succeeds perfectly; even though the ineluctable fatedness of Luzhin
(dare one say) makes the book a chess rarity rather than a universal
drama of human feeling. Hamlet no doubt played chess and one
might wish that Shakespeare had made passing mention of this

aspect of his character, if you see what I mean.

*Remember, dear, chess is a danger to family life.* Chess Fever

'Chess poisoning' may manifest itself, like any other fever, in various colours, many degrees of light or heat. I take, as a classic representation of this addiction in ordinary mortals – not players of genius, but people like you and me – the film *The Chess Players* made by the Indian director Satyajit Ray (1977). Indeed, many movies have used chess as a rich metaphor for life, sometimes head-on, as in Bergman's celebrated *The Seventh Seal*, when a knight plays chess against Death, in a potent recreation of mediaeval myth, down to light-hearted asides on the game, as in the James Bond films. Indeed the number of films which have taken the image of chess as a motif is too big to track down here, and also too elusive – some Soviet films, for example, have never found their way to audiences in the West. I can't resist quoting, as illustrating the wide span of films touching on chess, the following entry from the American Film Institute catalogue of films made in the 1960s: *Brainwashed, Les Créatures, Hide and Seek, The Magic Voyage of Sinbad, Torture Me, Kiss Me.* All human life is there!

The most comical view of the interplay between chess and real life is the classic twenty-minute *Chess Fever* by the celebrated Soviet director Vesevolod Pudovkin, co-directed with Nikolai Shpikovsky. On the pretext of making a newsreel, he managed to film the great Moscow tournament of 1925 in which Capablanca and other leading masters were playing; and then cut up this footage to interleave it in the narrative involving his own actors, to make a satirical comedy. The result would have greatly surprised the chess masters if they ever saw it, which seems unlikely (according to *Kino* by Jay Leyda) as the film was never shown abroad until the late thirties, though Capa himself may have been in on the joke as he (or a figure resembling him) is shown at one point escorting the heroine to the tournament. The hero's extreme preoccupation with chess, and the growing exasperation of his fiancée, are depicted in a series of running gags in the good old silent movies style (my three young sons laughed a lot when we saw it). Everyone in the snowbound city is playing chess – a policeman in the middle of apprehending a passer-by forgets his questioning in the excitement of working out a position on a pocket set; a peasant taking his bag of corn to market becomes instantly engrossed when a chess book, thrown from the window above, lands in his lap; even the children, heads bent over the board, are in thrall to chess fever – 'Kolya played a queen's gambit!' Some of the gags are delightfully visual, as when the hero, kneeling to beg his fiancée's forgiveness, spreads out a large chequered handkerchief on the floor, and while she is swooning away starts setting out a chess position on it; even the wedding cake is in the form of a chess board; while the lovelorn damsel herself, resolved to make an end of everything in her despair, finds that the pharmacist, distracted by the game taking place in his shop, has wrapped up, not the fateful bottle of poison as she ordered, but a chess piece. 'Maybe love is stronger than chess?!,' the sub-title suggests. Enter Capablanca. 'When I see a beautiful woman, I also begin to hate chess,' he says gallantly. He is shown sweeping the jilted heroine off to the great tournament. When the hero elbows his way through the crowd to reclaim her at last, all is made up. 'Darling,' she coos, 'I never realized it was such a fascinating game!' The lovers' tiff is over.

It is difficult to photograph chess in an interesting way: it's slow; and there is a limit to the amount of time the camera can focus on players' faces to convey their inner feelings. A modern film which succeeded rather well in photographing chess was *Black and White Like Day and Night* (1978) by the West German director Wolfgang Petersen. Yet another variation on the theme of the chess genius whose addiction leads to madness, the film tells the story of Thomas Rosenmund who, after learning to play chess at the age of seven, simply by watching the game, suffers a nervous breakdown and swears never to play again. He keeps his resolve for twenty years. But as a distraction he devises a computer program which, for publicity reasons, the advertising manager of his firm arranges to play in a challenge match against the world champion. The match is staged on TV and the champion wins in seventeen moves. Rosenmund feels he has been made to look ridiculous and humiliated and determines to take his revenge. He gives up his job to become a professional chess player. 'His iron will, extraordinary intelligence and single-minded fanaticism,' as the film synopsis puts it, 'enable him to overcome all obstacles.' He becomes the official challenger and eventually succeeds in defeating the world champion. 'But he has already become a prisoner and victim of his own obsession. He suffers from increasingly frequent bouts of paranoia and megalomania . . . destroys his social contacts, his friendships and love for his wife – and finally himself.' He ends up in an asylum. 'Several things,' the director explained, 'interested me in the subject. First, to draw the psychogram of an over-ambitious, morbidly eccentric, self-demanding character who sees himself as the centre of the world and who is no longer capable of any feelings except towards himself . . .' The study is certainly extreme, he adds, but it may serve as a warning in a society geared towards ruthless individualism and success. The chess games, staged in a theatre against a backdrop of lights and curtains, focus the drama.

Among modern directors I single out one, Stanley Kubrick, as using chess in his work, as a model, as a way of thinking, quite deliberately. Chess is Kubrick's favourite game, the first of two lifelong obsessions (the other being photography) which he acquired from his father, a doctor in the Bronx. 'In Kubrick's case,' as film critic Alexander Walker has noted in his excellent film-biography *Stanley Kubrick Directs* (1972), 'there appears to be a very strong creative link between chess and the camera – one is a mental discipline, the other an imaginative craft.' They are both, one might add, visual-spatial in their operation. The thought that goes into movie-making, as Walker puts it, both in the physical preparation of a production and in the conceptual structuring of the film, is closely related in the case of this director to the attitudes that chess playing develops. 'If chess has any relation to filmmaking,' says Kubrick, 'it would be in the way it helps you develop patience and discipline in choosing between alternatives at a time when an impulsive decision seems very attractive. Otherwise it is necessary to have perfect intuition – and that is something very dangerous for an artist to rely on.' Evidently he believes that the pondering of choices, as in chess, enables him to make more good decisions than if he had impulsively taken the first one that came to mind as attractive. There is a striking photograph in Walker's book of Kubrick standing, playing chess with George C. Scott, on the set of *Dr Strangelove*, that stunning film about the endgame of life itself. Kubrick is a good player, up to amateur tournament level and, so Walker told me, likes to test an actor's character over the board when casting a film. Kubrick finds an analogy between the rigorous framework of chess and budgeting a film on schedule: 'You have a problem of allocating your resources of time and money in making a film, and you are constantly having to do a kind of artistic cost-effectiveness of all the scenes in the film against the budget and time remaining. That is not wholly unlike some of the thinking that goes into a chess game.'

More to the point, the chessboard finds its way into scenes in several of Kubrick's films, almost as a trademark. One thinks of the mighty computer HAL 9000 in the space odyssey *2001*, the machine which has taken on almost human qualities in contrast to the highly mechanical conduct of the astronauts themselves. In *Dr Strangelove* the narrative is structured around the race against time and the consequences of 'moves' made by the characters or by objects virtually independent of the characters. 'But whether there is this kind of internal evidence or not in a Kubrick film,' Walker sums up, 'its whole feeling suggests it has been shaped by a particular kind of mind, intuitively aware of choice, consequences and the pattern of play – and chess has been a part of this conditioning discipline.' Kubrick also worked on and off with Nabokov, the master problemist, in transposing *Lolita* to the screen.

However, the film which reflects in the most everyday way, the most charming way, the common experience of chess is surely Satyajit Ray's *The Chess Players*. Here the fascination of the royal game is depicted in a domestic setting, as distinct from the stark patterns of self-destruction or mental breakdown, even though their fondness for the game in effect costs the players their birthright, their national independence; they pay the price willingly, almost unaware.

It is a beguiling film, set in the land where chess was invented. The scene is the kingdom of Oudh in the 1850s, one of the last of the Indian States to have evaded takeover by the British, thanks to a combination of good fortune and regular payment of tribute. Lucknow, the capital, appears as a sandy pink and yellow city, its walls crowned with minarets and turrets, clustered around the courts of the palace. The chess players themselves are two plump and pampered easy-going friends, gentlemen of leisure, Mr Mirza and Mr Meer. Their absorption in their games, conducted reclining on cushions in Mr Mirza's house, soothed by hookahs, stuffed with sweetmeats, is complete: yet so gentle, so easy and domestic is their fascination with chess that they hardly notice how it has taken over their lives, threatened their marriages and, in the end, made them oblivious of the imminent seizure of the kingdom of Oudh by the British. For the British, having taken most of India, have now set their sights on this one remaining plum. Oudh is ruled by a dreamer, a poet, who in his self-indulgent fondness for music and dancing girls and the pleasure of his concubines, is as lost to the real world as are the chess players in their play together.

What gives *The Chess Players* its special quality is the way it conveys the intensity of feeling for chess as experienced by ordinary players in any place and, no doubt, any age – not the intensity of a world champion as in *The Royal Game* (also filmed in West Germany in 1960, starring Curt Jurgens as Dr B.) or the obsession of a great master as in *The Defence*, but the feeling all of us amateur players share when we don't want to go to work or go home and see our families . . . *you* know. The tone is set early on as Mirza and Meer, lolling on their cushions, gaze dreamily down through the aromatic exhalations of their hookahs at the highly ornamental pieces set out on the bright square of cloth spread on the floor. 'You may ask,' says the narrator, '"Have they no work to do?" Of course not! Whoever heard of the landed gentry working . . .' The tone is gentle, indulgent, the pace languid; and it is notable that they play the slow Indian game, not the British version of chess. The queen is called 'minister' and stays close to the king; the pawns can move only one square, not two, from the starting rank. Chess, the king of games, the game of kings, originated in India, the friends muse, so why have the British changed the rules? It's a *faster* game: just as they have taken over chess, so they are taking over India. In other ways the two old friends try to be strict. 'If you touch a piece you must move it,' warns Mirza (played by Saeed Jaffrey). 'But I always – ' 'But you don't! Last time you touched a knight and then moved a pawn.' Tch tch.

But, as usual, there is trouble at home with 'this stupid game', as Mirza's very beautiful and very bored wife puts it, vehemently. She wants him to give up playing all day and all night, to leave the game and come to her. 'Now you sit hunched over that stupid piece of cloth, and jiggle around with those stupid ivory pieces, and I sit praying to God so you will finish early and come to bed. But the wretched game goes on and on and I go crazy sitting and waiting . . .' He fobs off her attempt to seduce him with a hurried embrace – 'I do love you! I'll prove it tomorrow!' – and hastens back to the game which mentally speaking he has never left. 'They don't say a word,' he complains to Meer, 'when you spend the night with a whore. But when you stay at home and play a clean game, they pester you all the time.' Meer's own wife, it turns out, is countering her husband's preoccupation with chess in a more practical way: having an affaire with his nephew.

Next morning, when the two friends meet as usual to play again, the elegant ivory chessmen are missing, vanished – and as it is Friday the shops are shut. The duo are disconsolate; what are they to do now? 'To think I'd worked out such a beautiful new strategy,' wails Meer. 'The entire day is ruined.' They are in despair until Mirza remembers something. Surely a certain acquaintance of theirs, an old lawyer, keeps a chess set in the corner of his drawing room . . .? A pressing reason for paying a call on him this very morning! As they wait to be received, the two friends, like naughty schoolboys, surreptitiously start to move the pieces on the board, hoping the servant won't spot what they're up to. The old acquaintance, however, is on his deathbed; the sight of his evidently not-so-welcome visitors finishes him off; and they withdraw in confusion, the game unplayed. And then an idea, a saving resource, strikes Mr Mirza like a shaft of truth from Heaven itself. 'For every problem there is a solution! One must know where to seek it. Let's go home.' He sets on the cloth of the chessboard in place of the missing chessmen, an array of vegetables. 'Let me see,' Meer rehearses the new formula, 'tomato is bishop, lime is knight, chile is rook.' Enter the lady of the house in a furious temper, to hurl the missing chess pieces in their faces – it was Mirza's elegant wife who had hidden them, to frustrate their interminable playing together. These little scenes of marital discord, immediately recognisable, are very funny and very revealing, too. For when the two friends retreat, in self-defence, to the house of Mr Meer instead, who does he find, hiding under the bed, but his nephew? His wife stammers out an explanation. The young man is hiding from the British. Why? Because the British are rounding people up, prior to their takeover of Oudh. Meer accepts this implausible account of his nephew under the bed completely – his only concern is where they can play chess in safety.

Meanwhile, on the big board, the board of *realpolitik*, the implacable British are carrying out their own plans. The British Resident, General Outram (played as a Scots martinet by Richard Attenborough), has determined to revoke the treaty and replace it by a total takeover of the kingdom; this is not chess but conquest by arms. Except that the King, in his dreamy realm of dancing and poetry, is quite unable to act to save himself: the response which comes to his mind at news of the ultimatum, given him by his faithful prime minister – as in Indian chess, close to the king – is a plangent stanza on the lost city of Lucknow. His voice as he sings is full of tears. To spare his beloved and loving people he orders that there shall be no resistance; the cannons are to be spiked, the soldiers to lay down their arms. The British will take the game, without a shot fired.

Not that this worries Mr Mirza and Mr Meer for more than a moment. Their sole concern is to find a place where they can play undistracted by their wives and undisturbed by the British. All the more ironic, their dedication to the game of war, considering that in their veins flows the blood of Indian warriors whose valour, in their great-grandfathers' day, earned them the estates off which they are now living. And they find a place, over the river beyond the city, in a field by a ruined house. Here all is calm and peaceful; they lay the cloth on the ground and set up the chessmen. What could be more pleasant . . . the mimic battle of the chessboard is far more urgent than the loss of their national independence, not that that thought troubles their minds. No, what upsets them is a personal quarrel, and a bitter one. Beneath their partnership at chess there burns, as always in such friendships, a sharper rivalry, already suggested in the pointed little rebuke about Meer having moved a piece once he's touched it. Stung to the quick, when Meer's new strategy leads to his beating him in the first game, Mirza makes a scarcely veiled reference to the infidelity of his friend's wife. Meer is incredulous. The accusation, he retorts hotly, is only because Mirza is losing. Mirza repeats it. The shaft sinks in. Meer loses his self-control and snatches up a silver pistol – the friends have packed a pair of elegant handguns to defend themselves against robbers in the countryside.

Mirza backs away a pace. 'You must be insane. Throw away that gun!'

Meer stands there quivering with rage and wounded pride. 'You're saying this to upset me, so I'll lose the game.'

'That's a vile thing to say, Meer.'

In the stillness, the boy who has been attending to their needs gives a shout, 'The British are coming!'

Meer fires. The shot shatters the tranquil scene. And at that moment, on the skyline, the redcoats come into sight, marching forward, like pawns. Mirza stands clutching his shoulder; the bullet has nicked the cloth at the edge of his tunic. Silence. It is a bitter moment of unspoken reproach and self-accusation. The friends are shooting at each other when they should be defending their kingdom. As Mirza stands holding his shoulder, Meer begins to realise what he has done, or so nearly might have done. He retreats, and stumbles away towards the deserted village, from which all the inhabitants save this young boy have fled, fearing the invasion. The boy has brought food. In the distance, Meer's figure re-emerges, winding slowly back. Mirza calls to him. 'The food is getting cold.' Evidently he is ready to forgive. 'I see you've been standing under a tree,' he adds. Meer, birdlime on his hat, looks utterly miserable.

'Even the crows despise me. The British take over while we hide in a village and fight over petty things. We can't cope with our wives, how can we cope with the British army?'

'Yes, you're right, so why worry?'

'I'm not worrying about that.'

'What are you worrying about?' Mirza asks quizzically, looking up from his seat on the ground. And here the film completes its gentle circle of irony, for Meer tells him: 'About who to play chess with.'

Mirza puts down his food and makes a soft reply. 'Here is one person, Meer.' His friend nods, approaches, sits. Mirza smiles again: 'Come, let's have a fast game!' he invites slyly.

'A fast game?'

'Yes, a fast game. Fast like a railway train.' He picks up a chessman. Move over Minister! Make way for Queen Victoria.' And the army bugles sound in the distance.

# 8

# VISION

*O Prince, from inattention to the humbler forces the*
*King himself may fall into disaster.*
*The Tithtattiva of Raghundana*, 15th century

As a poker player myself, I find the most fascinating thing about chess is that the game is all open. Each player can see everything that can happen. In that sense it is exactly the opposite of card games which also require some cerebral effort to play well, like bridge, or, where concealment and deception is everything, poker. At any stage of a game of chess all the possible moves are open and therefore analysable. Of course the variations proliferate to such an extent that no player can possibly work them all through. But the number of individual moves playable at each turn in the game is strictly limited. In that sense chess comes down to 'seeing' more than one's opponent. How often does one hear the lament 'I didn't see it!' This is not entirely a matter of seeing with the eyes – look at the feats of blindfold play – so much as seeing in the mind: *vision*.

The lack of such vision is what makes one a bad player. I mean, it is easy enough to play through hundreds of master games – one of the attractions of chess is that almost everything has been written down for the past hundred years or more, so that one can enjoy an instant replay of all the great tournaments – and still make no improvement at all. One is simply repeating by rote a certain opening or move order without understanding what it means, what it implies. There is no 'seeing' in this process. The age-old question, 'How far can or should you see ahead?' is misconceived. The question should be: 'How far can you make sense of what is happening?' And in practice it's more subtle than that because a good player often makes his moves not directly towards a visualised objective, but (to change the metaphor) because he has a 'feel' for the position. I was much taken by a comment made to me by Tony

Miles, who rather consciously tends to depreciate home study and hours of analysis – the opposite of a player like Portisch who spends eight hours a day at it – when he explained that, for him, 'Chess is all feel!'

In this sense Karpov has a fantastic feel for positions, probably more subtle and alert than anyone now playing. He has the ability, highly developed, to see into a given position, to assess its potential for either side. But even he can go wrong.

An amusing instance of how this kind of vision works occurred in full public view when Yasser Seirawan of the United States, a very strong GM and US Champion, played Karpov in the Phillips & Drew tournament in London in 1982. Viktor Korchnoi turned up during the tournament, as was his habit in those days, to protest about the continued detention of his wife and son in Russia. Obviously the great Viktor, who had won the tournament two years previously, was not invited this time because of the unwritten Soviet law that if he played, no Soviet GM would be allowed to come. This time the British organisers wanted Karpov. After causing a minor stir for the cameras by parading around outside the hall, Korchnoi came in to watch the play. Seirawan had been his second at Merano, and Korchnoi returned the compliment by spending some time the night before Seirawan's game with Karpov, preparing him for his encounter with the World Champion.

Korchnoi came up with a new move in the Queen's Gambit, 12 Rc3!

| | Seirawan | Karpov |
|---|---|---|
| 1 | Nf3 | Nf6 |
| 2 | c4 | e6 |
| 3 | Nc3 | d5 |
| 4 | d4 | Be7 |
| 5 | Bg5 | h6 |
| 6 | Bh4 | 0–0 |
| 7 | Rc1 | b6 |
| 8 | cxd5 | Nxd5 |
| 9 | Nxd5 | exd5 |
| 10 | Bxe7 | Qxe7 |
| 11 | g3 | Re8 |
| 12 | Rc3!? | |

There followed **12 . . . Na6 13 Qa4 c5!??** giving the position shown in Diagram 18a.

18a

Blunder or sacrifice? asked Raymond Keene in the tournament bulletin. 'Spectators stood around in droves, gawping at the possibility of Re3 winning a piece. Karpov, however, seemed to be very calm, chatting happily with Geller while awaiting Seirawan's reply.' Of course, White has to accept the challenge and the game proceeded:

| | | |
|---|---|---|
| **14** | **Re3** | **Be6** |
| **15** | **Qxa6** | **cxd4** |
| **16** | **Rb3** (not Nxd4? Qb4+) | |

and with a solid piece up, Seirawan went on to win – the only game Karpov dropped in the whole tournament.

A few weeks later the players met again, this time in a television spectacular, the World Cup chess tournament played in Hamburg. Though played in a rather pop atmosphere and at a faster pace than a major tournament, it was still a serious event. The prize money to the winner was on the same par as the London event. So they sat down to play, under the eye of the cameras, and reeled off exactly the same opening moves. The feature of this entertaining TV presentation of chess is that the players comment on their moves (recorded after the game, but relayed as the game is actually happening) by voice over. So the viewer gets in effect a triple mental image: watching the game, his own judgement is overlaid by what the players themselves think about their moves, and then modified again by an expert commentary from the resident analyst of the series, British IM Bill Hartston.

At move 12 Seirawan paused for thought: 'I've looked at this game so often, I've shown it to all my friends. I'm sure he's got something to surprise me with. But I can't chicken out . . .' So, 12 Rc3.

Karpov played the same move, 12 . . . Na6, repeating the earlier game.

Seirawan: 'Can it be I'll beat the world champion twice in the same system? No!'

## 13   Qa4

Karpov: 'I was surprised by this move in London. But now I'm not surprised because I've prepared something. Now I play b5 and win a tempo [gain a move] . . . The queen is out and I can sacrifice the piece again.'

18b

**13   . . . b5! (Diagram 18b)**
**14   Qa5?** (Qc2 is safer; Qxb5 Rb8 is good
       for Black)
**14   . . . Qe4!**

Seirawan: 'Oh Jesus! Oh, it's so simple. Oh no! He has a free attack. I fell into his preparation.'

## 15   Kd2

Karpov: 'It was the only move.'

Hartston: 'It looks like a really venomous piece of preparation, to bring the queen to e4. With the queen out of play and the king out of position . . .'

The game proceeded:

| 15 |      | Re6       |
|----|------|-----------|
| 16 | b3   | b4        |
| 17 | Re3  | Qb1       |
| 18 | Rxe6 | Qb2+      |
| 19 | Kd1 (if Ke3 Qc1+ . . . Qc3++) | Bxe6! |

Seirawan: 'It's getting hotter and hotter . . . why did I dress up in a tie? I wonder about these things. Here I am sweating horribly and I'm all nicely dressed. Next time I'll come in my underwear. At least it will be good psychologically. He will never expect that. Of course, I could come better prepared too . . .'

| 20 | Qxa6 | Qa1+ |
| 21 | Kd2  | Qc3+ (Black's last two checks are to bring his queen to c3 preventing White's queen from defending at c6.) |
| 22 | Kd1  | Bf5 |
| 23 | Ne1  |     |

Karpov: 'I must get my rook in the game. If Re8 then he has Qb5 . . . so maybe better Rb8.'

| 23 |      | Rb8! |
| 24 | Qxa7 | Rb6  |
| 25 | e3   | Rc6  |

Hartston: 'I've yet to see what Karpov's got in mind. I don't see it.'

Seirawan: 'Oh yes! He probably did not see that I can save the game! Let's first ensure the draw with Bc4.'

Karpov: 'I saw something . . . Oh yes . . . I have a trap after Bc4.'

**26  Bc4** (Diagram 18c)

**18c**

Hartston: 'I'm still not convinced he is winning . . . Karpov sounds as if he has got it all worked out. Seirawan and I still have to see what it is he's got worked out.'

**26 Qa1+**

'Now I must win for sure.' (No exclamation mark in his voice, he's a cold fish.) Seirawan: 'Now he will take the draw. I'll just allow him a perpetual now.'

**27 Ke2          Qb2+**

Seirawan: 'Fine, Kd1' (28 Kf1 Bh3+ 29 Kg1 Qc1 or 28 Kf3 Be4+ leave White defenceless).

Karpov: 'Now it's very simple. I take on c4 and sacrifice my rook. How can he protect d2?'

**28 Kd1 dxc4!**

Seirawan: 'Shrak! Oh Jee-eez. Oh my gosh . . . It's atrociously hot now. How come the little things bother you when you are in a bad position. They don't bother you in good positions. As Larsen said, "A chess player never has a heart attack in a good position." What does that mean about the opening? Qa4 is bad, I should have played Qc2 . . .'

**29 Qa8+          Kh7**
**30 Qxc6          c3**

And as Seirawan added, 'That's it, sports fans.' (There is no adequate defence against Black's threat of Qd2++.)

The moral of which is: seeing is in the eye of the beholder. In the first game the World Champion, taken by surprise, played the plausible thirteenth move . . . c5. He did not 'see' that his position was not going to be tenable. In the latter game he played the slightly but significantly different response . . . b5 and Seirawan did not 'see' that his own position was going to collapse.

I talked to Seirawan, who has a very easy-going and engaging personality, some time after this débâcle, and asked him how he could have tried to pull the same stunt twice on the World Champion. He told me: 'No way! I had seen Qe4 and prepared for it. But not in this line. Somehow I had completely overlooked it. I don't know what the hell I was doing. I had analysed Qa5, Korchnoi thought Qd1, and Qc2 was a sort of compromise.'

It's not a new move as such which floors an opponent, the so-called prepared variation, it's the idea. As Hartston put it, Re3 in the first Seirawan–Karpov game had not been seen before. The normal move is pawn to e3. He suggested a parallel in the rather unusual move which Spassky found against Fischer, a backward knight move, in game 11 at Reykjavik (Diagram 19).

Here's how Svetozar Gligoric, the amiable Yugoslav *éminence grise*, put it in his final account of the match: 'So it seemed that the end of the great Soviet chess empire was taking on the appearance of a strangely quiet, easy and uneventful death [Fischer was then leading 6½–3½] . . . Outwardly Spassky looked abandoned to his fate. Spassky's first move had a slightly electrifying effect. It was the king's pawn, the move which he had avoided against Fischer for twelve years [until this match] . . . after thirteen moves the position was still of a known type.

'Then Spassky took thirty minutes to decide what to do next. It is hard to guess whether the next move was prepared or not. Spassky said it was not.'

Here's the position after Black's 13th move . . . B-d7, preparing to put his king into safety by castling queenside. What do you play?

Spassky found Nb1!! This is a quite unexpected idea in this kind of position because it seems to retard White's development. Whether it was prompted from Moscow, dreamed up in the past couple of days in Spassky's hotel room, or discovered over the board in those

**19**

thirty minutes during which he thought about it, it had a devastating effect on Fischer who, as Gligoric adds, had never been in trouble with this line in his whole career. He resigned on move 31.

Sometimes on encountering a 'new' move, a player will rise to the challenge. Thus Capablanca, in one of the most famous games in the history of chess, played in New York in 1918, beat off the Marshall attack and finally won. It was the first time in a decade that Frank Marshall did not play the Petroff to avoid the Ruy Lopez.

| Capablanca | Marshall |
|---|---|
| 1  e4 | e5 |
| 2  Nf3 | Nc6 |
| 3  Bb5 | a6 |
| 4  Ba4 | Nf6 |
| 5  0–0 | Be7 |
| 6  Re1 | b5 |
| 7  Bb3 | 0–0 |
| 8  c3 | d5 |
| 9  exd5 | Nxd5 (Diagram 20) |

At this point, Capablanca noted afterwards: 'I thought for a while before playing this, knowing I would be subjected to a terrific attack, all the lines of which would of necessity be familiar to my adversary. The lust of battle, however, had been aroused within me. I felt that my judgement and skill were being challenged by a player who had every reason to fear both (as shown by the records of our

**20**

previous encounters), but who wanted to take advantage of the element of surprise and of the fact of my being unfamiliar with a thing to which he had devoted many a night of toil and hard work. I considered the position then and decided that I was in honour bound, so to speak, to take the Pawn and accept the challenge, as my knowledge and judgement told me that my position should then be defendable.'

And he played 10 Nxe5.

In short, a man must have the courage of his convictions! Frank Marshall, the great American player, really enjoyed his chess and played every day. He had saved up this variation for ten years to topple the mighty Capa, but in vain. The Marshall attack, nevertheless, based on 7 . . . 0–0 and quick development, has proved its value and has won a lasting place in chess theory.

Players recognise at once, of course, when a new move or new line comes up, designed to unhinge their normal play. Fischer, being Fischer, was the kind of player who was so interested in a new idea that he positively relished the challenge. An absorbing account of the layers of perception in chess vision came up in his one and only encounter with Botvinnik, at the Varna olympiad in 1962. This dramatic meeting between the generations, as Larry Evans termed it, took place on board 1, after it was rumoured that Botvinnik would take a rest day. But the lure of playing Fischer was evidently too attractive for Botvinnik to resist, especially as he had White and had prepared a new line, seventeen moves deep, in one of his favourite openings, the Gruenfeld defence. 'I could see by the glint in his eye,' Fischer observed after his third move, 'that he had come well armed for my King's Indian.' The position after White's 17th move is shown in Diagram 21.

**21**

'When I was preparing to meet Smyslov,' Botvinnik wrote, 'I, of course, made a thorough analysis of the Smyslov system in general and of the position on the diagram in particular! Here I reckoned that whether the Black Queen went to h4 or f5 it would be in danger . . . Alas, my opponent found a third continuation!'

17 . . . Qxf4! 'When I made this move, I felt sure he had overlooked it,' noted Fischer.

'A very unpleasant surprise,' Botvinnik continued; 'now White really has to start playing. Up to here I had only to remember my analysis . . . then suddenly it was obvious that in my analysis I had missed what Fischer had found with the greatest of ease at the board. The reader can guess that my equanimity was wrecked.'

Why didn't Botvinnik 'see' this tactical resource? The answer, presumably, is that there is usually, or anyway very often, something more in a position than appears, especially when a player has a psychological motivation for wanting to believe that his own analysis of his own chances is superior. Black won a pawn out of this manoeuvre and the game moved into a long and complex middle and end game, in which Fischer throughout had the initiative and, apparently, missed the win he was convinced was there. Botvinnik only saved the draw thanks to exhaustive overnight analysis of the adjourned position by the Russian team. 'Fischer spent the night asleep and in the adjournment session fell into the pitfall – there were tears in the young man's eyes,' Botvinnik recalled. When the game ended Fischer shook hands and fled the hall 'white as a sheet'.

In his own exhaustive account of what-might-have-been, Fischer demonstrated that he had the win, and that the analysis published by Botvinnik was wrong. In it, Botvinnik had concluded, 'after considerable soul-searching', that the game was drawn even against the best line. Fischer's analysis seemed to prevail. But there was a sting in the tail, which came many years later from a player who was not even born when the game was played. Botvinnik gave the position as an exercise to the pupils in his chess school. Thirteen-year-old Garry Kasparov found yet another way to draw it!

In other words a player can still be of world championship calibre and not 'see' everything going on. Here's another example of a new idea, which caught Karpov in the shortest defeat ever suffered by a player in the Candidates' series. It began in Moscow, when the English players Keene and Hartston went over to prepare a book on the Karpov–Korchnoi encounter. Keene was playing around with a pocket set over dinner and hit upon what seemed a stunning new idea in the Queen's Indian. Korchnoi was so impressed he immediately phoned David Bronstein, who gave the matter some further thought and elaboration. The position after move 10 is shown in Diagram 22.

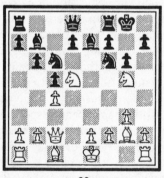

**22**

11. Qd2! The most effective method of transferring the queen towards the dark square weaknesses near the Black king.
. . . Nxd5?
12. Bxd5 Rb8?

13. Nxh7!! Re8 Tantamount to resignation, but acceptance of the sacrifice is quite hopeless.

14. Qh6. That Anatoly Karpov should be faced with calamity after a mere fourteen moves, with enemy units clustered around his king, shows just how difficult chess really is, the Hartston–Keene commentary rightly observes. The game concluded with Karpov resigning on move 19.

Karpov's own comment, recorded in his autobiography, was: 'How could it be?' with a bitter laugh. 'In one of my opening notebooks Black's twelfth move is given an exclamation mark, and yet immediately after White's reply he has to resign! Once again I was too trusting . . . Well now, let that be a lesson to me.'

Wise advice. Never take anything for granted. Players react very differently to defeat. Karpov has the strength of character not to be thrown. 'When a player loses, he suffers two thoughts: the first – he is angry with himself, how could he lose at all; the second – that he should lose to such a "twit".' It is reassuring to know that world champions have exactly the same reaction to losing as the rest of us. The point is, everyone loses at one time or another. And a strong player must have the resilience to bounce back. Karpov on the rare occasions when he loses likes to change his suit for the next encounter, implying perhaps that a new man is sitting at the board. I once watched Tony Miles lose to an unrated player, in a difficult game where Miles could have taken a draw by perpetual, but chose, characteristically, to go for a win. Though he seemed entirely at ease after the game, he must have been seething inwardly. 'How did you really feel after that loss?' I ventured to inquire, when he had subsequently won the tournament. 'Angry. How could I lose to such an idiot?' In a strong tournament the top rated players are likely to have at least one loss: the eventual winner is the player who has the will, as it were, to master himself.

Addressing the subject of defeats in his *Psychology of Chess*, Soviet GM Nikolai Krogius proffers the remedy of 'auto-suggestion'. 'Do not try to recall the ancient wise men and the mysterious magic of the Indian fakirs. It is all much simpler. These days hypnosis has become one of the main methods of psycho-therapy and education. It is a good thing when a trainer can cheer up "the sufferer" without too much moralising, bring a light-hearted touch to the subject of his misfortune and then direct his thoughts elsewhere. Often, though, there is no trainer, and whether you want to or not you have to face your emotions on your own. It is here that auto-suggestion can help . . .' He recommends 'self-orders' to forget adverse emotions in order to concentrate on thinking about something pleasant and happy . . . rather heavy-handed advice, it seems to me. Krogius himself, though a strong player, has given up active play and joined the ranks of the administration. I prefer the advice of Capablanca: 'Most players . . . do not like losing, and consider defeat as something shameful. This is a wrong attitude. Those who wish to perfect themselves must regard their losses as lessons and learn from them what sort of things to avoid in the future.' Both Karpov and Botvinnik before him have reacted amazingly strongly to losses, scoring around 67 per cent in games following a loss. Euwe, by contrast, tended to crack up, with results as low as 40 per cent after a loss. All strong players need this introspective bent, to find out what went wrong, with a trainer or without a trainer.

The role of a 'second' in chess is bizarre. According to Raymond Keene, who acted as a second for Korchnoi in Baguio, the task has little to do with chess. 'The main job is to keep the player happy, get him a drink when he wants a drink, cheer him up when he's miserable, calm him when he's angry, and try to keep him out of hassles.' Yefim Geller once observed that he was not interested in having a second. Why not? 'I don't have time during important tournaments to give chess lessons!'

To return to vision: 'seeing' is not just a matter of finding new moves in the openings, or unravelling the maze of the middle game. It applies no less to endgames and simple positions, when only a few pieces may be left on the board. As a case in point, here's a little puzzle shown to me by Leonid Shamkovitch (Diagram 23).

White to play and draw.

Shamkovitch has tried out this study on two or three world champions, with amusing results. Thus, he once showed it to Petrosian, who while a great player is perhaps a touch lazy. Petrosian gave him a wry smile. 'Hm . . . mm . . . Leonid, I don't want to break my head over it . . . just show me the answer, will you?'

Smyslov had quite a different reaction. 'Yes, now let me see, knight moves . . . no, knight moves there . . . no . . .' He spent ten minutes on it and then asked for the solution.

Only two players have cracked it. The first was Bobby Fischer,

**23**

during a lunch in Pasadena. 'Bobby, here's a tricky position for you. It's rather difficult so I'll show you the solution.'

'No, no, no! I'll find it myself.' Bobby took out a pocket set and cupped it in his large hands in front of his face, so no one could see what he was doing as he tried out various moves. He got the answer in a couple of minutes.

The other solver was Garry Kasparov, but this was really incredible because he didn't have a board with him. He found the answer immediately in his head. Tal who was watching gave a quizzical smile as if to say, 'You didn't know what this kid can do, did you!'

Shamkovitch was surprised himself. 'Garry, you've seen it before, haven't you?'

'No, certainly not, I understood how to do it. *I knew immediately what was the best square for the knight.*'

For the reader who might care to try his wits, I should explain that obvious moves with the knight are blocked by the Black king so that the pawn goes on to queen. The key move, as so often in such problems, is a logical but wholly unexpected third move. I give the solution at the bottom of the page,* just in case you are not as smart as Kasparov.

Vision indeed is everything, but it can also be influenced by extraneous factors. As I noted at the start of this chapter, chess is not like poker because it is all open. Yet there is bluff at chess which might be defined in this context as an attempt to distort the

*1 Nb4 h5 2 Nc6 Ke4 (best)

3 Na5!! h4 4 Nc4 and it is easy to stop the pawn by moving the knight around f1–h2–g4.

opponent's vision. Remember Fischer's opening move of pawn c4 in the sixth game against Spassky at Reykjavik? He had never made any secret of his conviction that pawn e4 was far and away the strongest opening move. Such a ploy by Fischer was not exactly a bluff but a way of throwing his opponent off balance – Spassky cannot have really expected it. And Fischer took the lead in the match for the first time.

I suppose the most outrageous piece of bluff in recent times was Miles's game against Karpov in the European Team Championship at Skara in Sweden, in 1980. Knowing that Karpov's opening repertoire was so complete as to be almost impregnable, Miles as Black responded to 1e4 with a6, which was greeted by incredulous smiles from the spectators, and followed up 2 d4 with b5 which provoked outright mirth. Miles had played a lot of games at home with this coffee-house type of defence and knew something about it. The World Champion got nothing out of the opening and blew the middle game. After this victory, the English players dubbed this defence the St George!

Shallow tactics? No, playing the man. An extraordinary kind of ploy in time trouble occurred in a game between Yuri Razuvaev, friend and helper of Karpov (on whom the incident made a lasting impression), and the Argentine Quinteros. Razuvaev was in tremendous time trouble, the position was far from clear, and his flag was about to fall. Quinteros did not have much time either, but he did have more than the Russian. As Karpov recounts the story: 'The Argentine moved quickly, hit the clock, and Razuvaev's flag crept higher and higher. But suddenly Yuri picked up his cup of coffee and began to drink ever so slowly, not making any move right away. Quinteros, watching all this, became stupefied, and his hands even began to tremble. Three or four moves later Quinteros resigned.'

Karpov attributes the Quinteros factor to his escaping with an invaluable draw in an absolutely lost position against Polugayevsky in the fifth game of the Candidates' in 1974 (*My Best Games*). Karpov had to give up rook for bishop or offer immediate resignation. 'What happened then seemed at first glance completely incomprehensible to those uninitiated in the secrets of chess and to those superficial thinkers who call such things "luck" or the result of hypnosis or, even more ludicrously, of witchcraft. During all this time, the words of a popular song kept running through my head over and over again: "Everything is so foggy . . ." . . . these constantly repeating lines from the song somehow lulled me, and I sat at the board as in a fog, thinking that everything was just fine. I was seeing a lot, in fact, but nothing was really any good. Polugayevsky also seemed to think I was rather subdued . . .

'It begins to sound almost funny – as though I had a psychological advantage. And this was what defeated him!' As Mikhail Tal has observed, good players make their own luck.

In Karpov's next encounter, in the semi-final of the Candidates', Spassky bluffed himself. Having won the first game rather easily, Spassky was evidently persuaded that his challenger was going to be something of a pushover. Karpov draws an instructive parallel with the World Cup soccer final of 1974. The Dutch team scored such an easy goal in the first minute of play against West Germany, it looked as if the final was all over bar the shouting. But the Germans won. Likewise Spassky's quick win lulled him into overestimating his chances.

I am not suggesting, obviously, that over-the-board play is not decisive. It is, even when a player has studied an opening in great depth, to the extent of writing an entire book on the subject. Two examples over the years have struck me as rather telling. First, the young David Levy wrote a book about the Sicilian Dragon, back in 1972. He then had the chance of testing his ideas out in practice against no less an opponent than Boris Spassky. The result was that Levy got crunched. 'I didn't follow the recommended line,' Levy explained. Why not? 'Oh, I just didn't feel like it . . .' Not quite the ideal approach in facing a world champion, perhaps. The other example came up at the Lucerne olympiad in 1982, when John Nunn, a distinguished mathematician, renowned at chess for his calculating ability, met Kasparov. Nunn had just published a book on the Modern Benoni, containing some 140 pages of analysis, the most up-to-date treatise on this tricky opening system that existed. One particular line, he noted, was suspect for Black. And Nunn found himself defending it over the board. In fact Kasparov varied on move 3, playing knight c3 instead of knight f3, which at that early stage might seem a relatively minor difference in move order, but in fact is very significant: Kasparov did not fear Nunn's known predilection for this system. It evidently had a profound impact on Nunn, who felt more than psychologically disoriented. Anyway, the author of the new book was sent back to do some more homework, losing a very clear-cut game in twenty-one moves. Such are the perils for opening theorists.

Bluff also exists off the board. I am not thinking here of the antics of Bobby Fischer so much as the demeanour of a player during critical parts of the game. Alekhine, as Botvinnik recalls, was a shrewd psychologist who knew how important it was to exert moral pressure on the opponent. In their first encounter, playing a prepared line in the Sicilian, 'right up to the critical moment he played at lightning speed, circling round the board (and his prey) and sitting down at the board only for a moment to make his move quickly. He had to try and suggest to his opponent that in the quiet of his study everything had been worked out to the end and resistance was therefore useless.' When Botvinnik found a line to draw, and paused to think, because there was no hurry, before repeating moves, 'My goodness, what came over Alexandr Alexandrovich . . . his tie became undone, his button-on collar curled up at one side, his thinning hair became dishevelled . . .'

The exemplary Botvinnik, who may be regarded as the personification of rectitude in chess, well appreciated the importance of the impression given to his opponent, as shown by his conduct at a critical moment during his return match for the World Championship against Tal. Adjourning the twentieth game in a difficult position for him, Botvinnik spent a sleepless night. He struggled on, but at the end of the adjournment session came into a lost endgame. Came a second sleepless night, and by morning he realised there was a stalemate possibility, if White did not play actively. 'I sat and thought: how can I let it be known in the enemy camp that it is really hopeless for me? Then they will not work hard at it, and it is possible they will overlook the stalemate. Should I phone somebody up? No, out of the question, that is pretty flagrant. I would have to wait until somebody phoned me for the message to get across by roundabout ways . . .

'Aha, a phone call from Yasha Rochlin, who has links with all the journalists, that's fine. "Well, Misha, are you working at it?" I gave a deep sigh, "Yasha, you yourself must realise how it stands . . ."

'Yet another ring – Salo Flohr, even better . . . I kept quiet and then in a broken voice said, "I shan't say anything to you, Salomon, I'm very tired."

'After two days of play and two sleepless nights I was thoroughly tired out, yet I did not take my usual thermos flask of coffee with me to the adjournment session – this would be the most weighty proof that I would make just a few moves and then resign the game. It was during just these few moves that Tal had to miss the stalemate.'

Normally, Botvinnik adds, recalling all this in his memoirs, he did not have recourse to such tricks. Later Tal denied that he noticed the absence of the thermos flask. Anyway, he saw the stalemate danger too late. Next day the return match ended too.

Decisive games, on which matches and titles turn, require special handling. Probably the 'unluckiest' player in the history of modern chess, and, some people would say, the most talented player too, was David Bronstein (born, as random fate would have it, with exactly the same name and in the same town as Leon Trotsky). In 1951 he was leading in the match for the World Championship with Botvinnik right up to the twenty-third game. With the greatest difficulty, Botvinnik with White managed to salvage what was in all probability a lost game, to level the match. And in the final game, Bronstein only managed, in another hard struggle, to draw again, which meant that Botvinnik retained his title. As he himself would recognise, Bronstein never really recovered from this blow which scarred his whole career. Thus in 1958 he lost in the last round to a weak player, so failing to reach the Candidates' tournament and suffered a similar experience in 1973 in the Interzonal.

According to Lyev Polugayevsky, who probably concentrates on preparation more than anyone, the worst danger in decisive games is excessive constraint. On the contrary, what is needed, so he says in his monumental labour *Grandmaster Preparation* (1981), is an inwardly light-hearted, even devil-may-care attitude to the game; in his own case, to reduce such encounters to the most ordinary level of games – the kind a player has played and won a couple of hundred times. At the same time, of course, to play thoughtfully, without weakening the combative edge, to play with all possible aggression – 'but on no account to associate each important step in the game with the sheen of the gold medal'. Every player must find his own method: some need a good sleep, others to take a brisk walk, yet others to get well and truly angry, or, by contrast, induce a state of deep calm. 'The secret is simple: you must conduct the game as though it were of precisely no importance, but at the same time instil in each move all of your internal energy, concentrate extremely hard, and attempt to foresee anything unexpected.' As he admits, easier said than done.

Every day for about six months, during one stage of his life, Polugayevsky confided, he spent several hours at the board studying positions from the opening which came (with some justification) to be known as the Polugayevsky variation of the Sicilian – he even dreamed about it at night.

| 1 | e4 | c5 |
| 2 | Nf3 | d6 |
| 3 | d4 | cxd4 |
| 4 | Nxd4 | Nf6 |
| 5 | Nc3 | a6 |
| 6 | Bg5 | e6 |
| 7 | f4 | b5 (Diagram 24) |

24

It became an obsession with him. Every time an opponent found a refutation of Black's tactics Polugayevsky went back to work. '. . . regardless of common sense, the decision was made: to seek again! To seek and seek until I found that fresh idea which in the critical position would instil the despondent Black pieces with life, and enable the situation on the board to be assessed differently.' The obsession with his variation persisted on and off for years. Like a difficult, much-loved child, he cursed it and coddled it and in a sense subordinated his own life to it . . . such are the fixations of chess. He had a recurrent duel with Bronstein over the board, putting his researches to the test. The Variation had long since been promoted to capital letters. 'How much time have I spent on this one single Variation, and on how many occasions have I found a defence for

Black! It would simply be unjust if all this work were in vain!' It was not enough for him that he understood so much more than his opponents that they would not know or discover a refutation that he himself knew existed . . . he did not, as he believed, have the 'moral right' to rely on his opponent's ignorance. And at just the point when he felt obliged to abandon The Variation as unsound, it became highly fashionable, and everyone began to play it. He became disillusioned, taking each defeat sustained by Black as a personal reproof, a demonstration of artistic failure.

Only after an interval of ten years did a 'miracle' occur. Checking over old games, both his own and other players', Polugayevsky was vouchsafed a revelation. The Variation suddenly took on a new aspect. 'A sensation, hidden in the depths of my emotional memory, was suddenly revived: what if . . . What if for me The Variation is not dead? If The Variation is alive?!' It was as if a dam had burst and the flood of inspiration carried him backward and forward, over and over, searching, studying, helping to revive his most difficult and beloved and seemingly unquenchable brainchild: 'The Variation lives!' This Sisyphean labour represents another aspect of chess vision. The wealth of ideas and the number of variations in this line are so great, Polugayevsky concluded, that all lovers of fighting play will always be able to find in The Variation – beginning with 7 . . . b5 – a boundless and fruitful field for exploration, experiment and discovery.

Vision at the grandmaster level is based on seeing the relationship between pieces, seeing the pieces in chunks on the board (see Chapter 1). In a computer, intuitive vision of a position is not (yet) built in, because we do not know what 'intuition' means and cannot therefore translate it mechanistically. 'The essence of the matter is that the conduits of sense in chess thinking are "virtual" images of the real situation, transformed, existing only in the imagination, created by a process in which visual perception, memory and thinking are joined into one' – thus Bronstein and Smolyan (a Soviet psychologist) in *Chess in the Eighties* (1982). The image is the necessary support for an idea. Many oversights and blunders, they say, can be explained by the inertia of the visual image, its post-action, for example when a piece is still seen on a square although several moves earlier it was exchanged.

A graphic description of the function of the image in chess is given in their account of how blindfold chess works. 'Your thoughts are precisely directed – you are attacking f7, and thus you see an enormous, flickering black pawn and practically nothing else, the remainder of the board is obscured in mist. Your thoughts pick out and illuminate isolated parts of the board, groups of interacting pieces. Then they are once again released into the dark. Your optical system, visual memory, and visualization mechanisms operate at full power. It is the continuity of transforming visual images that provides the rapidity of intuitive thinking in particular, and the high quality of creative thinking as a whole.'

I think vision in chess can be considered as an amalgam of intuitive perception, from the image, and calculation, from the variations open. The best players need both qualities, but the imaginative process of seeing in the mind takes precedence; calculating ability monitors it. 'A strong player,' according to Bronstein and Smolyan, 'requires only a few minutes of thought to get to the heart of the conflict. You see a solution immediately, and half an hour later merely convince yourself that your intuition has not deceived you.' Or *has* deceived you, as the case may be. It seems more reasonable to suppose that some chess positions do lend themselves to the kind of intuitive flash that Bronstein celebrates in the creative process, and that other chess positions, such as endgames, respond better to calculation.

We do not know what goes on inside the minds of grandmasters, or of anyone else for that matter, in the neurological sense. But we do know how people think, the rules which seem to construct the process of thinking. The distinction is an extremely revealing one. Here, as set out by one of the leading authorities on artificial intelligence, Professor Herbert Simon, is a rather beautiful metaphor on the ways of . . . the ant.

We watch an ant make his laborious way across a wind- and wave-moulded beach. He moves ahead, angles to the right to ease his climb up a steep dunelet, detours around a pebble, stops for a moment to exchange information with a compatriot. Thus he makes his weaving, halting way back to his home . . . I sketch the path on a piece of paper. It is a sequence of irregular, angular segments – not quite a random walk, for it has an underlying sense of direction, of aiming toward a goal.

I show the unlabelled sketch to a friend. Whose path is it? An expert skier, perhaps, slaloming down a steep and somewhat rocky slope. Or a sloop beating upwind in a channel dotted with islands or shoals. Perhaps it is a path in a more abstract space: the course of a student seeking the proof of a theorem in geometry.

Whoever made the path, and in whatever space, why is it not straight; why does it not aim directly from its starting point to its goal? In the case of the ant (and, for that matter, the others), we know the answer. He has a general sense of where home lies, but he cannot foresee all the obstacles between. He must adapt his course repeatedly to the difficulties he encounters, and often detour uncrossable barriers. His horizons are very close, so that he deals with each obstacle as he comes to it; he probes for ways around or over it, without much thought for future obstacles . . .

Viewed as a geometric figure, the ant's path is irregular, complex, hard to describe. But its complexity is really a complexity in the surface of the beach, not a complexity of the ant. (*The Sciences of the Artificial*, 1970)

Whatever its complexity in the microscopic detail of its cells or molecules, Simon adds, an ant, viewed as a behaving system, is quite simple. 'The apparent complexity of its behaviour over time is largely a reflection of the complexity of the environment in which it finds itself.'

There is a parallel here (one might suggest) with the progress of a chess player – slow, circuitous, directed towards an unseen goal. Chess masters do not have some special gift of visual imagery, Simon notes, citing the de Groot experiments on memory. Otherwise, why did their performance deteriorate at reconstructing pieces placed at random (instead of in chunks) on the board? The evidence is clear that the human information-processing system is basically serial in its operation (doing one thing after another); so that it can process only a few symbols at a time (some seven items) held in short-term memory; and that the most obvious limits on human beings' ability to employ clever strategies stem from the small capacity of short-term memory and the relatively long time (five seconds) required to transfer a chunk of information from short-term to long-term memory. Five seconds may not seem very long: it means, talking about human behaviour in general, that human beings do not have sufficient means for storing information in memory to enable them to apply the most efficient strategy, unless the presentation of information is slowed down or they are given external memory aids, or both.

The talent of the grandmaster, it would seem, lies in combining short-term and long-term memory. The good player is continually processing the chunks he sees in front of him on the board in relation to positions from previous games imprinted in his long-term memory, so that he can relate one to the other – as if the ant had stored up a record of his previous walks across the dunes. 'Intuitive' thinking at the board is simply this process carried through at lightning speed, so fast that the separate stages in the process of perception are a single flash. In short, intuition and calculation are opposite ends of the same mental prism.

# 9

# MISTAKES

*'What went wrong with your plan?'*
*'He didn't follow it.'*
Eight-year-old after a simultaneous
exhibition against Korchnoi

Why do you play so badly? Sorry, I'll rephrase that. Why do *I* play
so badly? It's a question which revolves in my thoughts from time to
time, usually as I drive back to work after losing another series of
five-minute games at the chess café where I pass an hour, or two, or
three, most days. Originally, the café was up in Hampstead, a large,
bare working-class caff serving mugs of tea and eggs on toast, with
wide plate-glass windows, through which passers-by could watch
the chess players. The same crew of players and kibitzers turned out
every day, morning, noon and night; and in their various quirks and
eccentricities, arising from their addiction to chess, they no doubt
resembled every other chess café in Vienna, Paris or New York.

Ah, Vienna! At the peak of their popularity, before the Second
World War, the city had about 4,000 coffee-houses. Even today
there are some 400, almost half of them within the Ringstrasse, the
inner city. Those were the days when Vienna, with its cosmopolitan
style, its taste for talk and fascination with diplomacy, and its
substantial Jewish community, was the hub of Central Europe. 'The
origins of the very first café,' noted a recent tribute to Das Wiener
Kaffeehaus as one of Europe's most civilised institutions, 'can be
traced precisely to 1683, when Vienna lay under siege from the
Turks . . . a certain Herr Kolschitsky, a coffee merchant by trade,
was helping the Austrians to achieve victory in a more subtle way.
Disguised as a pasha he traded among the Turkish camps, taking
detailed notes of their positions and numbers.' When the siege was
raised the Habsburgs did not forget their brave spy. A licence was
granted to establish a coffee-house. Kolschitsky's 'Kaffee-Shrank'

proved addictive. In Vienna, and to a lesser extent Budapest, Prague and Trieste, the café still plays the role of office, library and club, a meeting place for students, artists, businessmen and of course 'revolutionaries'. According to this account by Richard Bassett in the London *Times*, it was in the Central Café, in 1913, that a certain Herr Bronstein would regularly take coffee and play chess. 'A harmless activity, the Viennese secret police observed, even if Bronstein's real name was Trotsky and his chess partner better known as Stalin.' Alas for left-wing legend, there is no record whatever of Stalin playing Trotsky at chess. (But there is the delightful one-liner from an habitué of one of New York's lower East Side chess clubs: 'Trotsky? Hmmf! I could give him knight odds.')

The most celebrated of all coffee-houses was the Café de la Régence in Paris, where the great players of the golden age of chess played and talked and argued – Philidor, Deschapelles, La Bourdonnais, McDonnell, Saint Amant, Staunton, Kieseritzky, Anderssen, Harrwitz and, of course, Paul Morphy. Engravings of the Régence show a warm, dark-panelled room lit by globe lamps, the chess players formally attired in cravats and white shirts, waiters pushing by the thronged tables. This was the scene of Morphy's immortal triumphs of blindfold play which, even at this distance, breathe all the ardour of romantic chess. Recounting the end of his blindfold display against eight of the strongest players of the day, his secretary F. T. Edge caught the moment:

Morphy stepped from the arm chair in which he had been almost immovable for ten consecutive hours without having tasted a morsel of anything, even water, during the whole consecutive period; yet as fresh, apparently, as when he sat down. The English and Americans, of whom there were scores present, set up stentorian Anglo-Saxon cheers, and the French joined in as the whole crowd made a simultaneous rush at our hero. The waiters of the café had formed a conspiracy to carry Morphy in triumph on their shoulders, but the multitude was so compact they could not get near him, and finally they had to abandon their attempt. Great bearded fellows grasped his hands, and it was nearly half an hour before we could get out of the café. Père Morel fought a passage through the crowd by main strength, and we finally got into the street. There the scene was repeated; the multitude was greater out of doors than in the café, and the shouting, if possible, more deafening . . .

But, as I was saying, the question is: why do we all play so badly? Yes, all of us! There is a pecking order in the chess cafés – there always is – from the better players who are up to strong club or county standard, maybe even above it, descending the scale through the middle order of competent players, down to patzers of the lowest rank. None of us ever improved our play at the place I play at. Of course one picks up a point or two of technique, from bitter experience, or occasionally assays a new opening. But so far as the fundamentals of chess ability go, one could scarcely observe any difference from day to day and month to month. Win some, lose some . . . and then lose' some more. It seems extraordinary that different levels of ability can be measured so accurately, with such a high degree of probability as to who is going to beat whom in any particular game.

In one way, playing badly does not matter because one is playing with the same motley group of fellow addicts every day – people in casual or part-time jobs (no one seemed to work very much), mittel-European intellectuals, the occasional writer or painter, professional layabouts – and if they all play the same sort of standard, it works out fine for everyone. But in another way it is downright frustrating that one can't do better. The first chess café I frequented was run by a Greek Cypriot who played worse than any of his customers, which was some consolation. But then he sold out to a pizza parlour. All the players were in a state of acute anxiety, facing withdrawal symptoms as the day and the hour and the minute approached when the regular life-support would be cut off – where would we go? Playing at home is no satisfaction when you've got used to café life, with its well-worn jokes and jibes, its familiar rivalries and arguments and occasional fights – 'You touched the knight!' 'I touched nozzing!' 'Did he or didn't he touch the knight?' 'I am never playing mit ziss man again . . . *NEFFER!*' Then at the very last moment, in mid-afternoon just as the place was closing down, one of the players, like a magician, found a combination to save the spirits and sanity of the assembled company . . . he opened up a new café just down the hill . . . and the players trooped off without a backward glance, carrying their chess sets and clocks with them, to start their arguments anew.

Games were played for money, naturally – 25 or 50 pence a game, with the interesting proviso, adapted from backgammon, that a player could double the stakes by announcing '*Contra*'. If the challenge was refused, the game was ended there and then, and the winner pocketed the stake. But if the challenge was accepted, the doubler had to win the game outright – a draw was not enough to save his bet; and as the game proceeded it remained open to the second player to double back – '*Re-contra!*' – if his chances improved. In case you are not familiar with this shocking form of gambling at the royal game, the general rule is that if you reckon your chances of saving the game are no worse than 3 to 1, i.e. once in four times you can make it, take the bet! The calculation is that by refusing a double, it costs the loser one point each time, which over four games totals four units. But if the player can *save* one game in four, even by a draw, he wins two units and loses only six, giving the same net loss of four, so he is no worse off. And in taking the challenge, he has the further chance that he may save the game and re-double at some stage to win four units. In fact, because of the draw, it's miles better odds than at backgammon. What's more, if you never take a challenge players will always take advantage of you by doubling, so it is sound tactics to fight back. Playing on the clock, with all the opportunities afforded for swindles of one kind or another, it was, and is, common practice to accept doubles in normally losing positions, even a whole piece down. Not chess? There are many rooms in my mansion, saith Caissa. Even in serious play, understanding of the odds can be important. The reason that Bent Larsen takes such high risks in playing dubious or unorthodox moves lies in a simple estimate of his true chances. Over, say, three games, where the position is unclear, if he plays safely and correctly, he can expect to take 1½ points. But if he takes risks not strictly justified by the position, he may come unstuck now and again but would expect to win two games out of three, giving a net result of plus 2.

Hustling is the word. In such chess cafés there are always sharp-witted players on the look-out for mugs. Sometimes a very strong player will drop by and tempt the sucker with outrageous odds – say five minutes to one. Such an advantage is an illusion. The strong player knows the opening traps and tactics inside out and can play, if necessary, 50 or even 100 moves in a minute. There's a nice story about Lasker going into a chess café, unrecognised, and being offered knight odds by the pundit in residence. After the World Champion contrived to 'lose' the game, he argued that actually it was an advantage to give knight odds, because the player could then develop the queen's rook quickly and work up a strong attack. He persuaded his opponent to play him again, with Lasker giving a knight odds. And the World Champion duly won. After alternating games in which the player giving a knight always won, Lasker proved his point. (Some versions of the story make it a king's rook odds, which meant the player could not castle and win by a kingside attack.) According to another story it was Lasker, incognito, who was recognised by a blind player. After a series of powerful moves, the blind man nodded his head in appreciation: 'Ah, Dr Lasker I presume!' Steinitz used to play all-comers at Simpson's coffee-house in the Strand for half a sovereign a game. (Now an old-English style of restaurant noted for its roast beef, Simpson's still has on display the board and pieces used by such legendary players as Staunton, Zukertort, Blackburne, Tarrasch and of course Morphy himself. The board is a big one, 60cm square.) One of Steinitz's regular customers was a woodpusher who lost game after game, week after week. As chess writer Irving Chernev tells the story, a friend advised Steinitz to let him win just one game, so as to avoid killing the golden goose. Steinitz took the advice, played as badly as he could, left his queen *en prise*, and when his opponent finally saw it, resigned. He began setting up the pieces for a new game but the jubilant victor ran out of the café shouting the amazing news that at long last he had defeated the World Champion, and never played him again.

It's not just the moves that matter, in coffee-house chess it's *how* you make the moves. The object is always to disconcert, intimidate or infuriate the opposition. Some well-known moves noted by Norman Lessing (*The World of Chess*, Anthony Saidy and Norman Lessing, 1974) include 'The Hammer' – the piece is lifted high in the air and brought down on the square with great force, designed to terrify the opponent; it is exceeded only by 'The Sledgehammer', used only in dead lost positions: the piece is slammed down so violently that the other pieces are sent flying, foiling all efforts to reconstruct the game. The answer to 'The Hammer' is 'La Déli-catesse' – finger outstretched in the air, the piece is not lifted at all but delicately slid into its new square, just so. In 'The Screw', designed to give an air of solidity and permanence, the piece is screwed firmly down into the square as if it will never be shifted (favoured, so it is said, by former world champion Vassily Smyslov).

Any kind of verbal or procedural distraction is permitted, provided it is not actually cheating. Seizing a black-squared bishop, for instance, and banging it down on the opposite side of the board on a white square is going too far. Leaving a pawn half-way between two squares, pending a decision on future tactics, is rather more than careless. But staring very hard at one corner of the board, to divert your opponent's attention from the other corner where you intend to conduct some surprise manoeuvre, is quite in order. Blowing cigarette smoke over the board is vulgar: but offering a light at a crucial moment of thought might be considered as much helpful as distracting. The same applies to studious inquiries about your opponent's health, financial prospects, or amorous entanglements. As for kibitzing . . . that is a vocation in itself. The rule is that kibitzers must not speak or make any comment about the game in progress. But the judicious sip of coffee, the anguished roll of the eyes, the stifled groan, the knowing smirk – these are all part of the kibitzers' code designed to insinuate their own superiority to either player while annoying both. All this, reprehensible in the extreme, is part of coffee-house chess. So if you can't stand the heat, stay out of games which begin:

'You call that an opening?'
'I'm making it up as I go along.'
'Pin and win!'
'Knight on the rim, future looks grim.'
'Karpov found this move.'
'Ask him to take it back.'
'What kind of plan is that!'
'Against you I need a plan?'
'Always give a check, it might be mate.'
'Contra!'

Yes, anything is permitted, by fair means or foul, in coffee-house chess, except violence. Violence, however, I have seen several times, including one occasion when an infuriated loser cracked down with a chair leg on his unsuspecting opponent's head. The latter had to retire to the hospital, fortunately just across the road. It was not many months before the perpetrator of this incident was back, pacifically helping rent out chess sets. Men have died at the chess board, witness many tales in mediaeval verse and romance. Such games always start in a friendly spirit, as shown by these lines from *Guy of Warwick* (*c*.1450) based on events in the age of Vikings four hundred years earlier.

> 'Faber', quod Sowdan, 'y bidde thee
> To playe at the chesses wyth me.'
> 'Syr', quod he, 'wyth myn entente
> I shall do youre comawndement' . . .
> They sate downe frendys in all wyse,
> But they were wrothe ere they dud ryse . . .

Sowdan, the younger man, called Faber the son of a whore, and cracked him so hard over the head with a rook he drew blood. Faber kept his temper, because his opponent was the son of the lord to whom he owed allegiance; but the headstrong young man went for him again, whereupon Faber retaliated in kind.

> On hys fete dud he stonde
> And took the chekur in hys honde.
> He smote Sowdan undur the ere
> He felle to grounde and dyed there.

'Chekur' being the chessboard, in mediaeval times a heavy weapon.

But why all the bloodiness, why the apparent malignancy in chess, Arthur Koestler once inquired? 'The reason is intuitively felt by every chess player, yet difficult to explain without giving the impression of indulging in artificial profundities.' In the first place, each chessman embodies a dynamic threat, he pointed out, as if it were alive and animated by the desire to inflict the maximum damage on the opponent's men. 'When a chess player looks at the board, he does not see a static mosaic, a "still life", but a magnetic field of forces, charged with energy – as Faraday saw the stresses surrounding magnets and currents as curves in space; or as Van Gogh saw vortices in the skies of Provence.' Lewis Carroll was aware of the animism and magic in the game when he chose chessmen as the characters for *Alice Through The Looking Glass* – the Queen of Hearts' 'Off with his head!' 'Off with her head!' is apt.

People who think of chess as a quiet, peaceable game have

obviously never visited a chess café. In our own day, hustling has become more refined. When a new player walks into a chess café or club the assembled company soon sizes him up, but it may take a little time before a good player is smoked out. Yasser Seirawan told me of his success in one or two New York City clubs in the early days before he became so well known. 'Hi, fella, wanna game?' some basking shark would casually inquire. 'Siddown right here, have a cuppa coffee! So here's how we play, a dollar a game, two bucks if you double, two-fifty if you win inside twenty moves . . .' or some such elaborate come-on. 'Okay, I'll give it a try,' says Yasser, sitting down. The hustler narrows his gaze: 'Say, where ya from?' 'Seattle', confesses Yasser. 'SE-attle! We-e-ell! Give ya knight odds, kid.' Whoever heard in NYC of a chess player from way out yonder! (American players do live far apart – they are like isolated pawns, in a beautiful simile by Larsen.) But how can a strong player win a coffee-house game and give the impression that he is, in reality, just lucky? 'Promoting a pawn one move before your opponent gets his,' Seirawan explains. 'You count the moves in an ending, and just scramble your pawn home first with a tempo. The other guy can't believe it, that he's lost! It seems a complete fluke, like playing a drop shot at tennis.' The loser is rocked out of his seat. 'Wh-a-at! Didja see that? I've never had such an easy win . . . Okay, awright, tell ya what I'll do, five bucks this time, and you can play White again.' Some GMs, like Walter Browne, are renowned for their fondness for skittles games at high stakes, and will spend their whole night taking on all-comers, in the intervals of serious tournament play. Karpov himself used to play a lot of five-minute games at the start of his career but came to believe that it was too distracting. Now he does not play blitz during tournaments at all. Botvinnik was always against it.

Do you feel it goes slightly against the grain, offends the *purity* of chess, to set odds in order to even up an unequal contest? Well, maybe so; but once again, there's nothing new in it. How about this for exactitude in calibrating the giving of odds at the board – it comes from an early Arabian manuscript, as noted by Murray.

A true Chess-player ought to play with all sorts of people, and in order to do so he must make himself acquainted with his adversary's strength in order to determine what odds he may give or accept . . . It is only by equalizing the strength of the combatants that both of them may reap amusement and edification . . .

The smallest degree of odds, then, is to allow the adversary the first move. The second degree is to give him the Half-Pawn, which consists of taking either Knight's Pawn off his own file and placing it on the Rook's third square. The third species of odds is the giving the Rook's Pawn; the fourth, that of the Knight; the fifth, that of the Bishop; the sixth, that of the Queen. The seventh degree of odds is to give the adversary the King's Pawn, which is the best on the board. The eighth species of odds is the King's Bishop. The ninth is the Queen's Bishop. The tenth degree of odds is the Queen. The eleventh, the Queen and a Pawn; or what is equivalent, a Knight; for though the Queen and Pawn be slightly inferior to the Knight at the beginning, yet you must take into account the probability of the Pawn becoming a second Queen. The twelfth species of odds is the Knight and Pawn. The thirteenth, the Rook. To give any odds beyond the Rook can apply only to women, children, and tyros.

Talking of playing for money, the unfortunate distinction of incurring the most expensive loss on record, in a serious modern tournament, falls to Soviet exile Lev Alburt, at Lone Pine 1980. Alburt was then in the initial stage of trying to make a living under free enterprise, so what happened must have been quite a shock.

25

With a first prize of $15,000 at stake (these events at Lone Pine were sponsored by a wealthy American chess enthusiast, the late

Louis Statham), the lead was being contested by two ex-Soviet players, Alburt and Dzindzihashvili. Paired against each other in the last round, the winner would take all. But a draw would guarantee each player a healthy $10,000. Spurning all offers of a draw, Alburt reached the position in Diagram 25 after 43 moves. A pawn up, with the time control coming on move 45, he faced a big decision. Should he swop knight for bishop and race his passed pawns in the queen ending, or press on with the attack against the Black king? Queen and knight are better than queen and bishop, as every Russian schoolboy knows (commentary by Michael Stean). So, 44 Qd8?? An error costing $4,167 since the game is now a draw and he can only share first prize. The threat is 45 Qc7 winning, but in between Black has a move. Instead 44 Nxb7 Kxb7 45 h4 would win, e.g. 45 . . . a5 46 h5 a4 47 h6 a3 48 h7 a2 49 h8=Q a1=Q 50 Q(g5)g7+ Kc6 (50 Ka6? 51 Qa8+) 51 Qf6 changing one pair of queens with a comfortable win as Black has no passed pawn.

44 . . . Qe5+

45 g3 Qe2

46 Qf6?? And this last move cost Alburt $6,933 as White still had a draw. 46 Nxb7 Qxf2+ 47 Kh1.

46 . . . Bf3! and now White is lost. Over the last three moves Alburt's winnings had plummeted from $15,000 to £3,900 – a rather sharp if salutary introduction to capitalism. (On the other hand another Soviet chess exile, Dimitri Gurevich, told me that getting his visa to leave the Soviet Union was, for him, better than winning a million dollars.)

Some time afterwards I asked Alburt, who is a very amiable character, how he felt about this reversal of fortune. 'Not too bad,' he observed stoically, 'and not nearly as bad as I felt when I overlooked a win against Tal and missed a GM norm.' Such are the hazards of the modern chess circuit. Alburt now earns his livelihood by teaching. He advertises his services in New York with portraits of himself, like a glossy ad for whisky, seated at the chess board wearing a ruffled shirt and dinner jacket, promising pupils that he will teach them to 'forget about blunders'.

Alburt's error at Lone Pine was caused by time trouble. In playing for the win he was true to the spirit of chess. The essence of coffee-house chess (which I suppose led to the word 'coffee-housing') is the swindle. You don't know what a swindle is? A resource which – quite against all the odds and natural justice – turns the position around and saves a lost game.

The starting point of a swindle is to recognise that, all things being unequal, one has a lost game. Failure to take some kind of remedial action will lead, inescapably, to a loss. Something has to be done (since we are not talking here about resigning gracefully). One technique is for the losing player to make unclear moves, very quickly, to complicate the position – such is the advice of the young English player Simon Webb who reviews this disgraceful practice in his amusing *Chess for Tigers* (1978) – in the hope that the opponent will lose time and find a way of going wrong. Webb calls his method 'Controlled Desperation'. You play quickly to give your opponent something to think about, not worrying about giving him a pawn or the exchange. He may have a forced win, but he still has to find it. 'Look at it from your opponent's point of view. He has a number of possibilities, all of which look good, so he must analyse it in detail. If you can confuse him by making the position complicated enough, he won't be able to analyse it out to the end. Instead he'll have to play the move which looks best and hope, and that is exactly what you want, because he's more likely to make a mistake when he's not in control of what he's doing . . . the more you can confuse him, the more likely he is to go wrong. It doesn't matter if you confuse yourself – you've got a lost position anyway!'

It was Sammy Reshevsky who was the victim of a celebrated swindle at the hands of Larry Evans, dubbed 'the swindle of the century'. Black is a knight ahead in the position given in Diagram 26 and can win as he pleases. Instead of resigning, Evans offered a little prayer. Can you see why the move he was praying for was such a blunder?

**48   . . . Qxg3??**

As so often, the obvious move, played quickly and unthinkingly, is fatal. Simply 48 . . . Qf6 would have done the trick; if 49 gxf4, then . . . Qxh4+

Evans unleashed

**49   Qg8+!!**

**26**

'Reshevsky still had no inkling of the plot. He actually thought I was reaching out to shake his hand, which is a customary gesture when resigning.'

**49 . . . Kxg8**
**50 Rxg7+!! Draw**

Of course it takes a master to see this kind of resource in a crisis. Black must either recapture the rook, giving stalemate, or face perpetual check after 50 . . . Kf8 51 Rf7+ Ke8 52 Re7+ etc. 'Reshevsky's face turned a delicate shade of scarlet [this was the US Championship of 1964]. He laughed wryly at his own stupidity, but otherwise there was no departure from his customary aplomb.' Bravo, Sammy. Perhaps he was steeling himself to this kind of calamity, because ten years later an even worse fiasco engulfed him, missing a forced mate against Soviet GM Savon. I give this story because it illustrates that on occasions when justice is *not* done in chess (cf. Lasker's dictum 'On the chessboard lies and hypocrisy do not survive long; the merciless fact, culminating in a checkmate, contradicts the hypocrite') everyone feels badly about it, even the winner. The position is shown in Diagram 27.

It was the 40th move and Reshevsky had only a few seconds left. He played Qxg6+?? – the Black bishop on b1 had slipped his mind for a moment, backward captures always being the hardest to visualise – and Savon replied 41 Bxg6, leading to instant resignation. The forced mate is not easy to find – if you can do it in thirty

**27**

seconds, count yourself an expert (solution at the foot of the page*). This is the eyewitness account given by Burt Hochberg, quoted in *Chess Panorama* (William Lombardy and David Daniels, 1975). 'Werner Hug, the Swiss international master, came tearing into the room like a bull elephant, yelling "Reshevsky blundered! My God, what a blunder! He had a mate and sacrificed his queen! . . ." a few minutes later, Reshevsky was pacing the press room looking absolutely distraught. In that atmosphere of general excitement at the approaching end of the tournament, Reshevsky stood alone – God only knows what was in his mind. No one had dared to speak to him. Savon, looking sheepish, his blond hair carelessly draped over one eye, followed his compatriots around as they examined the other positions on the demonstration boards. No one was speaking to him either; he looked like a little boy who had done something bad and was sure to be punished later, but for the moment was on his best behaviour.'

Does one attribute mistakes to lack of vision, time trouble or money pressure? – or a combination of all three? The time factor is, of course, crucial, 'merciless' in Nabokov's verdict. The usual time for master games is 40 moves by each player in 2½ hours, followed by 16 moves an hour in the adjournment sessions. But why shouldn't chess, in practice, be played faster? Time is the third dimension in the game. There is a case, so some players believe, for shortening the time of tournament games. Ljubomir Ljubojevic, the Yugoslav GM, puts it this way: everything has been speeded up

*40 g5+ Kxg5 (40 . . . Bxg5 41 Qg7++) 41 h4+ Kxh4 (41 . . . Kh6 42 Qg7++) 42 Qf4++.

in the modern world – people used to cross the Atlantic in six weeks, then it became five days, now it's a few short hours; in the olden days, people used to travel by horse, live by daylight hours, take a bath once a week; now it's just a few moments to take a shower, raid the fridge, drive off in the car. The chess clock is an invention of the nineteenth century. Why not speed up chess games to one hour! Wouldn't this attract the public, like the World Cup tourney on TV? And why not run the World Championship, like the motor racing grand prix, on an annual basis? As things are, it's all too long drawn out and too slow. The public, on whom the welfare of chess and the livelihood of grandmasters depend, would like it and understand it. And wouldn't chess players themselves adjust to the faster pace? Wouldn't the game be just as good if played in a shorter time span? In a more precise variation of this argument, Fischer has been reported as saying he would return to chess if 60 moves were played in 2½ hours, i.e. no adjournments.

Support for this approach comes from Bronstein and Smolyan who maintain (*Chess in the Eighties*) that it is in rapid play that the intuitive mind triumphs. 'Time provides an additional weapon for the player who is inclined towards slow, calculating play, and allows knowledge and factors of preparation to reveal themselves, rather than intuition, fantasy and daring.' With slow play, they say, does not chess lose its intrinsic fascination, the ability to surprise with the unexpected, the ability to create? 'Multi-hour games are monstrous, like dinosaurs from past ages . . .' As for adjournments, they are in general contrary to the spirit of chess.

It is true that adjournments are the exact opposite of hand-to-hand combat. Players know that if they can safely get up to the time control on move 40, they can have a respite for home-brewed analysis, with the bonus of a fresh mind or even a team of other players to help them through. Botvinnik spared no effort in the prodigious study he made of adjourned positions and often reaped a valuable reward at the cost of his sleep. In our day Polugayevsky, amongst others, has demonstrated the worth of adjournment analysis. It is an integral part of chess, and in its inner or unspoken dialogue, a very fine part of chess. But it is not the same as over-the-board struggle. Iakov Damsky, a chess commentator for Soviet radio and TV, taped some of the analyses he conducted with Polugayevsky during one of the USSR championships. 'Only a chess beginner will be unfamiliar with the pressing, obsessive sensation of an impending adjournment,' reported Damsky. 'It is fine if a win is in prospect. But if not? If one has to try to save a game, or attempt to realise a slight advantage? Then day and night, when eating, and sometimes during another game, the mind involuntarily returns to the position in question, and considers the hundredth or even thousandth variation with which one can continue the struggle.' It has been estimated that if the first session was extended to seven hours, it would probably reduce by a factor of five the number of sealed moves. On one adjourned game in the 1969 championship, Polugayevsky spent some seven hours' work – to reproduce his analysis in full would take at least three normal tournament bulletins. (He got the draw.) Perhaps Bronstein with his exalted conception of creative intuition overstates his case. There is probably ample justification, in terms of the originality and excitement of play, for playing both long games and shorter games.

It is important to master the clock, otherwise the clock will master you. Some players always seem to fall into time trouble; perhaps, like Korchnoi, they are stimulated under pressure. The commonest mistake of weak players is to rush at their moves, to gain a time advantage, and hope by such means to hustle their opponents. Any half-way good player will defeat this tactic, by the simple method of getting a winning position – after which he will not need time to win. It is a standard ploy to consume a lot of time in the opening to conceal a prepared variation. But it is also true that in complicated games players are bound to use up time and risk getting into a scramble. Larsen says, rightly, that if a player has a time advantage at the end of a game, he should not then rush at his moves: on the contrary, just because he has the advantage of time to think, he should use it well. If in time trouble, the point is to keep your nerve by playing any move which does not immediately lose out of hand – and keep it going, bang, bang, bang.

Although a chronometer was used to record the amount of time taken over each move in the Staunton–Saint Amant match of 1848, it was not, apparently, until 1861 that any kind of time limit was enforced (*Encyclopedia of Chess*). This was the Anderssen–Kolisch match in London, the first known occasion when timing by means of an hour glass for each player was introduced, with a time limit of 24 moves in two hours. The first tournament in which the players had to face a time limit regulated by sand glasses, 20 moves in two hours, was held in London next year, 1862. Mechanical double chess clocks arrived in the 1880s, making their formal debut at the great London tournament of 1883. It took almost a century before the next major innovation came on the scene, the electronic digital clock. Up to now tournament play has remained faithful to the push-button double clock. Personally, I like the digital clock because it shows to the precise second how much time is left, sparing one that agonising sideways squint to estimate the gap before the little red flag falls. (I once played a 60-minute game on a digital clock which was won by one second!)

Timing is the standard way to fix handicaps at chess, when matching strong against weaker players. A time limit of, say, five minutes against two and a half, helps compensate for differences in ability. Of course there are many heartbreaking stories of won games being lost on time. Karpov himself once (but only once!) lost a won game by leaving his 40th move too late, when he had two minutes on the clock, against Belyavsky. He made his move but his flag fell with his finger on the clock. One of the strangest cases in modern times was Vlastimil Hort's 'freeze' in his decisive game against Spassky in the World Championship quarter finals played in Iceland in 1977. The Czech grandmaster had a minute in which to make five moves . . . he saw a forced win . . . and staring at the board, in excitement or surprise, in a kind of trance, completely forgot about his clock. 'The blackest day of my life,' was Hort's verdict: he gave vent to his frustration by taking on the amazing total of 550 Icelandic youngsters in a simultaneous display. He began with 201 at the first sitting, increasing the total in batches of 50. Result, after 24 hours' play: won 477 (at an average of 2 minutes 14 seconds per game), drawn 63, lost 10. The German master Fritz Saemisch reputedly forfeited 15 games in a row on time, allegedly as a protest. He was in the habit of dawdling for an hour as early as move 4. Asked what he was thinking about, Saemisch explained that he was analysing a sacrifice on move 23 of another game. Yes, but what did that have to do with his fourth move? 'Oh, I always think about what interests me at the moment.'

The longest pause for thought ('big think' in Fischer's phrase) is not recorded. But one of the longest in modern times was Wolfgang Uhlmann's reflection over his twelfth move in a game against Tal in Moscow, 1971. The East German grandmaster thought about it for one hour and fifty minutes! The point I want to make, so far as we patzers are concerned, is that playing longer games does not improve the quality of the chess. On the contrary, we perpetrate as many idiocies over the board, as it were in slow motion, as we commit in blitz games. The nature of the errors may differ, fewer gross oversights in slow play as distinct from more positional errors, but the mistakes, in Tartakower's witty phrase, are all there, waiting to be made. So I return to the issue raised at the start of this chapter, which is why do I/you play so badly? Talent at chess, so far as we know, is not directly related to IQ. Morons often beat intellectuals. Einstein, though sufficiently interested in the game to write an introduction to the life and career of Emanuel Lasker, was not a chess player (and according to hearsay had a reputation at Princeton of not being able to keep time in the string quartet!).

So here are twenty-five things which bad players tend to do wrong, and repeat game after game. *Openings* 1. Not developing the pieces. 2. Trying to win a pawn quickly at the cost of organising the position. 3. Neglecting control of the centre. 4. Leaving the queen in a pin. 5. Ignoring opponent's threats. 6. Weakening pawns around the king. 7. Playing an opening from the book without understanding its point. *Middle Game* 8. Swopping off pieces because it seems easy. 9. Pursuing a tactical manoeuvre after the opponent has prevented it. 10. Failing to guard against discovered checks. 11. Playing too quickly when there is plenty of time. 12. Putting a piece out of play, usually on the edge of the board. 13. Leaving a pawn, or even a piece, loose. 14. Playing without a clear plan. *End Game* 15. Haste in pushing pawns. 16. Failing to bring the king into play. 17. Confusing the nature of the position. 18. Failing to guard against opponent's passed pawn. 19. Missing opportunities to play for a draw. 20. Getting into a time scramble. *General* 21. Playing obvious moves too quickly. 22. Conversely, looking for elaborate brilliancies. 23. Getting annoyed with oneself because of a previous inaccuracy. 24. Conversely, getting over-confident because of opponent's error. 25. Overestimating one's own chances and abilities.

I wrote this list down very quickly and no doubt most people could find twenty-five more. So I will add another one, which covers all the above: *Not doing anything to remedy this catalogue of known and highly correctable weaknesses.*

Some of the above points overlap, but dividing them into categories one gets, roughly speaking, the following result: Lack of basic technique, 10 out of 25; blindness, greed and human error, 10; lack of self-control 5; or, rounded into percentages, say 40 per cent technique, 40 per cent character, 20 per cent self-control.

Yes, well, it's only a game, isn't it? Should one take games so seriously? 'We have a deep ambivalence about games,' observes no less an authority than the Wykeham Professor of Logic at Oxford, Michael Dummet. 'In all places and at all periods a large proportion of men's time is spent in playing games of one sort or another, or in watching others play them; they absorb a large proportion of men's energy and attention, and, nowadays, consume a great deal of money. And yet because we have at the back of our minds a contrast between play and work, because we think of a game as something that by definition is not serious, we are loth to allow that games are worthy of serious investigation . . . a game may be as integral to a culture, as true an object of aesthetic appreciation, as admirable a product of human creativity as a folk art or style of music; and, as such, it is quite worthy of study . . .' The game which preoccupied Professor Dummet was the abstruse and ancient form of cardplay known as Tarot, but the comment seems especially apt to chess.

So far as advice is concerned, there is nothing new under the sun. This, for instance, comes from an early Arabic treatise, quoted by Murray in his *History of Chess*, which could be embroidered into a sampler over chess players' beds: 'Never snatch at an offered piece until the consequences have been fully weighed. Do not sacrifice a piece unless you see your way clear to regain it shortly, or a certain win. Do not let your *Shah* be hemmed in . . . Never play a move without a reason . . . When you see a good move for a piece, look out for a better . . .'

It is surely possible to improve one's game by a little application. I mean, one can't improve at tennis without coaching or at the piano without a music teacher. The inherent difficulty with chess is that one *knows* already what one *should* do, how to play correctly, at least in a macro sense, so what is really required is not so much a trainer as self-analysis. Perhaps a behavioural psychologist might provide the remedy: 'Attach this wire to your right hand, and wind it up your sleeve to the back of your head. Now every time you leave a piece *en prise*, you will receive a small electric shock, gradually increasing in intensity until . . .' 'AAAAgh!' Or psychoanalysis? 'Doctor, I have this overwhelming compulsion to sacrifice, I just can't help it, every time I play I throw away my queen!' 'Hm . . . why don't you tell me about your *mother*?' It's not just patzers who

**28**

throw away pieces, of course, but that does not make one feel any better.

Diagram 28 is a classic case of zero-zero vision, involving one of the finest players of our time, former Soviet champion Leonid Stein, who alas died prematurely, from the chess master's 'occupational disease', heart failure. (The phrase is Korchnoi's but I have not found any evidence showing that chess masters are especially prone to heart disease; the strain of competition could be a factor, but one must bear in mind that many kinds of people enjoy stress, and actually thrive on it.) This is the position which arose at Mar del Plata, 1966. Stein, not in time pressure, spent more than twenty minutes pondering his move, and produced 34 . . . Qc2??

This kind of blunder is probably caused by intense concentration, getting wound up trying to find a forced win. But his opponent, an Argentine player named Emma, instead of snapping off the queen with his knight, played 34 Rd7??, a reflex action to the rook being attacked. The game, poetic justice, was eventually drawn.

Explaining mistakes, GM Nikolai Krogius, who is a professional psychologist, distinguishes between three types of image – retained, inert and forward. The retained image is the transfer of part of a previous position into a new position, without the player realising that the position has changed. His perception has become static, fixed on a previous pattern. (See Diagram 29 below.) By contrast, the inert image describes the mental state of a player who has formed a firm impression of the course of an entire game, usually, perhaps correctly, that he has a won game, and fails to adjust it to changed circumstances; and the reverse can also be true, in failing to appreciate that what was a lost game can not merely be saved, but won. The forward image occurs when a player is so absorbed by possible future threats or moves, that they become a present reality in his mind, before they have happened: over-attention to Tarrasch's dictum that the threat is stronger than its execution.

29

In Diagram 29 Tal has just taken the Black queen by 37 Nxd6+ but is badly down on material. As Tal himself said after the game, it seemed vaguely to him that this move simultaneously attacked the Black rook on e8 – he reckoned on winning the rook and pawn ending after recovering the exchange. But two moves earlier the rook had moved from e8 to e1, with the threat of mate. Tal had failed to update the retained image, assuming the piece was still on its old square. If this can happen to a player like Tal, one may say, it can happen to anybody. 'No matter how strong the visual imagination, it is quite clear that the mental picture is paler than the visual impression,' Krogius quotes another psychological observation. 'Therefore, after the opponent has made a move, even if it was anticipated, one should never make one's reply without thought, (except of course during extreme time pressure).'

It may be objected to all this that in the end, after much hard work, the consequence is merely that you reach a new threshold at a slightly higher level of ability, and will continue to lose games. Maybe so: but there might be some satisfaction in losing to new faces and, even more gratifying, beating the players who previously beat you. Although self-control is the key to improvement at chess, or a large measure of improvement, what about technique itself?

The skill of the master lies in securing an advantage. After that, it is simply a question of exploiting it, 'a matter of technique'. In amateur play, it seems to be the other way round. Thanks to the high incidence of error, one side or the other may secure an advantage quite early in the game. But the advantage often swings to and fro, because weak players do not have the technique to convert their plus into a win. So how can this technique be acquired? Most weak players make the mistake of boning up on opening play, hoping to get an edge that way. And in theory this method does yield results. But the advantage tends to fizzle out in the middle game: many a slip 'twixt cup and lip. It is in transposing from the middle game into a winning endgame that technique really counts. It is essential to get a grip on the basic endings – king, rook and pawn against king and rook; or king bishop and pawns against king, knight and pawns; and so on – so that having arrived at the desired ending, you are able to clinch it. When one looks at a handbook on endgame play, the winning method is, in many standard cases, quite straightforward. Of course, analysis often leads to incredible depth and subtlety, displaying 'art' in chess in its most rarefied form. But when you come down to it, *this* is the drillsquare on which recruits to chess must learn their paces.

The essential characteristic of the endgame, it has always seemed to me, is that the chess pieces *change their value*. Everyone knows that 'the king is a fighting piece', but in the ending the king, normally so weak, becomes a giant-killer; a pawn with the imminent threat of promotion, the chess version of reincarnation, is often more powerful than all the other pieces combined; and giving up or gaining a tempo may make the difference between winning and losing the whole game. All sorts of new concepts such as 'bad bishops' – a bishop obstructed by its own pawns – and 'good bishops' – when the piece has lines open to operate freely – come into play. And the possibilities of achieving a draw, through stalemate, or blocking the opponent, or reducing the forces on the board to an unwinnable configuration, are manifold, sometimes simple, sometimes mysteriously complex.

I give one example, a famous study by Richard Réti, the Hungarian-born grandmaster and moving spirit of the hypermodern school, which shows how the king can subvert the laws of mathematics: namely, by disproving the axiom that the shortest distance between two points is a straight line. Diagram 30 shows how the king may cross from one side of the board to the other in seven moves: and how it can also proceed diagonally or in a zigzag, to reach the same objective in the same number of moves.

**30**

It is this quality in the king which enables White to save himself in the seemingly hopeless position devised by Réti in Diagram 31, White to play and draw; the king cannot catch the Black pawn before it queens, nor move over fast enough to protect its own pawn from the Black king. So how is it to be done? The answer lies in pursuing both these unattainable goals simultaneously.

**31**

1 Kg7! h4 2 Kf6! h3 Now what? 3 Ke7! White can support his own pawn now, because if 3 . . . h2 4 c7! h8=Q 5 c8=Q+ and with queens on each side this position is completely drawn. Whereas if Black tries to thwart this manoeuvre by 2 . . . Kb6 then 3 Ke5! Kxc6

4 Kf4! and White overtakes the Black pawn before it gets home. 'The Black pawn is like a comet slowed down by the gravitational pull of a distant body,' as has been well said. Note that if Black tries to forestall White's plan by first making a move towards the White pawn and then, instead of capturing it, reverting to pushing his own pawn again by 3 . . . h3, then White also changes course by 4 Kd6! h2 5 c7! Kb7 7 Kd7! and again the two queens draw. Such is the magic of the endgame.

'When I advise beginners that the best way to improve is to study this phase,' Larry Evans once observed, 'they consider me frivolous and usually retort that since there are a thousand ways of being slaughtered before they even reach an ending, they will continue to concentrate on the openings. To this, I can only reply that it is just as well they be slaughtered in the opening as that they reach an ending and misplay it.' As John Nunn, the English GM, justly remarks, introducing his study of endings, whenever a game is played containing an important opening innovation, it is immediately published all over the world: but if a game contains an interesting ending it may appear in one magazine and then sink into obscurity. The reasons are primarily that chess columnists are short of space, so they prefer short games to long ones; and while there is a vast demand for opening theory, catered for in specialist publications, there is no magazine devoted to over-the-board endgames.

Technique . . . self-control . . . endgame theory . . . all these elements of the game have their place. But if there is one overriding quality which is all-important, which I could wish a good fairy would bless me with, it is what I would call *knowing what one is doing*. By which I mean understanding the essence of the position at each point. It is the quality which I find so immensely impressive in Fischer's analysis of his games. He knew what he was up to, which squares he was heading which pieces for, and why. And he explains it so directly. One must know not just the opening as per the book, but the logic behind it, not just the characteristics of the middle game, closed or open, tactical or strategic, but the implications of playing it; not just the practical possibilities but the limitations of endings; it means . . . oh well, if one knew half of this, one wouldn't be the patzer one is, would one?

Some of the finest minds of our civilisation have gone through the same process of self-doubt and self-knowledge, if it is any consolation. Here is Jean-Jacques Rousseau (1712–1778) who described how, after he learned chess, he made such rapid progress he thought he could soon beat the man who taught him, Bagueret. 'I went frantically mad with chess,' he wrote in his *Confessions*. 'I bought a chess-board. I bought *Il Calabrese* [a French collection of games]. I shut myself up in my room and spent days and nights there with a will to learn all the games by heart, to cram them into my head willy-nilly, to play alone without end or remission.

'After two or three months' working in that fine way, and after unimaginable endeavours, I went to the Café with a lean and sallow face, and nearly stupid. I made a trial, playing with Monsieur Bagueret again. He beat me once, twice, twenty times. My head was all of a muddle with those chess combinations, and my imagination had become so dull that I saw nothing more than a cloud before me.'

Rousseau continues, reporting on his progress at chess: 'Whenever I took Philidor's or Stamma's book and wanted to train myself by the study of games, the same thing would occur, and after being worn out with fatigue, I found myself weaker than before. Besides, whether I gave up chess or trained myself by play, I have never progressed one step since that first sitting with Bagueret, and always found myself at the same point as I was when it ended.

'Were I to train myself for thousands of centuries, I should only succeed in the long run, in giving the odds of a rook to Bagueret, and nothing more.

'A pretty use of your time! you will say . . .'

The café he referred to was, of course, La Régence. It has kept its lustre and its fame long after many richer and royaller palaces have faded into dust. I can't resist repeating that old anecdote about the man going into the café to watch Voltaire and Rousseau play at chess. Mere scribblers, those two, sniffs an acquaintance. 'True, but today they play with Philidor!'

A final piece of advice: when taking exams at school, there is a truism, inculcated in vain by generations of schoolmasters, which says it all: 'Read the questions!' One might adapt this invaluable but frequently ignored precept to chess, with the following dictum: *'Look at the board!'*

# GLOSSARY

*Adjournment* Unfinished games are adjourned, to be continued at a later session or day. In international competition, each player usually has 2½ hours for 40 moves; and then a further hour for each 16 moves (see *Clocks*)

*Algebraic notation* The most effective way of designating chess moves; each square on the board has its own letter and number, corresponding to its rank and file, running from 1 to 8 and a to h, as shown in Diagram 32. Moves are indicated by taking the initial letter for King, Queen, Rook and Bishop, and N for Knight; and the lower-case letters for the pawns, according to which file the pawn is on. A capture is indicated by *x*, check by +.

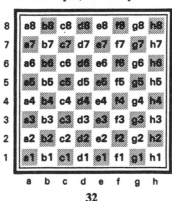

**32**

*Candidates'* The play-off matches between the winners of the regional tournaments (see *Interzonal*) to produce the final challenger to meet the World Champion.

*Clocks* The standard chess clock consists of two clocks linked together. Each player uses his own time when making his move; he then presses a button to start his opponent's clock, when it is the latter's turn to move; and so on. Failure to complete the stipulated number of moves within the time limit forfeits the game.

*Correspondence* Chess played by post.

*Grade* The British system of calculating a player's strength, based on his tournament results in the past year. The British grade × 8 + 600 = the FIDE rating. (see *Rating*)

*Interzonal* The regional tournaments, organised by geographic zones, held to enable the best players to qualify for the Candidates'.

*Olympiad* Team tournaments, held every two years, between member states of FIDE.

*Opposition* A term defining the relationship between the kings in the endgame, whereby the player who does not have to move 'has the opposition'; by forcing the opposing king to move, the player with the opposition has the advantage.

*Rating* The system of calculating a player's strength, relative to other players, based on tournament results over a period of years. Titles are awarded on achieving the requisite 'norms' in tournament results.

*Tempo* The gaining (or losing) of a move; e.g. in the opening, moving the same piece twice wastes a move, thus giving the opponent a tempo in development.

# INDEX